Finding a Job on the Internet

Amazing new possibilities for
jobseekers everywhere

Internet Handbooks

Books & Publishing on the Internet
Building a Business in Cyberspace
Chat on the Internet
Email for Beginners
Find It on the Internet
Finding a Job on the Internet
Free Stuff on the Net
Gardens & Gardening on the Internet
Homes & Property on the Internet
Internet for Schools
Internet for Students
Internet for Writers
Kids Stuff on the Internet
Law & Lawyers on the Internet
Medicine & Health on the Internet
News & Magazines on the Internet
Personal Finance on the Internet
Privacy & Security on the Internet
Shops & Shopping on the Internet
Travel & Holidays on the Internet
Wildlife & Conservation on the Internet

Other titles in preparation

Finding a Job on the Internet

Amazing new possibilities for
job seekers everywhere

Brendan Murphy

Internet Handbooks

Copyright © 1999 by Brendan Murphy

First published in 1999 by Internet Handbooks, a Division of International Briefings Ltd, Plymbridge House, Estover Road, Plymouth PL6 7PY, United Kingdom.

Customer services email: cservs@plymbridge.com
Editorial email: publisher@internet-handbooks.co.uk
Series web site: http://www.internet-handbooks.co.uk

All rights reserved. No part of this work may be reproduced or stored in an information retrieval system without the express permission of the Publishers given in writing.

Brendan Murphy has asserted his moral right to be identified as the author of this work.

Note: The contents of this book are offered for the purposes of general guidance only and no liability can be accepted for any loss or expense incurred as a result of relying in particular circumstances on statements made in this book. Readers are advised to check the current position with the appropriate authorities before entering into personal arrangements.

Case studies in this book are entirely fictional and any resemblance to real persons or organisations is entirely coincidental.

Produced for Internet Handbooks by Deer Park Productions.

Typeset by PDQ Typesetting, Newcastle-under-Lyme

Printed and bound by The Cromwell Press Ltd, Trowbridge, Wiltshire.

Contents

List of illustrations		8
Preface		9

Part One: information and guidance for job seekers

1	**Internet basics**		**11**
	How it all began		12
	The world wide web		13
	Internet service providers		15
	What it costs to be online		16
	Which ISP?		17
	ISPs and cybercafés		18
	Browsers		19
	Searching for information		21
	Search engines		22
	Explorer or Navigator?		25
2	**Contacting employers by email**		**26**
	What is email?		27
	Creating effective emails		28
	Making and sending copy emails		29
	Avoiding pitfalls		30
	Reading your email		31
	Storing email		33
	Points to ponder		34
3	**Your online CV**		**35**
	Finding CV sites		36
	Emailing your CV		38
	Attaching a CV to email		39
	Automated CV selection		41
	Checklist		42
4	**Home pages for job hunters**		**43**
	Creating HTML documents		44
	Using HTML tags		45
	Testing HTML in a browser		46
	Uploading a document		47
	Expanding your CV		48
	Forms		49
	Web creation resources		50
	Netscape page composer		52
	Talking points		53

Contents

5	**Choosing a career online**	55
	Starting points	57
	Careers services	58
	Bookmarking interesting web sites	59
	Further and higher education	60
	UCAS	61
	UK academic sites	62
	Postgraduate education	63
	The Open University online	64
6	**Finding out about jobs online**	65
	CareerMosaic	67
	Email job opportunities	68
	Questions	70
7	**Exploring employers online**	71
	Employment agencies online	73
	Job sites on the internet	75
	Jobs in IT	76
8	**Newsgroups for job seekers**	79
	Newsgroup names	80
	Accessing newsgroups	81
	Using your browser to access newsgroups	82
	Joining a newsgroup	83
	Accessing newsgroups via your browser	84
	Newsgroups for job seekers	86
	Examples	87
	It's OK to lurk	88
9	**Checklists for getting that job**	89
	Composing a covering letter	90
	Approaching an interview	91
	Interview checklist	92
	After the interview	93
	Points to think about	94

Part Two: key web sites for job hunters   95

10	**Top job sites and careers services on the internet**	95
11	**Top UK employers on the internet**	124
12	**Recruitment agencies on the internet**	135
13	**Overseas jobs pages**	153
14	**UK examination boards on the internet**	185

Contents

15	UK professional bodies on the internet	187
16	UK educational and professional bodies	193
17	Internet newsgroups for job seekers	195

Glossary of internet terms   199

Further reading   205

Index   207

Illustrations

Figure	Page
1. The information superhighway	12
2. The home page of Number 10	14
3. America On-Line's log-in page	15
4. The main menu of AOL	16
5. Netscape's home page	19
6. Microsoft's home page	20
7. The AltaVista search engine	21
8. Excite home page	21
9. Infoseek's home page	22
10. The Lycos home page	23
11. Webcrawler's home page	23
12. The Yahoo! home page	24
13. Sending an email	28
14. AOL: 'You have post'	31
15. An email message	32
16. Email folders	33
17. AOL's 'personal filing cabinet'	33
18. Sample CV site	36
19. TAPS	37
20. Monsterboard	38
21. Sending email attachments	39
22. Composing an email	40
23. HTML file in a browser	46
24. Uploading your pages	47
25. An HTML form page	49
26. Netscape HTML form	49
27. HotDog	50
28. HTML Writer	51
29. Microsoft FrontPage	51
30a. Netscape's HTML Writer	52
30b. Netscape Page Composer	53

Figure	Page
31. Career Builder Network	56
32. Career Mosaic	56
33. Plan It	57
34. Prospects Web	58
35. UCAS Admissions Service	61
36. Clickable UK university maps	62
37. AGCAS Occupational Profiles	66
38. CareerMosaic's jobs database	67
39. CareerMosaic International	69
40. Job Hunter	72
41. Jobsite	73
42. Monster Board	74
43. Taps.com	75
44. JobServe	77
45. Accessing newsgroups using Netscape browser	78
46. Messages in a newsgroup	80
47. AOL newsgroup page	82
48. Viewing a list of newsgroups	83
49. Messages in a newsgroup	84
50. BP home page	126
51. Cadburys	127
52. Disney recruitment page	128
53. Railtrack's home page	131
54. The Austin Knight home page	137
55. M&M Recruitment	147
56. Young Scientist	152
57. VSO	183
58. Royal Society of Arts	185
59. The ACCA	188
60. The British Computer Society	189

Preface

Just about three years ago I started to think about the internet. In my first couple of months of surfing the net I felt that, although it was fun, it didn't really serve any particular useful purpose. I've come a long way since those early days and I now conduct lots of personal, educational and business communications via the internet. Put simply, the internet has revolutionised the way that I conduct both my business and private life. From ordering CDs, browsing home shopping pages, having computer programming queries answered from a Canadian help-line, through to communicating weekly with a friend in Australia, the internet has become a truly indispensable tool. More recently, I couldn't help but be impressed with the number of online resources available to those looking for a change of job or career. Indeed, since signing up with a number of computing employment agencies on the internet, I've realised the amount of jobs that are available on a daily basis from this new source of opportunity.

In this book I'll hopefully pass on to you some of the enthusiasm that I have for the employment resources and educational opportunities that are available, ensuring that your usage of the many job-related services available is both rewarding and fun.

Hopefully I've organised my book in a nice easy to follow way, allowing you to get the most out of it in the shortest space of time.

At this point it's probably worthwhile clearing up a little bit of confusion. With the increased usage of the internet for academic, business and personal use, the terms used are becoming mixed up. As far as you are concerned the 'internet', 'net', 'world-wide-web' and 'web' should be considered synonymous.

The first part of the book contains a very brief history of the internet as well as describing the browsers that you need for job searching. This section is followed by a look at the creation of an effective electronic mail message to professional recruiters. Just as the letter of application or the telephone call is the first moment of contact traditionally used with a prospective employer, so the first email is the first point of contact on the internet.

The following sections then cover key areas of employment and career opportunity. By addressing the needs of all types of job seekers, a compendium of online sources will be introduced. Near the end of the book some useful advice is given to the basics of applying for and securing a job – still every bit as important on the internet as they are in conventional situations. The book includes a large section of internet sites for job seekers, as well as a glossary of internet terms for the nerdy.

Preface

Throughout this text there are numerous references to company uniform resource locators (URLs). The nature of internet page design is such that changes in design and layout will be inevitable. In some extreme cases companies may change the server where their site is held necessitating a complete change of URL. This could mean that some of the pages listed, although existing when the book was printed, may no longer do so. In normal situations you will be able to find the pages that you are looking for by dropping off the last part of the URL, the part referring to a particular file. For example:

http://www.somecompany.com/index.htm

becomes

http://www.somecompany.com/

If this proves unsuccessful then use your favourite search engine to look for the missing site.

As a committed internet user and an author who loves to know the views of his readers then I hope that you'll begin communicating with me online. My email address for correspondence is

BrendanEd@aol.com

Those that use this service will become part of an élite group of readers to whom I'll gladly send any interesting internet stuff that I come across during my technological travels.

I hope that you have fun with this book and have success in using the internet for job hunting. Good luck!

Brendan Murphy

1 Internet Basics

In this chapter you will discover:

▶ *the importance of the internet*
▶ *the history of the internet and the world-wide web*
▶ *what an Internet Service Provider (ISP) does*
▶ *how to choose an ISP*
▶ *what a browser does*
▶ *how to search for information on the internet.*

Why is the internet so important?

The rise in usage of the internet over the last two or three years has been explosive. Whilst it is very difficult to quote definitive statistics, recent figures suggest that there are over 40 million users world-wide, a figure said to be growing at a rate of one million per month. From hobbyists, educationists, through to business users, the internet is fast becoming a form of modern-day communication that has some relevance for just about everybody.

Getting access

Access is world-wide, inexpensive, visual, and instant.

All you need is a:

▷ standard PC or Apple computer
▷ modem
▷ telephone line

and away you go. The neat thing about the internet is that everyone can have their say or publish some pages of information. You don't have to be a big business, or a large college or university. Anyone can have the same presence as the big boys – and it's all done from your home computer.

Using the internet for a purpose

If you've used the internet for any reasons you can't help but notice the number of business transactions that are now being carried out online. These range from home shopping for books or music CDs through flight reservations to the transfer of huge business-to-business funds – the rise in transactions has been dramatic. In 1997 their total value was estimated at just under $10 billion. In 1998 it was forecast to turn out at $100 billion – and could multiply tenfold again in the next two years.

Another important and ever-growing usage of the internet is by

How it all began

employers looking to recruit staff, or those looking for a particular job or career (which, as you are reading this book, probably includes you!) The internet provides a powerful means of matching those who want a job with those who are offering them.

With sophisticated programming routines hidden behind user-friendly pages, the internet provides a very focused method of looking for, and securing, a job. No more waiting for the phone to ring, or the letterbox to rattle. You can now take the initiative. You can 'surf the net' (browse potentially millions of web pages) to make sure you get the job that you want. For job seekers the internet is the greatest personal marketing tool available, something that you'll come to discover in more detail in this book.

Explaining the history of the internet

Many people are confused as to exactly what the internet is. The internet is not one thing in one place, any more for example than the printed word is one thing in one place. It literally means the world-wide network of computers all connected up by telephone lines and satellite links. This network includes your own PC, if it is connected for example, via a modem. Being connected by a common method allows everyone ease of access both for visual and voice communication, and for sending or receiving data of every kind.

The internet covers all four corners of the world and can therefore be considered truly global. Conjuring up visions of fast cars heading off down the freeway, the internet is also known as the 'information superhighway' and you'll soon see why this name fits so well.

But where did it all begin? Well, back in 1969, at the height of the Cold

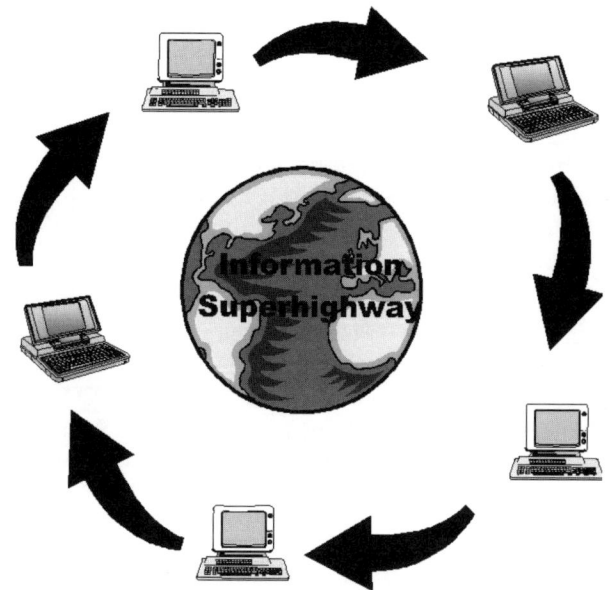

Fig. 1. The information superhighway. The internet refers to all those millions of computers linked together so they can receive and send all kinds of messages and files to each other. As soon as you link your PC to an internet service provider, you too are part of the internet.

The world wide web

War, the American Department of Defense devised a system whereby communication could still take place through the telephone network across the USA even if a nuclear attack disrupted the telephone system. This system was called ARPANet, or Advanced Research Projects Agency Network. It is generally considered to have been the birth of the internet and had taken around ten years to develop.

Although today's internet is highly sophisticated, this first version simply saw messages between two computers find their way through the telephone lines, trying different routes should some not be available, until they reached their destination. The foundations of this system saw the basic technology develop. The standard protocol is still used today to allow us access to the network. In case you are interested it is called TCP/IP (transport control protocol/internet protocol). But don't worry – you don't need to know about the technology!

Development soon followed, and by the mid 1970s the internet was becoming big in universities and research institutions, giving academics a great means of sharing research information. Things sailed along pretty much happily over the coming years until around 1980, when control of this network was taken over by the Internet Architecture Board (IAB).

In 1989, the internet was to change forever. In the CERN laboratories in Switzerland, a group of researchers came up with the World Wide Web. Today control of internet technology rests with a number of organisations all with impressive titles. To the average internet user however, it belongs in practice to you. You can use it to communicate effectively, you can publish on it, and you can transact a fair amount of your daily business on it. So in practical terms you are as much in control of it as anybody else!

The world wide web

The world wide web (WWW, or web, for short), was developed so that physicists world-wide could communicate easily on the internet using simple hypertext access to information sources. Over the following years, this concept evolved – often to the dismay of the stuffy academics – to produce jazzy-looking documents that included sound and even video.

Hypertext links

Hypertext documents allow users to click on **hotspots** on the screen; these hotspots commonly take the form of a word or picture. Clicking on them lets you access further detail regarding the information identified by the word or represented by the picture. This method of usage can be thought of as 'drill down'. By simple mouse clicking a subject is expanded and extended, on each click. Where this method of access leads to different documents then it's known as hyperlinks.

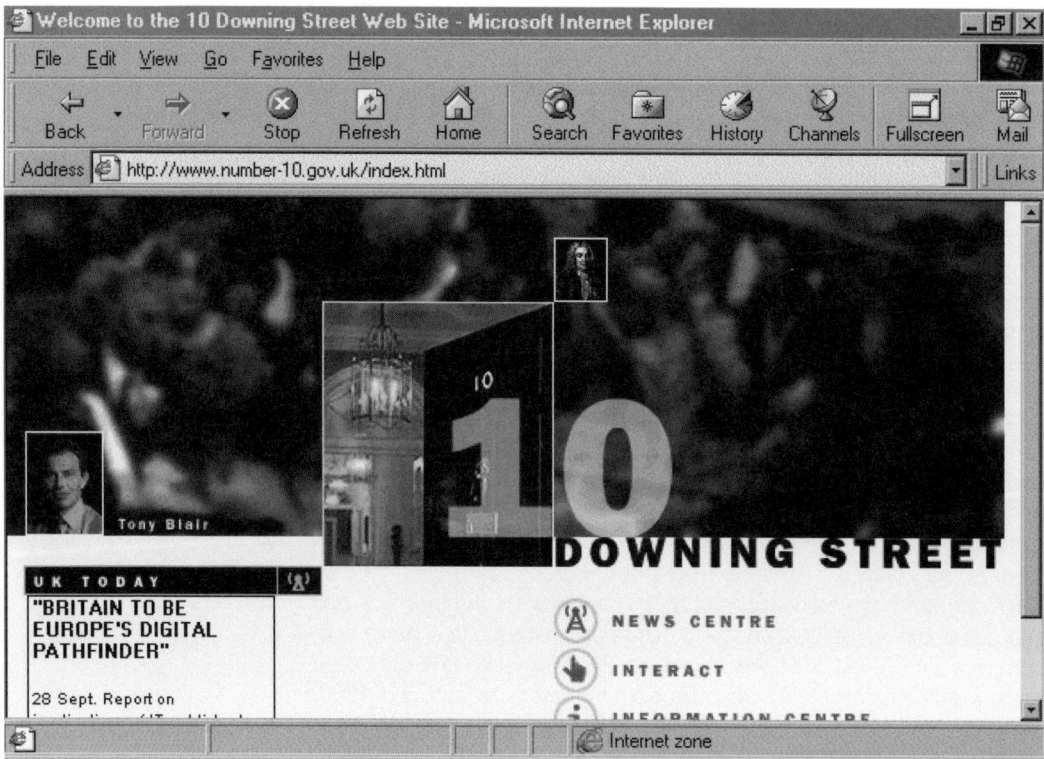

Fig. 2. The home page of Number 10 Downing Street, London.

Figure 2 shows the home page details for number 10 Downing Street, the home of the British Prime Minister.

If you click with your mouse on the 'Inside No. 10' icon, you will be invited to enter a further page of details relating to the British political system. If you've got a **browser** to hand, have a try looking at this site now.

Understanding HTML

Web documents are known as 'pages'. 'Home page' is the term used to describe the first page of details, usually an index or advertisement, that companies or individuals have on the web. This home page is rather akin to the cover and first few pages of a book. All the pages that you see whilst browsing the web are known as hypertext mark-up language, or HTML, pages.

HTML is nothing more than a very easy programming language that works on the basis of **tags**. In essence, an HTML document is just a fancy word-processed document. Indeed you could create a very simple HTML document on your own word-processor in a matter of minutes!

The following example illustrates the point:

```
<HTML>
<B>This is an example of an HTML file.</B>
</HTML>
```

Internet service providers

The **tags** – the instructions shown inside the angle brackets – all have special meanings. For example, each document must start with the <HTML> tag, and finish with the </HTML> tag. In the example shown, the <B> tag turns on bold typeface, whilst the </B> simply turns it off again. Simple!

Questions and answers

Where and when did the internet originate?

The internet originated in the USA in the late 1960s and its original purpose was to allow telecommunication of messages throughout the USA even in the event of a nuclear attack.

What is the WWW?

The WWW is the World Wide Web and is the user-friendly face of the internet accessed via personal computers.

Discussion points

1. Do you think that the rise in use of the internet for business purposes will continue to grow dramatically, or do you think it is all exaggerated?

2. What sort of problems could result from increased reliance on the internet by people whether at home or at work?

Internet service providers

An Internet Service Provider (ISP) is simply a commercial organisation that sells people access to the internet. So, just as you choose a telephone provider that you believe will offer the best service to meet

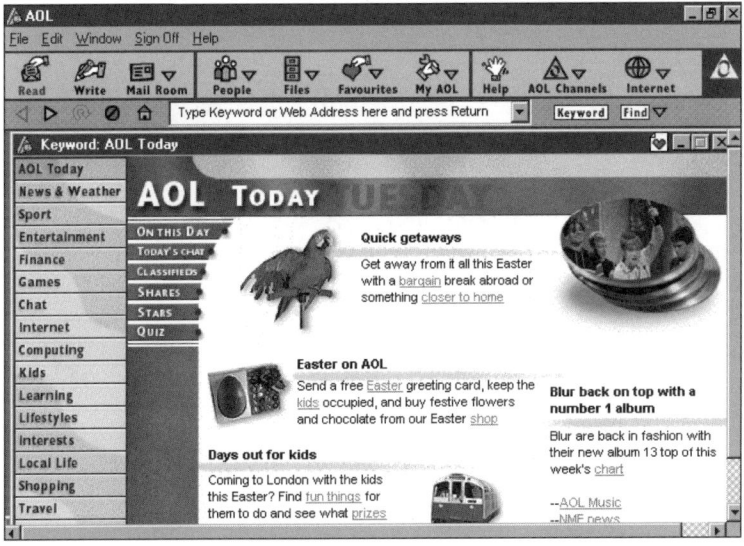

Fig. 3. The main menu page of America Online, familiar to millions of AOL subscribers. A new-look design was introduced in 1999.

What it costs to be online

your particular needs, so you choose an ISP that does the same. When you buy into an ISP, you normally get:

▷ some software (diskette, or nowadays usually a CD Rom)

▷ a user identification (which you can probably choose yourself)

▷ a password that allows you to sign-up and access the internet (log on).

Recently, ISPs have also begun to offer high-speed modems at very affordable prices, so as to provide a complete internet start-up kit for people without a modem in their PC.

What it costs to access the internet

It's also common for ISPs to offer a 'try before you buy' option. This normally gives you either a free trial period, usually one calendar month, or a number of free hours (say 50), to let you try out their services. A word of caution: to get your free trial you'll have to give your credit or debit card details, and after the free period has expired your bank account will continue to be charged unless you specifically cancel the agreement.

ISPs usually operate by charging a monthly subscription. This typically includes:

▷ a certain number of free hours access to the internet

▷ usually between three and ten separate email addresses

▷ some free web space for when you are ready to create your own web pages

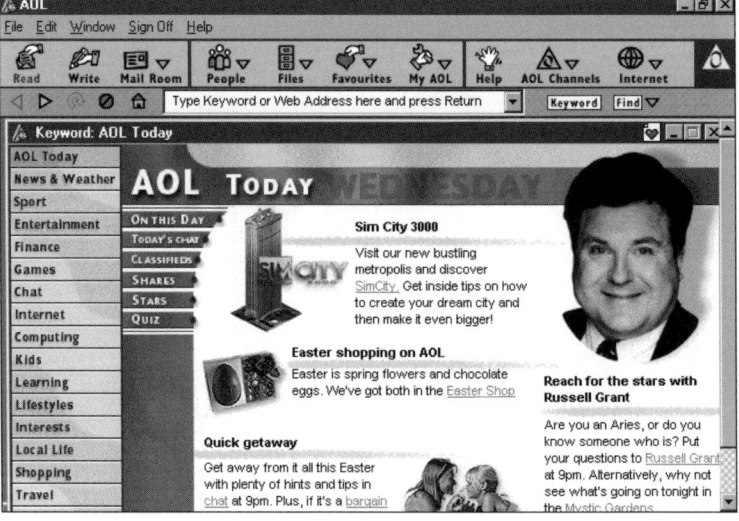

Fig. 4. The main menu page of America Online as used by millions of subscribers. The design was changed in 1999, giving a more businesslike appearance.

Which ISP?

▷ a telephone helpline

▷ a number of other 'unique' services on their own private network, such as weather reports, news updates and specialist interest areas for children and adults. Indeed some ISPs offer so many private services that you can often meet all your needs by simply surfing in these areas!

Should your monthly usage of the internet be higher that the agreed package, there will be a surcharge to be paid. Access to some restricted areas may also incur charges. As the number of ISPs have risen, so the competition has become more fierce and now, you can almost certainly have a perfectly suitable package for between £5 and £10 per month. Some ISPs are now offering free access!

Your checklist for choosing an ISP

▷ ensure that there is a standard monthly charge

▷ find out what's included in this charge

▷ check whether there is a set up charge (usually not)

▷ ensure that your access will be charged at local phone call rates

▷ check out the free web space provided (allowing you to create HTML pages) – typically it is 3 to 15 megabytes and this is generally quite ample

▷ ensure that you have enough email addresses included (e.g. one per person)

▷ make sure it comes with a browser (e.g. Netscape, or Internet Explorer)

▷ make sure that a fast access speed is available for your modem (e.g. 56K)

▷ ensure adequate support is provided (especially telephone support)

▷ find out what value added services are provided.

Major ISPs in the United Kingdom

Here are the home page addresses for the major ISPs in the United Kingdom:

America OnLine (AOL)
http://www.aol.com
Welcome to one of the internet biggies. AOL offers you up to five individual email addresses which could prove useful should you want to distinguish between, for example, private and business mail. AOL provides a number of interesting value added services. The monthly rate is competitive if you only plan to use it a few hours a month, but relatively expensive for 24 hour a day access.

ISPs and Cybercafés

Compuserve
http://www.compuserve.com
Another biggie. Compuserve has some great forums where information on every conceivable subject is available. Rates are comparable to AOL, with which the company is now associated.

Demon
http://www.demon.net
No longer an independent company, the UK's first internet service provider still offers some great sign-up deals. But there is an extra set-up fee for some facilities such as newsgroups. There is a telephone helpline.

Freeserve
http://www.freeserve.net
Now the UK's biggest internet service provider.

Line One
http://www.lineone.net
Administered by British Telecom, Line One is a new kid on the block, but has already received rave reviews. Offers very competitive monthly packages for personal use.

Microsoft Network (MSN)
http://www.msn.com
MSN, developed by Microsoft, offers all the development and support that comes with being a product of the world's biggest computer company.

UUNet
http://www.uunet.pipex.com
Another biggie in terms of ISPs, with extra email accounts as standard.

VirginNet
http://www.virgin.net/
Any product developed by Virgin is sure to be geared towards great customer service and value for money. There is an excellent 24 hour helpline.

Cybercafés

Apart from ISPs you can also access the internet through visiting a cybercafé or internet café. Just as the names suggest, these are indeed cafés that offer internet access along with a cup of coffee and a bun! Many bookstores are now offering internet access and again this may be an option for those who do not have access to a personal computer. In fact, using the internet in a specialist centre is often very relaxing and sociable, turning on its head the frequently quoted anti-social nature of internet use. Some smaller locally based companies also act as ISPs. However, they don't generally offer any value added services. These centres can sometimes offer faster internet access speeds, as they have fewer users.

Browsers

▷ *Caution* – when using a small company, should they go bust you could find yourself not only having to hook up with a new ISP but your email address may also have to change causing some confusion to those friends and organisations who may have your details held on their address book files.

Discussion points

The number of ISPs providing services that enable you to access the internet is increasing rapidly. Due to the highly competitive nature of this market, do you think that there is merit in waiting until the monthly access price reduces to a remarkably low rate before joining, or do you think that it's better choose an ISP, sign up, choose your email addresses and commit yourself to them for the forseeable future?

Browsers

You could think of a browser as a mini telephone system.

▷ You've got your phone (your PC).
▷ You know the number of the person or organisation with whom you want to talk (their address or URL – **Uniform Resource Locator**).

You just need some means of dialling them up (the browser software). Connect all the bits together and there you have it, instant access to a world of information. Shown in Figures 5 and 6 are the common entry screens that you'll find with both Netscape Navigator and Microsoft Internet Explorer, the most widely used web browsers.

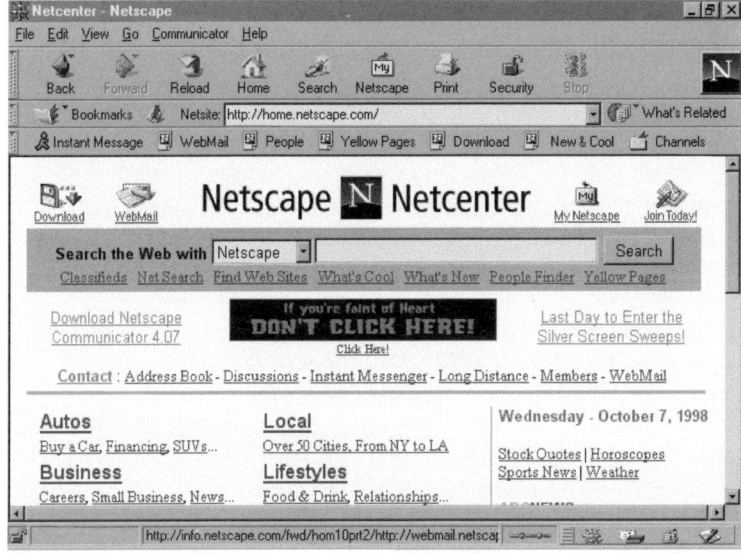

Fig. 5. Netscape Navigator. The illustration shows what the Netscape browser looks like. It also shows the Netscape home page in the browser window.

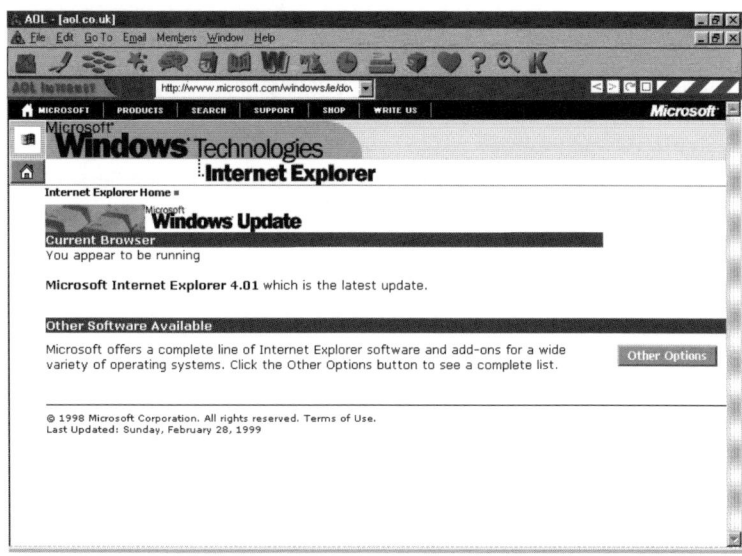

Fig. 6. Microsoft's browser, Internet Explorer. This has now become as widely used as Netscape, largely because Microsoft have persuaded so many PC manufacturers to load it on all their new machines. This has led to a big anti-trust case against Microsoft in the USA.

Choosing your browser

You don't really have to worry about purchasing browser software. The ISP you join will normally provide all the browser software you need to access the internet.

The only time that you might choose browser software is if you had some personal reason for favouring a particular product, or perhaps obtaining a more recent version. It's fair to say that Microsoft have the lion's share of the market, so you're most likely to come across Internet Explorer. But Netscape Navigator – its great rival – is just as good, and many people think has better features. But for the beginner, it really does not matter too much which you have.

Searching for information on the internet

The web has literally millions and millions of pages of useful information (and some not so useful). To remember the URLs – addresses – of all the pages that you want to access would be like memorising a telephone directory. Impossible!

Never fear, all those geeks at the many software companies that write programs for the web have provided an array of tools (**search engines**) that let you look for just about anything.

All the search engines are free, and they operate in a similar way. You type in a keyword, for example 'jobs'. This keyword is then taken by the search engine and all the associated pages containing the keyword in their description are then displayed on your screen (if there are thousands, as there can be, the pages are displayed a few at a time). The process usually takes a matter of seconds.

Let's have a look at some of the more common search engines.

Searching for information

AltaVista
http://www.altavista.digital.com/
AltaVista, from the Digital Corporation, will probably return the most pages from the keyword(s) that you enter. The main screen, shown in Figure 7, allows you to enter the term that you wish to search on, choose whether to search on the complete web or only certain sites, and choose the language to be searched on (so choosing 'English' will return only those web pages composed in English – great for filtering unnecessary pages).

Fig. 7. The AltaVista home page.

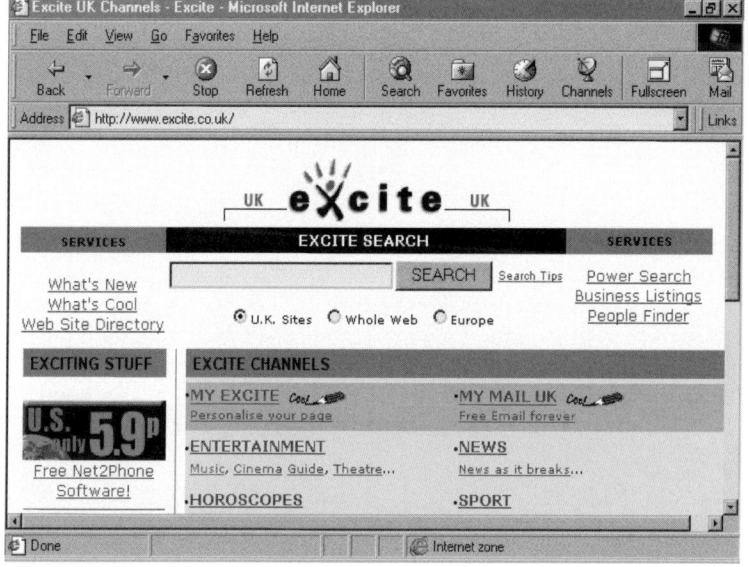

Fig. 8. Excite home page.

Search engines

Excite
http://www.excite.co.uk/
Excite does all the same things as the other search engines. You type in a keyword, choose where to search, click and away you go. However, Excite goes a little bit further – it looks for pages that are closely linked to the keywords that you enter. For example, if you enter the keywords 'secretarial recruitment', Excite recognises the link between secretarial and secretary and will provide details of pages associated with secretary and secretaries as well as the requested pages associated with 'secretarial recruitment.'

Infoseek
http://www.infoseek.co.uk/
Using Infoseek is a piece of cake. By simply entering suitable keywords Infoseek trundles off and returns the pages that you are looking for, simple! Infoseek also marks over 500,000 web sites, designating them as 'Infoseek Select Sites', these sites being, in the opinion of Infoseek, particularly interesting.

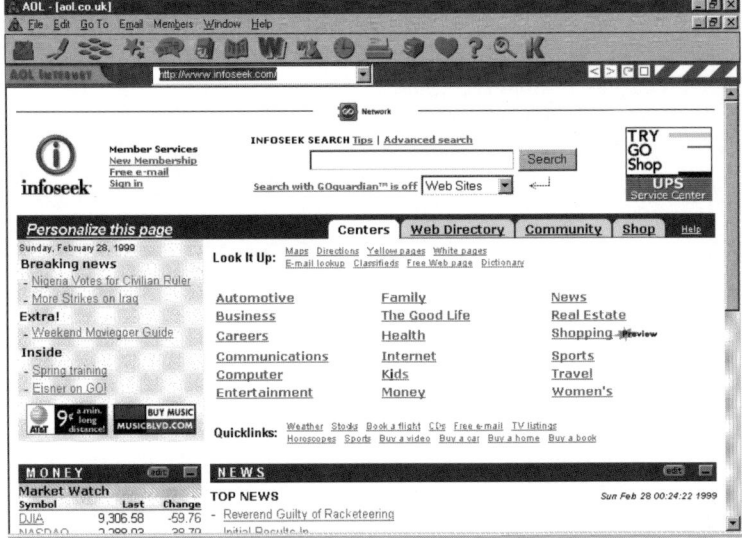

Fig. 9. Infoseek's home page.

Lycos
http://www.lycos.com/
With the Lycos search engine you enter your keyword(s), then you can choose where to look for it. Lycos is particularly easy to use. It has a useful utility that allows you to click on whether you want to find documents containing all of your keywords, or documents that contain any of your keywords. See Figure 10, the Lycos home page.

Fig. 10. The Lycos home page.

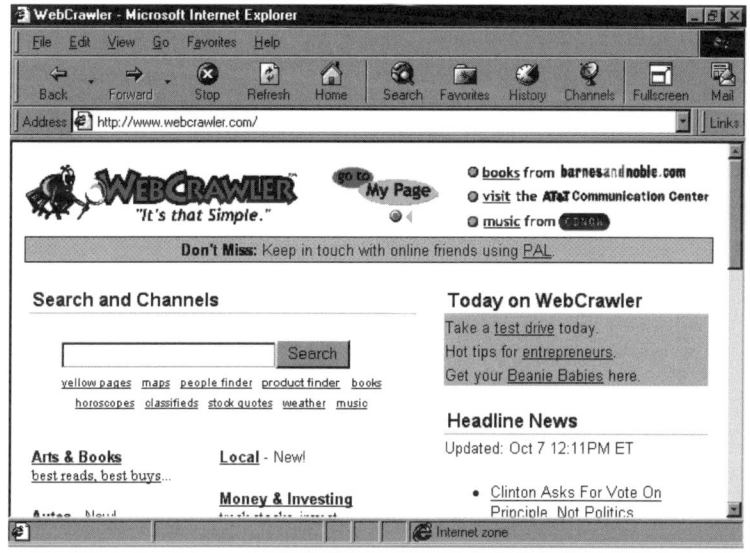

Fig. 11. Webcrawler's home page.

Webcrawler
http://www.webcrawler.com/
Webcrawler uses 'natural language searching'. This allows you to key in just what you are looking for, without having to learn any of the more annoying little tricks required to search any more than one word in other search engines.

Fig. 12. The Yahoo! home page.

Yahoo!
http://www.yahoo.com/
The enormous and hugely popular Yahoo! database has four main categories which it searches through upon entry of a keyword. Documents are then displayed in order of relevance. Yahoo! also has a 'yellow pages' option that allows you to easily locate business user home pages.

Give it a try!

The above explanation can only touch the surface of using search engines. They really are amazingly powerful. The only way to understand what each can do for you is to jump in to their home pages and have a look. Try typing in some of these key words and phrases, for example:

> recruitment
> jobs
> careers
> vacancies
> employment
> secretarial jobs Scotland
> law graduates London
> business training USA.

You will be amazed at the enormous amount of information searches like these will trigger.

Explorer or Navigator?

Questions and answers

Why do you need a browser?
A browser is a piece of software which allows you to access world-wide web pages and retrieve useful information. A browser is essential. Without one, you could not access the internet.

Which browser is better – Netscape Navigator or Internet Explorer?
The two browsers are broadly similar in layout and functions. Both have tool bars across the top of the screen and many of the features are much the same. For example you can type in the URL of a web page you wish to view, save ('bookmark') your favourite pages, search the internet, view a history of the pages you have visited, click back or forward, adjust some of the settings, and so on. Netscape have been around the longest and cornered the market early on. Microsoft, however, have been very successful, largely through shipping a copy of Internet Explorer with every copy of their Windows 95, Windows 98 and Office 97 products.

2 Contacting employers by email

In this chapter you will discover:

▶ *the importance of electronic mail*
▶ *what an email address consists of*
▶ *tips for creating effective emails*
▶ *how to read and store your email.*

....

The importance of electronic mail

Email is short for electronic mail. When using the internet, electronic mail is definitely the 'killer application.' It really has been the lifeblood of internet usage. You can think of an email as an electronic letter, and your PC as a post-box, just like the one on the front door of your home. Instead of simply receiving mail, you can also use it to send mail.

Today, more than 100 million emails a day are crossing over the internet. Emails are used by almost every kind of person and organisation imaginable, and transmitted in many different languages.

It is important to appreciate that email is not quite as private as some people imagine. Your email may be visible to:

▷ your internet service provider
▷ any computer through which it passes during its journey across the internet
▷ hackers
▷ your employer (if you are using a computer at work)
▷ your school, college or university authorities (if you are using an educational computer)
▷ anyone with whom you share a computer
▷ governments (including the UK and USA) who with very little public awareness have begun to conduct massive internet surveillance.

> **Hot Topic**
>
> Police authorities in many countries including the UK are pressing for new laws to enable them to read all emails at will. Do you agree they should have this power?

You can make emails secure using various popular forms of **encryption** such as **PGP**, which is legal in the UK and most developed countries. PGP ('Pretty Good Privacy') has been developed by a prominent American mathematician who has made it freely available worldwide in support of people's rights to privacy on the internet. It is quite simple to use, and involves a private key and a public key (the keys are automatically generated encryption codes). Few people as yet use encryption, and the topic is outside the scope of this particular book. To find out more, do a search in Yahoo! or another search engine or directory, using the key words 'encryption' or 'PGP'.

What is email?

What an email address consists of

Each individual who uses email has a unique ID which identifies him or her on the internet. Email addresses follow a certain general pattern. They normally take this form:

> username@domainname

The next line shows an example. Let's imagine the person's name is Frank Hughes:

> HughesF@cbridge.ac.uk

1. In the example, Frank chooses the form 'HughesF' as his **user name**. Alternatively he might choose some other variant such as:

   > frank-hughes
   > frank.h
   > FrankH

   and so on, depending on the formats allowed by his ISP.

2. The '@' symbol separates the user name from the rest of the address which identifies the provider of the web account. All email addresses include this 'at' sign.

3. The 'cbridge' is the name of the **server** (host computer) where your email account is managed from, or the name of the ISP who provides the service.

The last part of the address ('ac.uk') identifies both the organisation type and the country that the email account is managed from. So, in the above, 'ac' means that it is an academic institution and 'uk' is the two-digit country identifier, in this case, the United Kingdom.

Organisation and country identifiers

The table below shows some of the main organisation and country identifiers you see at the end of email addresses:

.ac	academic institution in the UK
.com	commercial organisation (international)
.co	commercial organisation (national, eg in the form co.uk)
.edu	educational institution
.gov	Government
.net	an internet services company
.org	public sector organisation
.uk	United Kingdom
.fr	France
.de	Germany
.hk	Hong Kong
.nl	Netherlands
.nz	New Zealand
.us	United States

Creating effective emails

Email provides a very rich source of communication. Senders take time to think out properly the message to be sent, and receivers generally study incoming mail at a time when they are ready to digest and understand it. For job seekers email is a godsend!

Tips for creating effective emails

The basic structure of an effective email is much like that of the old tried and tested memo. Emails include:

▷ sender details

▷ recipient details

▷ a subject heading (optional)

▷ lines of textual information

▷ a signature

▷ details of persons to whom the message is to be copied (although they're organised a little differently from a standard memo).

Sender details

Your recipient will automatically receive details of who has sent the email. However it's always better to include this information in the main body as it's often lost in the technical garble at the top of the message.

Fig.13. Microsoft mail message creation.

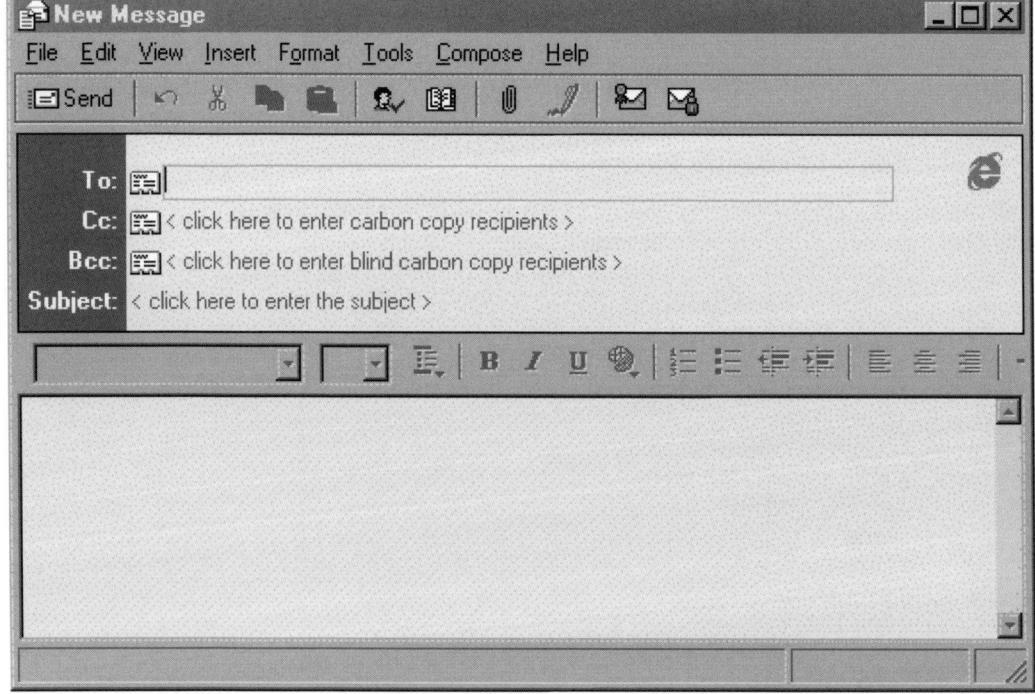

.... Making and sending copy emails

Recipient details

Here, enter the email address of the person to whom you wish to send the message. In job advertisements this will normally be shown on the advert and will take the form described in the previous section.

Making and sending copies

With most email software you can carbon copy someone ('cc'), and blind carbon copy someone ('bcc'). If you choose to 'cc' someone, then the main recipient of your message will also see the 'cc' details in the message.

When job hunting it's probably better to 'bcc' your message. This means that the 'bcc' recipient is kept hidden. The original recipient – a prospective employer, for example – will then have no knowledge that your message is being copied to anyone else.

> *Tip* – When you are job hunting, always 'bcc' your career adviser or job centre manager. It will show the efforts that you are making to secure a job (and if you are a school, college or university leaver always email your folks – just to let them know that you are taking life seriously!)

Inserting a subject line

The 'subject line' is where you summarise, in a very few words, the purpose of your email. Make this space work hard for you! Picture the scene: a large and busy employer receives more than 100 emails a day. Which ones will they choose to pay particular attention to in their screens full of information? Bet you it won't be the one that says

JOBS

or

REPLY TO ADVERT

No, they'll look at the ones that make it clear what they are concerned with, such as

APPLICATION FOR AREA MANAGER JOB REF: 0012

Message area

This is where you can really let loose – but use a nice concise, clear and simple manner. Don't ramble, just tell the employer who you are, what you want to know about their company and why you are writing. Just as large memos are tedious so are large emails. If you want to say lots - write a book! And remember, although emails are often very informal, you don't know who you are writing to, so a degree of formality is a must.

Avoiding pitfalls

Adding a signature

Some email software allows you to add a pre-stored **signature file** that gives your name, address, telephone number and similar information. This is very handy and saves typing it in each time.

Working offline

One last bit of advice – always create your emails offline. If your email software doesn't let you create messages before you dial up your modem then change your ISP – or face the cost of huge phone bills caused by unnecessary time spent typing on-line.

Checking your spelling and grammar

You may have heard the expression: 'You have only one chance to make a first impression.' It's very true. Your first chance to make an impression might be that first exploratory email into the jobs jungle – so really make it count.

Poor spelling and grammar are a real problem among job applicants today. Unfortunately most email packages lack a spell checker or thesaurus, and so the opportunity for poor English is always present. Even spell checkers have limitations. They won't usually tell you that you should have written 'then' when you mistakenly typed 'the'. As far as the spell checker is concerned, both words are correct.

> *Tip* – Get into the habit of cutting to the clipboard your email message. From there, pop it into your favourite word processing package, spell check it and generally fix it. Only when you are completely satisfied with its content and presentation should you paste it back into your email message.

Failing this it is worth spending a few pounds on a decent dictionary. You could also enlist the help of a friend, colleague or relative to scan your emails before you send them off.

Avoiding common pitfalls

The following checklist will help with emails being created to send to prospective employers:

▷ ensure that you follow the recognised format of email creation
▷ provide a clear and meaningful subject line
▷ make sure your message is clear, with the key points made at the beginning
▷ check your spelling and grammar with care
▷ use a formal but simple style of writing
▷ make sure your return address details are clear
▷ avoid the USE OF CAPITAL LETTERS – in internet mail and news messages it's the equivalent of SHOUTING and may not be appreciated.

.... **Reading your email**

A couple of other points are worthy of mention.

Netiquette

Netiquette is the name given to the rules and language commonly used to simplify and enhance messages sent via email across the internet. The symbols used in this language are called **emoticons**. They shouldn't really be used when communicating with those who are not personal friends, but it is still worth knowing the following symbols and their meanings. You decide whether to use them or not. If applying for a job within a bank, the recruitment manager would be very unlikely to appreciate them. On the other hand, if you are applying to a youth products marketing company there might occasionally be a place for them. Here are some well known examples:

```
:-)     = happy
:-)))   = very happy
:-(     = sad
:-(((   = very sad.
```

Spam

Good netiquette means you should avoid sending **spam**. Spam is the popular name given to unsolicited emails or junk email, and to sending them across the internet. So, when you are writing to a prospective employer pay them the courtesy of addressing your message to them and *only* them. The term 'spam' comes from a Monty Python sketch!

Reading your email

When you log-on to your ISP, new mail may be waiting for you. You will either get some form of audible reminder such as 'you have post', or a message similar to the one in Figure 14 will be displayed on your screen:

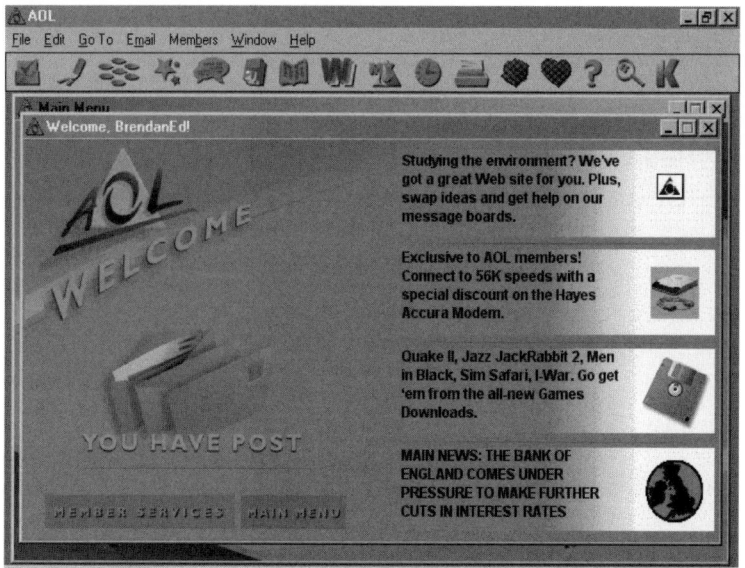

Fig. 14. The AOL mail receipt screen.

31

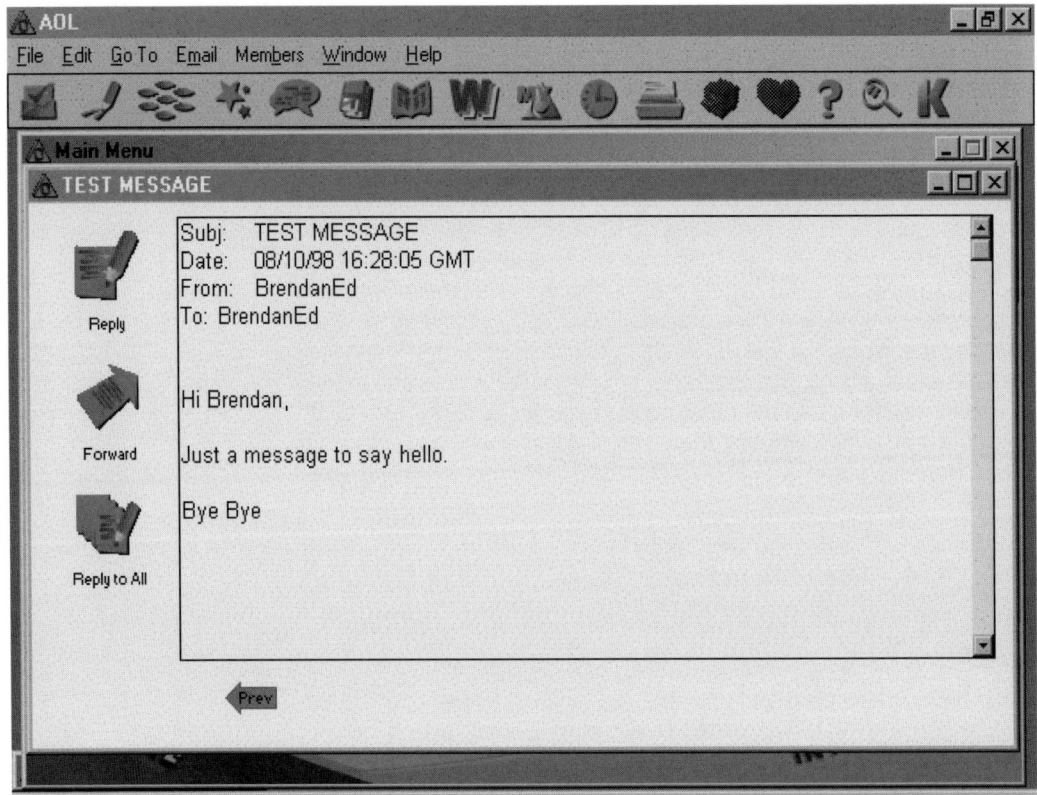

Fig. 15. Reading an email with AOL.

To read your email just double click on the message, and its contents will appear on your screen. It is as easy – if not easier – than opening a letter. If you wish to make an immediate reply then your email software will allow you to do this. You won't even have to key in the address of the person to whom you wish to send the message.

Also, don't be surprised if the reply you receive from the employer is a bit automated and impersonal. Many companies set up automatic email handling systems designed to answers email without human intervention – this inevitably leads to slightly robotic reply messages being received.

Storing your email

Your ISP will have some **electronic mailboxes** (folders) already set up for your use. You're likely to have two ready-made folders:

▷ an **out box** – to store messages you have written until you are ready to go online and send them

▷ an **in box** – to store newly delivered mail until you want to read it.

If you are planning to use your email system effectively to secure a job, then you really need to add a couple of extra areas. You can easily create a filing system much like the old filing cabinet that we all know and love.

Storing email

In the electronic world of the internet you do the same kind of thing. Most email systems will let you create folders where read email can then be stored. This way you can keep tab on who you've sent mail to, and who has replied. Shown below are two examples of filing systems that you might use.

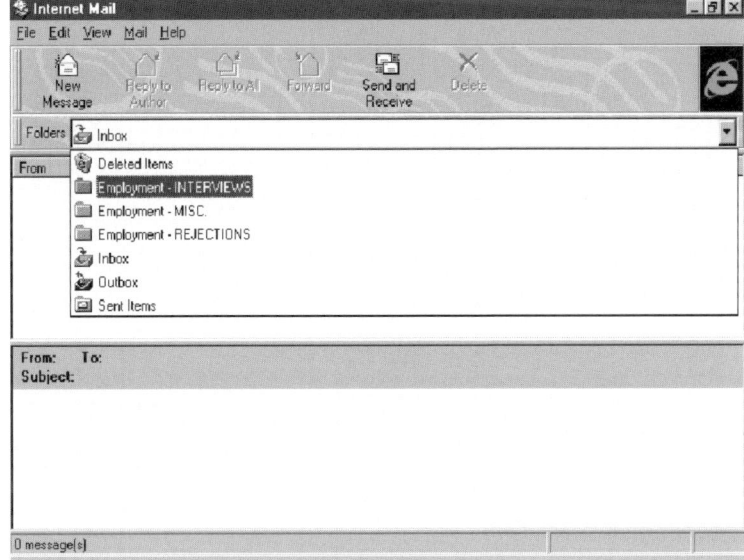

Fig.16. Microsoft Mail Folders.

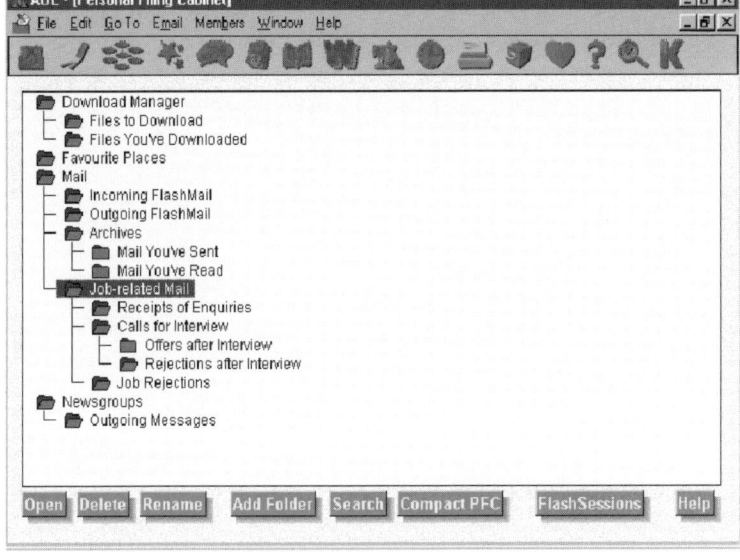

Fig.17. The AOL Personal Filing Cabinet.

33

Points to ponder

Questions and answers

What is netiquette?

Netiquette refers to the accepted etiquette you use when composing email messages. It includes various symbols (emoticons) and commonly used abbreviations. It is fine for using with friends, or when you want to be informal, but is best avoided in the serious business of job applications.

Why is it important to record your email address in the body of the messages you send?

If someone prints out your email message, there will usually be lots of irrelevant technical stuff at the top of the page. Sometimes your email address gets lost in this – better to include it to make it clearer for the recipient to reply to you.

Points to think about

1. Spelling is not everyone's favourite subject. You may be surprised to find a lack of spell checking facilities with your email software package. How will you ensure that your email messages are free from spelling errors?

2. Suppose you decide to set up an effective online filing system for your email messages. How will you go about setting this system up?

3. Is there a danger that internet users could face the same problem dealing with unsolicited email messages as is currently being experienced with postal mail?

4. An email address is much the same as a telephone number in that it uniquely identifes you. What would happen if you decide to change your ISP resulting in your email address being changed? Would this especially cause a problem if you had your email details printed on company stationery such as headed notepaper and business cards?

3 Your online CV

In this chapter you will discover:

▶ *how to create a great online CV*
▶ *how to find and use online CV-build routines*
▶ *the best way to sell yourself online.*

....

Creating a great online CV

What makes a good online CV? The answer, unfortunately, is not that simple to define. Some will say it should be very detailed; others will say it should be brief; others will say it should be somewhere in between. The actual meaning of the Latin curriculum vitae is 'the course of one's life'. Taken literally, such a document could reach many volumes. A good CV must be factually true and to the point. It must also be created with some effort as it is a document that really could change the course of your life.

For job hunting purposes, and reflecting the needs of most employers, the following sections should appear in a good CV:

Personal details – full names, date of birth, sex. Full address with postcode. Phone number with dialling code. Email address. Marital status. Nationality. In addition it should cover:

▷ education – where, and when

▷ qualifications – dates of examinations, subjects, grades or awards achieved

▷ working experience – names and addresses of employers, start and finish dates, job titles, duties, skills and experience gained

▷ additional information – major achievements, prizes, positions of responsibility held

▷ referees – two referees, at least one of whom knows you professionally.

The above information is probably best presented in a tabular form and kept to between two and three A4 size pages.

With the emergence of sophisticated desktop publishing software, there is a real temptation to present your CV as a very flashy document. Think of all those amazing fonts, background colours and special effects, and imported images. Resist this at all costs. The presentation of your CV should be kept simple, very functional and businesslike, and created using one standard font such as Arial or Times New Roman. Avoid all fancy fonts.

Finding CV sites

Have a look at the following internet site to view good examples of the kind of CVs recruiters want to see:

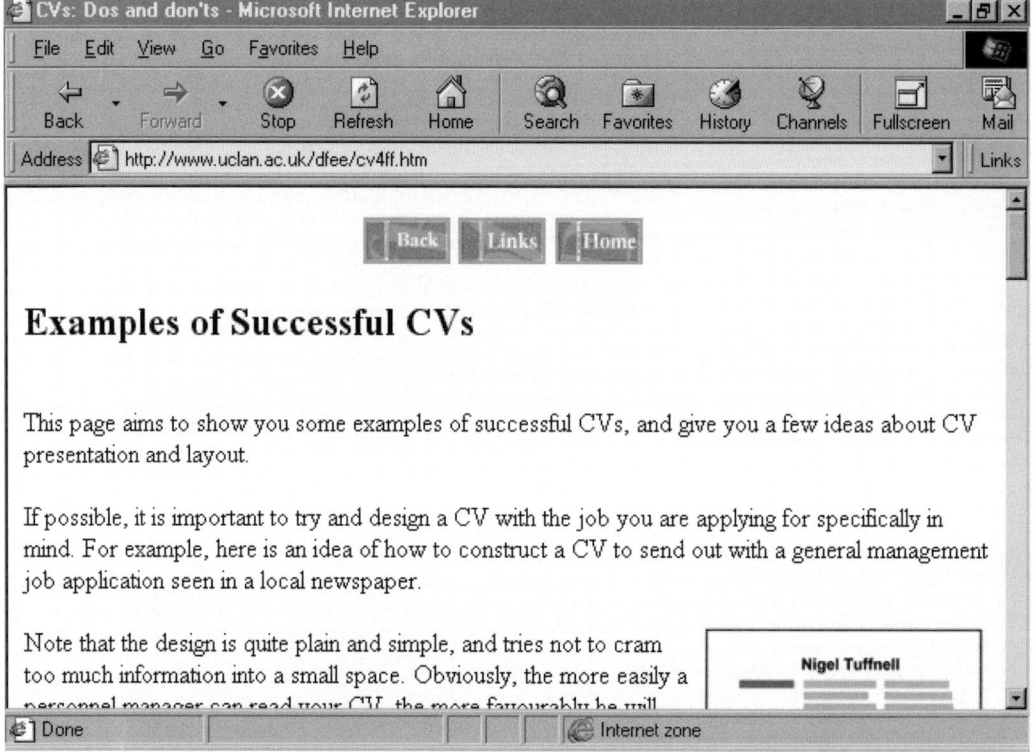

Fig. 18. Sample CV site.

Finding and using online CV-build routines

The internet has many sources for creating online CVs. Detailed below are a small number of the better sites where you can create your CV.

International Appointments
http://www.taps.com/misc/database.htm
TAPS (The Appointments Section) offers a very intuitive CV builder. There are easy to enter screens which much resemble the format of a paper CV. Once completed, your CV can then be available either within the TAPS database or externally, available for access by anyone on the internet.

JobFinder
http://www.infolive.ie/jobfinder/
For those looking for employment in Ireland, JobFinder provides a fantastic resource to create and store your CV but it does not provide open access to all CVs. This means you must sift through jobs available and choose who sees your CV. This gives you complete control over your job searching.

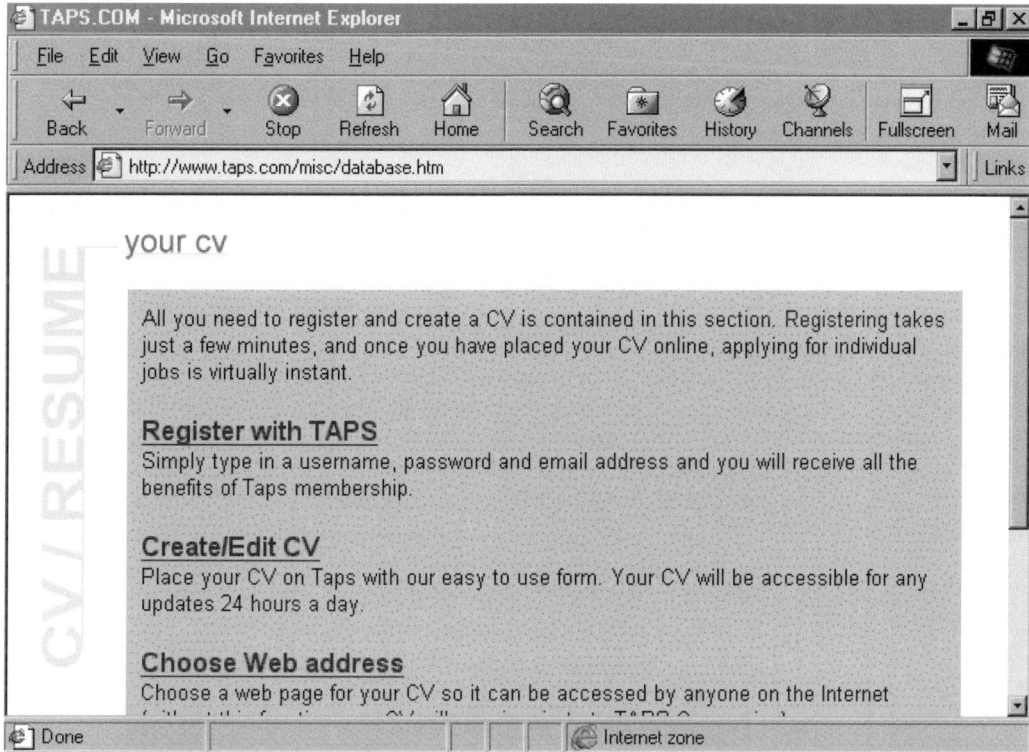

Fig. 19. The TAPS registration and CV creation page.

JobSearch
http://www.jobsearch.co.uk
JobSearch allows you to create a CV that will be available for access by prospective UK employers accessing the JobSearch database. Again, JobSearch is very easy software to use, and your CV will be created in quick time. The JobSearch system allows you to choose the employment category where you would like your CV to reside (for example Catering, Childcare) thus ensuring that employers have a reduced number of CVs to sift through.

Monster Board UK – CV Builder
http://www.monsterboard.com
Monster Board is a great source of jobs in the UK. Their CV Builder page allows you to either complete a pro-forma CV, or to submit your own by cutting and pasting. The layout of the Monster Board pro-forma CV is shown in Figure 20. Most of the other CV resource builders on the internet require the same information to be entered. Once created, your CV then gets added in 'CV City', an area where prospective employers can match skills to job requirements.

Workweb
http://www.workweb.co.uk
WorkWeb is the internet access to the 'UK Vacancy Database'. This database has been in existence for three years. It comprises a collated list of available candidates and jobs which is downloaded daily to many companies and employment-related organisations. To send your CV to WorkWeb you simply send your text document with a few simple rules and it's added to the WorkWeb database.

Emailing your CV

Points to remember when using online CV builders

▷ Ensure that there is no cost before completing your CV. Some organisations may charge fees.
▷ Look around the site and make sure that your CV isn't sold or passed on to other services without your consent.
▷ Many organisations will allow you to post a CV without divulging your name. This can avoid embarrassing situations should your current company use the service and inadvertently select your CV!
▷ Unfortunately, for each site that you choose, it is likely you will have to re-create your CV.

Emailing your CV

Another very effective way of getting your CV out to a prospective employer is to include it as part of an email. This method of sending a CV ensures that you are getting to the person you want to get to without getting caught in the electronic rush of other CVs. This method of CV management is most likely to be useful when sending your job enquiry to smaller companies which would not normally expect to receive a huge number of CVs from job applicants.

Remember – an unsolicited CV is every bit as likely to end up in the electronic garbage bin as any other piece of unwanted spam – so give careful thought to how you present it.

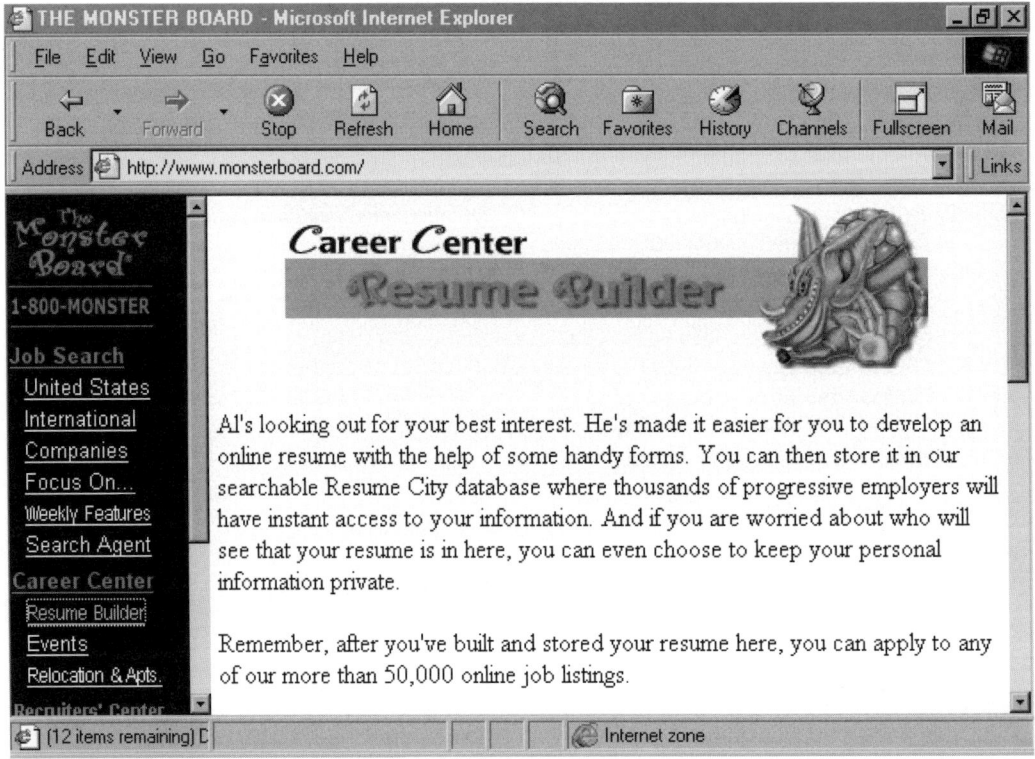

Fig. 20. The Monster Board CV Builder.

Attaching a CV to email

Creating your email-friendly CV

Well it's really quite simple. Crank up your favourite word processor and start typing! Add in all the sections mentioned earlier in this chapter. Ensure that text and fonts are kept relatively simple. That means little or no bold or italic text, and probably sticking to one basic functional font such as Arial or Times New Roman.

Once you've created your CV remember to save it carefully.

> *Tip* – do not just save your CV in your own word processor file format. Save it as a plain text or ASCII (American Standard Code for Information Interchange) file. This ensures that no matter who receives your CV they will be able to read it using a simple text editor such as Wordpad or Notebook. If you make it hard for people to read your CV they'll simply give up and move on to someone else. All word processors, in their *save* options, have a file type box which allows you to save the active document in a pre-defined format.

Attaching your CV to an email message

An **attachment** just means any file that you decide to send with your email message. This file can be a spreadsheet, a graphic file, a database or a simple text file. Indeed, you can even send sound files or video clip files as attachments.

Each type of email software has its own particular ways of attaching files to email messages. Figure 21 shows the menu item for doing this using America On-Line's email software.

Fig. 21. The AOL email attachment menu.

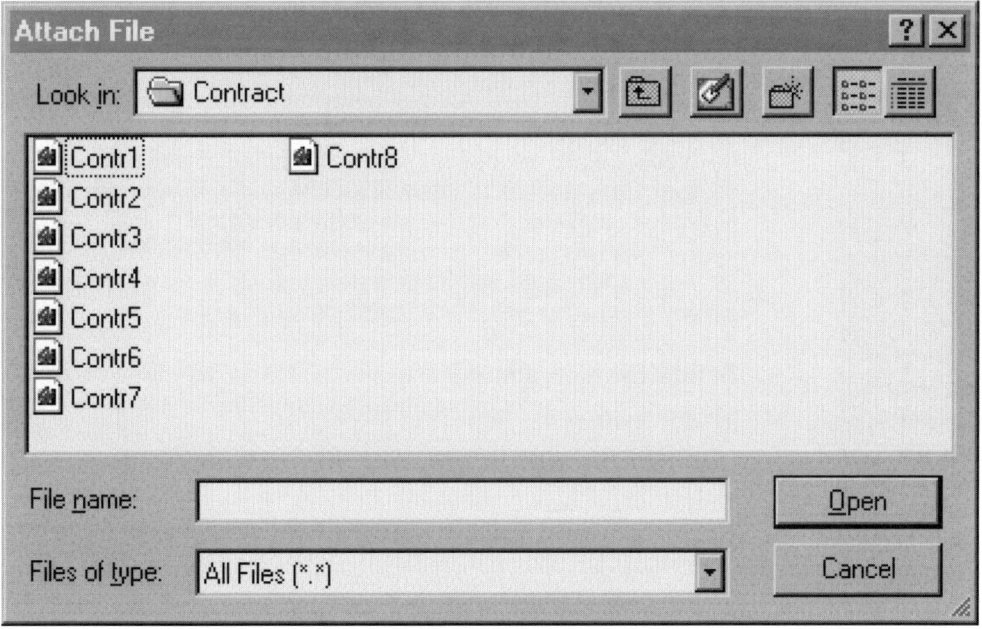

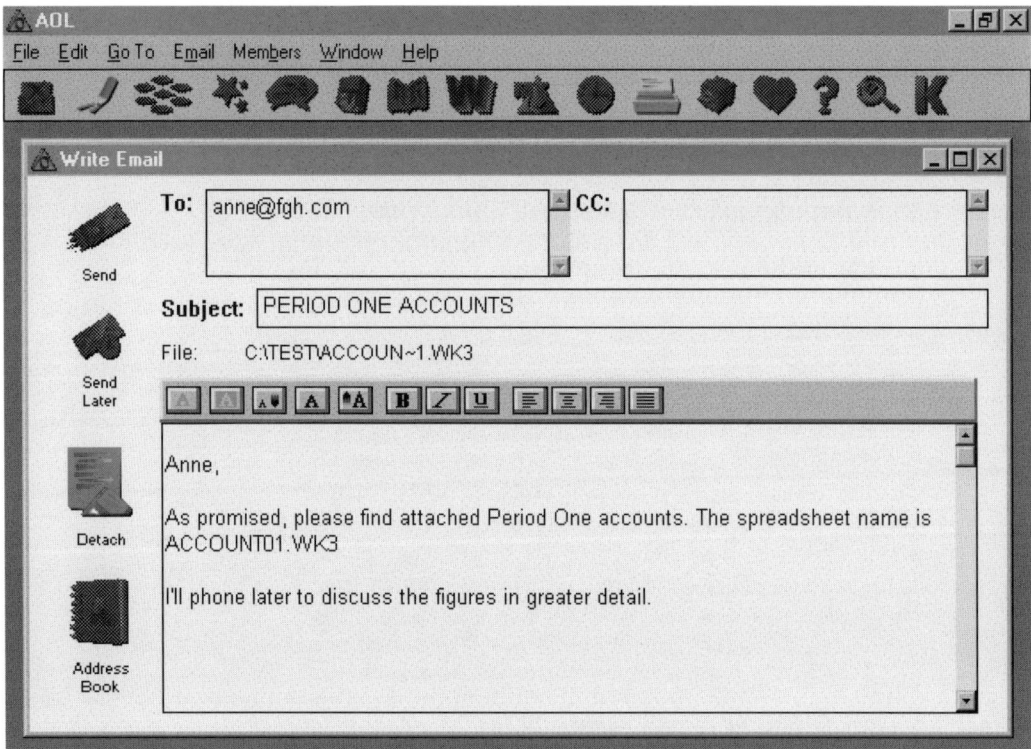

Fig. 22. The AOL email body describing the attachment.

The basic concept usually involves deciding that you do actually need to attach a file. You then simply browse (click through) the file directories on your computer until you find the one you want, such as 'myfile.txt'.

▷ *Example 1* – Gillian has just purchased some desk-top publishing software. As she is looking for a new job she's decided to put her newly found skills to use and create an all-singing, all-dancing CV. Gillian hopes to attach this CV to email messages and send it off to prospective employers. Is Gillian following a sensible route?

▷ *Example 2* – Angela has managed to build up a group of useful contacts within the personnel departments of some small to medium sized businesses. Hoping to secure employment, Angela has talked with each organisation and has arranged to send her up-to-date CV as an email message attachment.
To enure that each organisation has easy access to this file, Angela has saved her CV as a plain text file allowing access via any text-based editor or word processing package.

Points to think about

1. Should online employment agencies have the right to sell your CV details on to other companies without your agreement?

2. What are both the advantages and disadvantages in creating a CV that is detailed and that describes every educational qualification, job activity and work-based training courses that you have completed?

Automated CV selection

Selling yourself online

The important thing to remember when registering your CV with large companies or recruitment agencies on the internet is that this is becoming a very popular method of applying for a job. A large organisation may be deluged by hundreds of CVs every day, as candidates rush to use the power of the internet themselves.

Automated CV selection

An added problem which has recently emerged is the trend towards CVs being selected by computer software, rather than by human eye. When a prospective employer is looking to create a shortlist of candidates for further consideration or interview, instead of sifting through hundreds of application forms the selection is done automatically by a special computer program.

Whilst many different programs are used around the internet to do this, they generally fall into one of two categories:

1. text-based systems
2. artificial intelligence systems.

In text-based systems, the computer program searches all the CVs for pre-defined keywords. It then grades and sorts the CVs according to a number of categories. This means for example that any misspelt words can ensure that your CV instantly disappears into the electronic garbage bin, never to be seen by another human being.

The other method of automatic selection is by the use of artificial intelligence systems. Here, the program looks for more meaningful phrases such as 'I am a competent people manager' and proceeds to interpret them in a more detailed manner.

Your electronic CV checklist

The following checklist will help you when creating an electronic CV.

▷ Ensure that you use only standard text – no (or very little) bold, no wild type sizes, no colours, no italics, no fancy fonts.
▷ Give a detailed breakdown of your abilities and experience, concentrating on meaningful words, for example:

    Accountant *wrong . . .*
    Management Accountant *better . . .*
    Public Sector Management Accountant *excellent!*

▷ Check your spelling and grammar with great care.
▷ Have your CV checked over by an experienced friend or colleague.
▷ Avoid the use of the first person (I, me).
▷ Avoid lengthy, boring sentences. Short, factual, relevant phrases are a must!

Checklist

▷ List your qualifications and work experience chronologically, putting your most recent activities first, and concentrating on them.

▷ Show the prospective employer that you thoroughly understand the job that you are applying for, and that you know the industry.

▷ Create a few different versions of your CV, tailored to particular jobs you are applying for.

▷ Take control and sell yourself: write your own CV. Your objective is to get that job, and your CV is far too important a task to leave to someone else!

Tell me again

What is an online CV?

An online CV is one which is created online and which is available to prospective employers via the internet.

How can CV details be sent via email?

By adding your CV text file as an attachment, you can send your details direct to companies who have an email address.

The employment agency dilemma – protecting your personal data

Before signing-up with an online employment agency, Christopher feels that he should find out just who will have access to his personal information. After failing to find any relevant information on the home page of the prospective agency that he has signed up with, Christopher is unsure how he should proceed with his quest for employment. Should he take his chances and simply sign-up with the agency?

4 Home pages for job hunters

In this chapter we will explore:

▶ *the benefits of creating a job-related home page on the internet*
▶ *how to use basic HTML commands*
▶ *on-line software that can be used to help create HTML pages.*

Creating your own career page on the internet

As previously described, all pages that you come across on the internet are written in hypertext markup language, or HTML. HTML documents are simply fancy word-processed documents! As you look around the internet you'll come across pages that really jump out at you – there's video, sound, animation and lots more besides.

The objective for the job hunter, however, is not to confuse the issue by showing off with fancy tricks.

▷ The aim is to create an information area where you can set out a lot more relevant detail about the jobs and experiences of your working life.

The only concession to 'fancy design' you should allow yourself is the inclusion on your home page of a suitably smart photograph of yourself. Resist the temptation to include a photo album – complete with grannies, mother-in laws and pets! The employer will want to assess your effectiveness in the workplace, not what you look like in your domestic environment.

You might think of your own home page as an adjunct to your CV – if an employer wants to find out more then he can look here. If your home page contains a great deal of non-work related personal information, you may want to think twice before letting prospective employers view it. Your CV, however, should still be the main reference document for prospective employers.

What to include in your home page

Well, it's really up to you. The style you adopt for your home page should reflect both the industry you want to work in and the actual job vacancy that you are applying to fill.

▷ *Example* – graphic designers or those wishing to be employed in public relations or marketing, might want to create a home page which illustrates a good use of creative elements such as colour, design and typography.

However, for the great majority of job seekers, the old 'keep it simple'

Creating HTML documents

rule is the one to follow, because it is most likely to pay off in practice.

As explained above, the main aim of your home page, and its most likely use, is to assist employers who would like to know a little more about you than is readily available either on your CV or on a completed application form. From this perspective it is important not to repeat – but rather to expand – upon CV details.

However, if you choose to work as a contractor, it may be vital for an employer to access your updated CV as quickly as possible. Your home page is the ideal vehicle for this type of instant access to your latest CV type information.

It is vital that both types of enquiry can be satisfied. You could, for example, include two sections within your home pages:

(a) one giving basic CV type information

(b) one giving expanded details of your major work achievements.

Have a look at a guide to writing HTML, or look through your HTML developer software to find how to create this effect. One piece of essential information that is easily included in the simplest of home pages, however, is the placing of clear instructions (navigation links) at the top of the page guiding visitors to the appropriate parts of your site. It's very easy to get bored when visiting a poorly signposted site and simply click away to somewhere more favourable.

Creating HTML documents

Designing internet, or web pages, is a bit like driving a car – you can choose to understand the workings under the bonnet, or just drive the car until something goes wrong and then get someone else to fix it.

Creating HTML pages can be done in two ways:

▷ by using easy to use software

▷ by learning the basics of HTML yourself.

HTML documents are not really computer programs as such. Although they do have certain dynamic capabilities – for example in allowing emails to be sent – they are best described as 'smart' word-processed documents.

HTML operates using a number of **tags**. These tags are defined inside a pair of angled brackets, such as:

< >

which normally surround the text that they affect. The closing tag is normally preceded by a slash:

/

Using HTML tags

For example, to make some text appear bold, the <B> tag is used:

<B>Now is the time for all good men to come to the aid of the party</B>

This will appear as:

Now is the time for all good men to come to the aid of the party

The structure of HTML files

HTML files must have the following structure:

```
<HTML>
<HEAD>
<TITLE>
</TITLE>
</HEAD>
<BODY>
</BODY>
</HTML>
```

The following examples shows these main tags being used:

Headings <H1> – <H6>

```
<H1>Biggest</H1>
<H5>Smaller</H5>
<H6>Smallest</H6>
```

Bold <B>

```
<B>This tag makes text appear in bold type.</B>
```

Italics <I>

```
<I>This tag makes text appear in italic type</I>
```

Underline <U>

```
<U>This tag causes an underline to appear with text.</U>
```

Paragraph break <P>

This tag causes a new paragraph to be taken, and displays a blank line</P>

*Line break
*

This tag causes the text to jump to the start of the next line.</BR>

Horizontal ruler <HR>

This tag inserts a horizontal line in your document.

Testing HTML in a browser

Bulleted lists <UL>

```
<UL>
<LI>First Item in List.
<LI>Second Item in List.
<LI>Third Item in List.
</UL>
```

Tables <TABLE>

```
<TABLE BORDER>
<TR>
<TD>School</TD>
<TD>Year</TD>
<TD>Exams</TD>
</TR>
<TR>
<TD>Columba High</TD>
<TD>1989-1995</TD>
<TD>Maths, Physics, English</TD>
</TR>
</TABLE>
```

Fig. 23. A sample HTML page viewed in Netscape Communicator.

The following screen shows how the above tags might look when loaded into a browser.

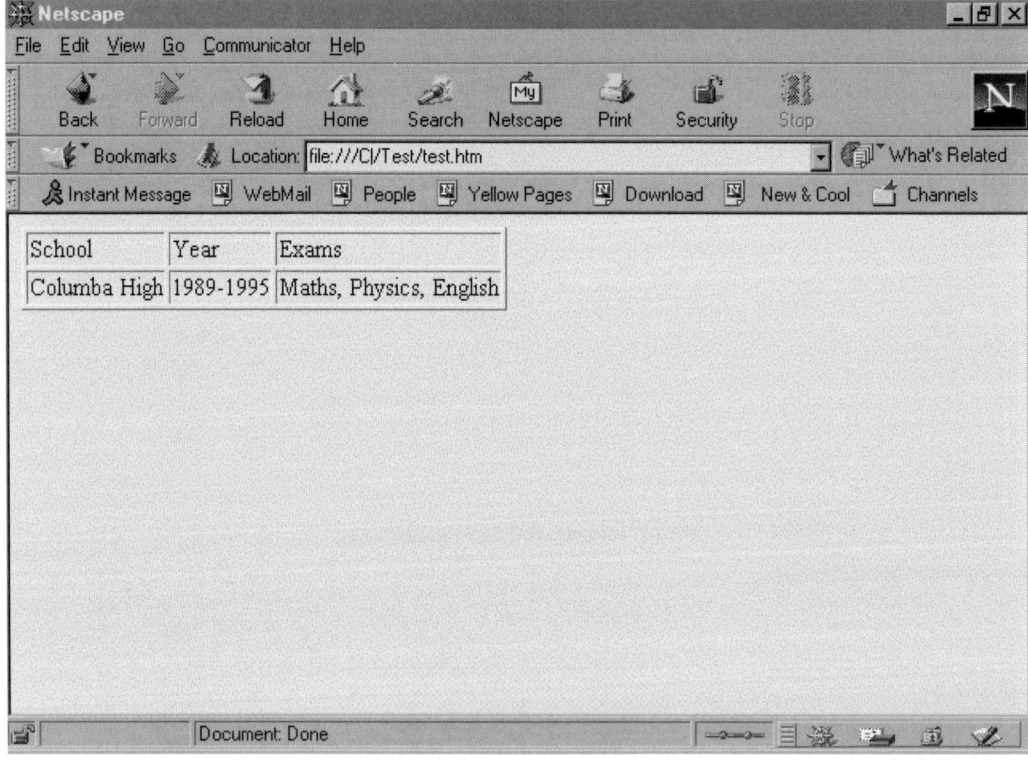

....**Uploading a document**

Loading your pages to view

Once you have created your HTML document on your PC, you will want to view how it will look using an internet browser. Simply follow these steps:

1. open your browser
2. choose *file, open*
3. choose the appropriate directory and HTML file
4. watch and be amazed...

Uploading your HTML document onto the internet

All being well, you will have chosen an ISP that gives you some free space on the internet in which to upload your own files. You can place any of your own HTML documents in this free space area. Then other internet users from all over the world can gain access to them.

▷ *What is 'uploading'?* – All it really means is that you copy a file from one area to another. It's just as you would do in Windows95, for example, when you copy a file from your A:\ drive onto your C:\ drive. The only difference with uploading to the internet is that you copy the file from your own computer to another computer at the end of your telephone line!

Your ISP's software will enable you to upload your files. This software is normally known as **file transfer protocol**, or **FTP** for short. Despite this rather off-putting name, transferring files is really very simple to do. Figure 24 shows AOL's FTP software screen.

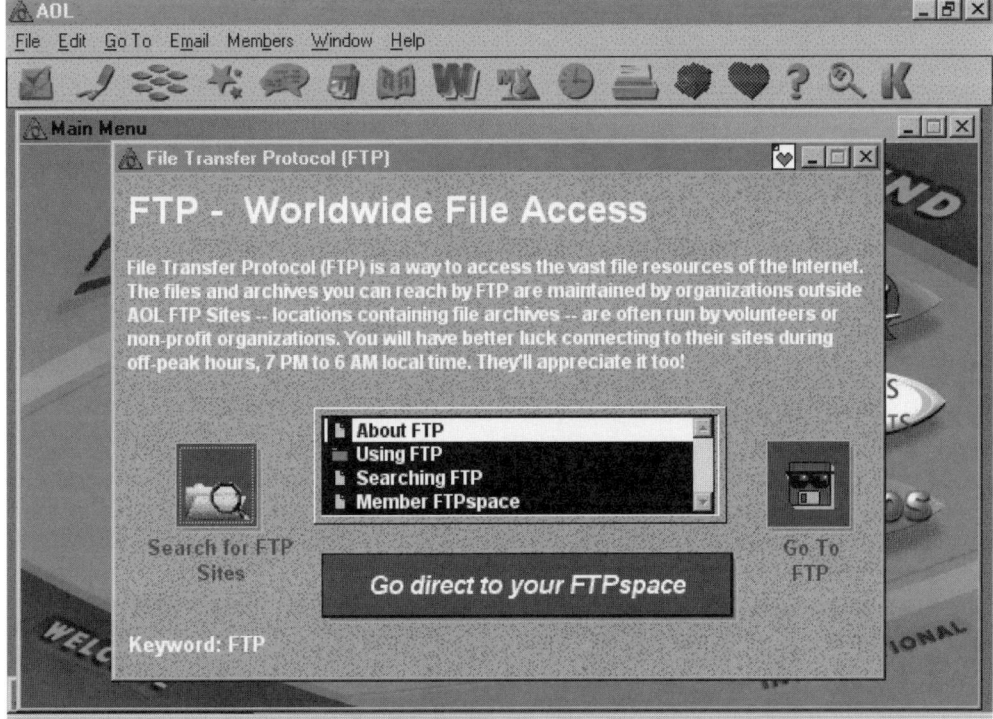

24. The AOL FTP screen. You can upload your pages to the internet from here if you are an AOL member.

Expanding your CV

Adding job-related information

As previously mentioned, the best CVs are strictly factual. The art is to set out as much relevant information as you can into an economical space.

Using web pages you can do quite a bit more, because you can easily link lots of your own pages together. For example if your CV includes a heading "Administration Experience" then your web pages might break this down into a detailed list of all the different types of administration carried out, for example sales administration, production administration etc.

Here is a checklist to help you when expanding your CV on your web page or pages:

Education
Describe major pieces of work or projects successfully carried out.

Postgraduate education and training
Detail any courses of study successfully carried out either at academic institutions or in the workplace.

Work experience
Describe in detail any major work-based achievements and the roles that you have played in these projects.

Membership of professional bodies
List the names of the organisations to which you are affiliated, and state your grade of membership and date achieved.

Additional information
Expand the text material and maybe even show the odd picture provided it is relevant in some way to your education and employment background, industry or profession.

Referees
Maybe you can persuade your referees to let you include details of the likely response that they would make if requested to issue a statement of your skills, strengths and abilities. Include your referees' telephone numbers, and email addresses. Some of these referees may have professional home pages of their own to which you could provide a link. Work or home address details would also be considered appropriate here, providing you had received prior agreement.

> *Tip* – remember to include the web address (URL) of the HTML page containing your employment detail in any emails you send to prospective employers. Your web address would typically look something like this:
>
> http://www.myISP/freespace/myname/index.html

Forms

Inviting prospective employers' feedback

There's not much point in prospective employers getting all this extra information about you unless they have a means to comment on what they see. That means using 'forms' – and yes, you've guessed it, some more HTML tags:

(<FORM>)

Rather than go into great detail here, there are lots of books that can help with this, or software packages will do it for you. Figure 25 gives an example of an HTML form page in Netscape. The details were simply created with the HTML code illustrated in Figure 26.

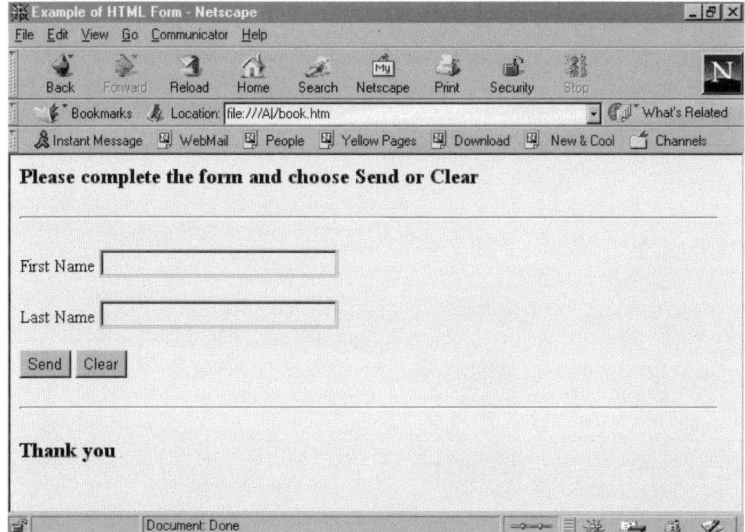

Fig. 25. Netscape HTML form page.

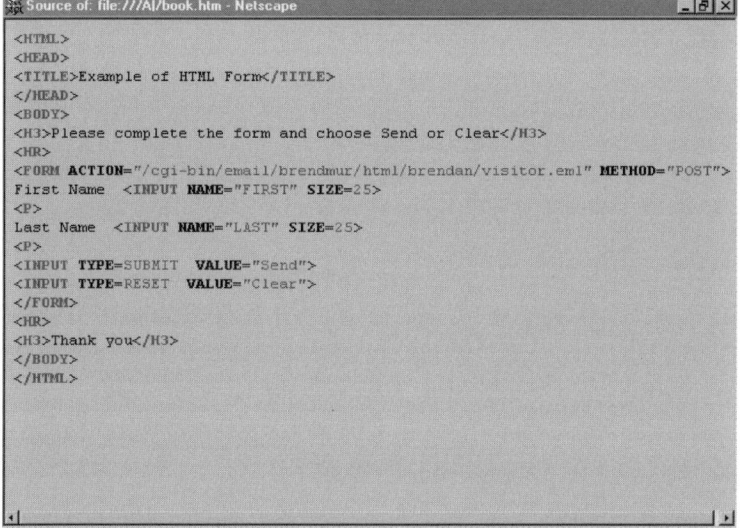

Fig. 26. Netscape HTML form page source code.

Web creation resources

Guide to online web page creation resources

If all of the HTML examples above seemed like a strange form of medieval torture to you, then maybe web creation through writing HTML is not for you. The smart software writers around the internet have (as always) come up with many resources to take the difficulty out of things. The following sites are definitely worth visiting.

HotDog
http://www.sausage.com/hotdog.htm
HotDog is a truly wonderful HTML writer. You can download software from this site, have a free try with it, and if you like it, a small cost must be paid. Try it, you'll love it! See Figure 27.

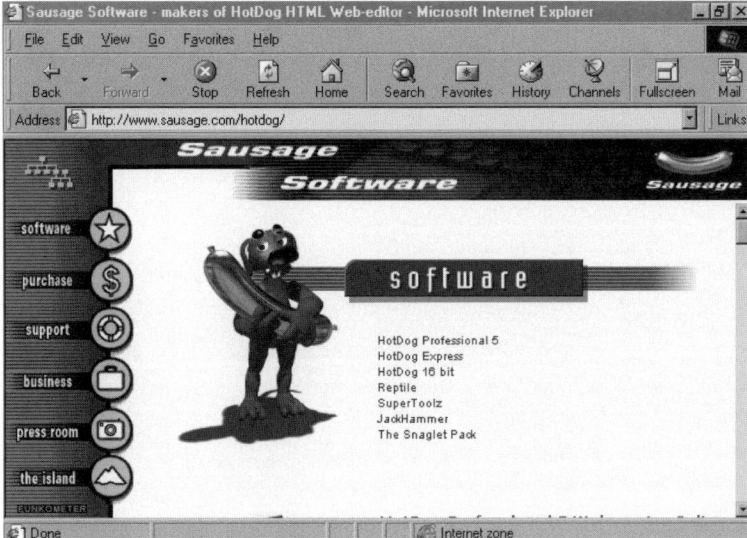

Fig. 27. HotDog home page.

HTML Writer
http://www.lal.cs.byn.edu/people/nosack/
HTML Writer is a no-cost, excellent piece of software. Created by an enthusiast, HTML Writer takes the drudgery out of basic web page HTML creation. The author asks only that a small donation is sent should you decide to continue use of the software (Figure 28).

HTML software free with browsers

Internet Explorer
Internet Explorer is now shipped with a cut-down copy of Microsoft's FrontPage web design software, called FrontPage Express. FrontPage Express is a very good package. In particular it makes the creation of tables and forms very easy indeed – some good advice if you fancy yourself as a bit of an HTML design guru.

Have a look at the full Microsoft FrontPage package (Figure 29). For

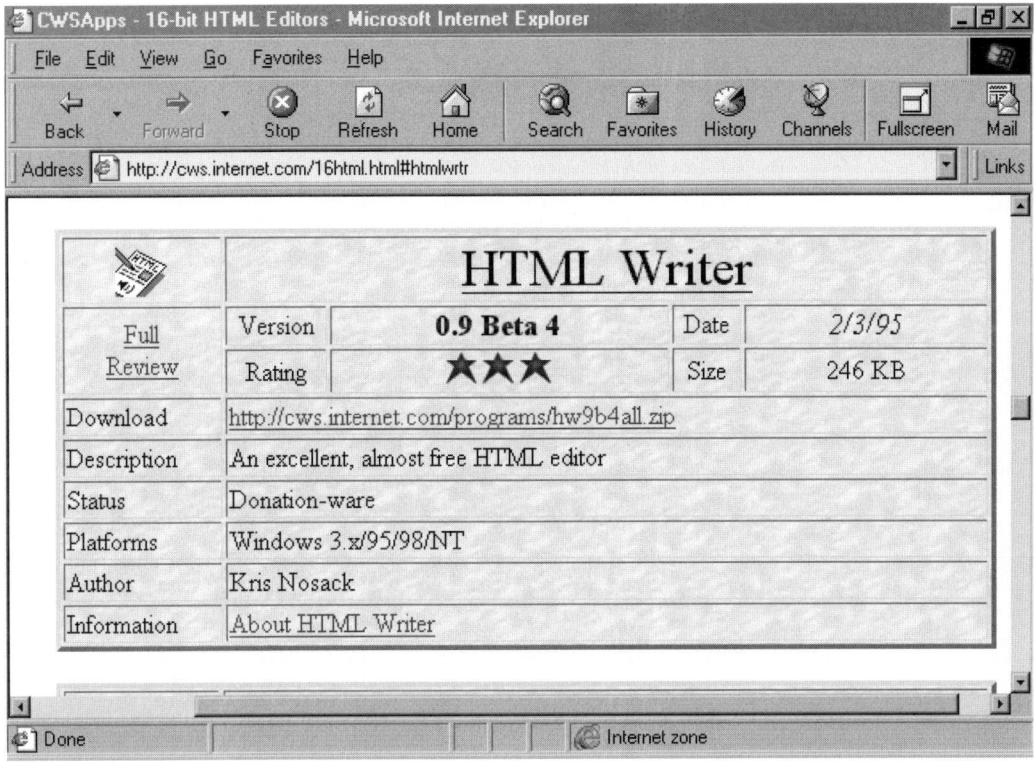

Fig. 28. HTML Writer home page.

under £100 it provides very easy methods of creating great looking home pages, plus a pre-loaded set of themes which provide wonderful backdrops and add a highly professional image to your completed web pages. You can design your pages using **frames**. If you use Microsoft FrontPage, you will have to check that your internet service provider is equipped with the required 'Microsoft FrontPage extensions' – not all are.

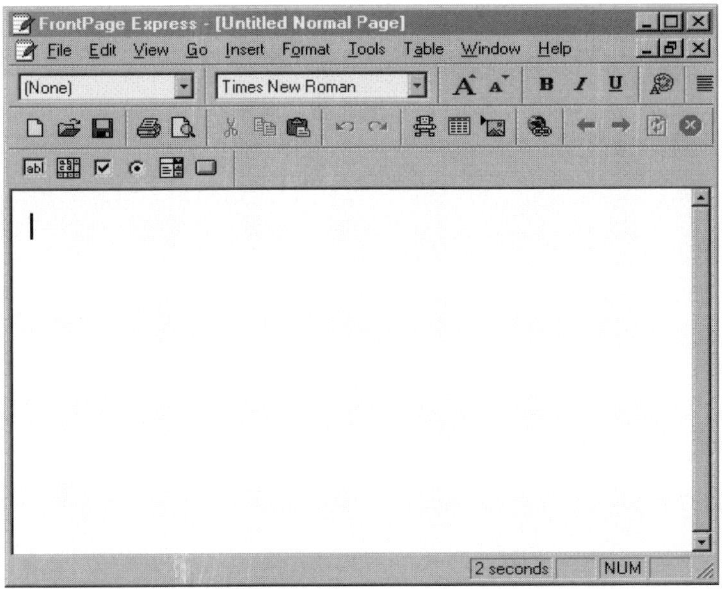

Fig. 29. Microsoft FrontPage Express. This is one of the most popular web authoring tools available, with over half a million copies supplied.

Netscape Page Composer

Netscape HTML editor

Netscape HTML editor is found in Netscape 3.0 (Netscape Gold) and Netscape 4.0 (Netscape Communicator) Page Composer. Both these versions of Netscape can be downloaded free from the internet, and you can sometimes find them on the CD-Roms given away with the glossy internet magazines. If you have Netscape 2.0 or earlier it is definitely time for you to upgrade.

These editors make creating web pages very easy. With the help of on-line wizards and templates, Netscape Page Composer in particular takes the pain out of creating web pages. You can easily change fonts and colours, insert images and clip art, and create hyper text links with the click of your mouse. Unfortunately this editor as yet has no tools for creating forms, or framesets, but you can create tables (Figure 30).

▷ *Example 1* – Jennifer has decided to start a night class studying computing. She has done some word processing, using Microsoft Word, and feels very confident in a number of advanced topics such as mail merge and the use of macros. Should Jennifer create her home page on the internet using raw HTML?

▷ *Example 2* – Brian has decided to buy a software package to help him design his new web page. Although he understands HTML, Brian feels that he just doesn't have the time to design a complete web page. He feels that this is not good use of the online time that he has job hunting. What choices might Brian have?

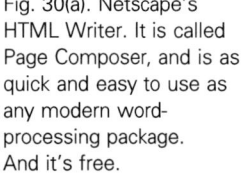

Fig. 30(a). Netscape's HTML Writer. It is called Page Composer, and is as quick and easy to use as any modern word-processing package. And it's free.

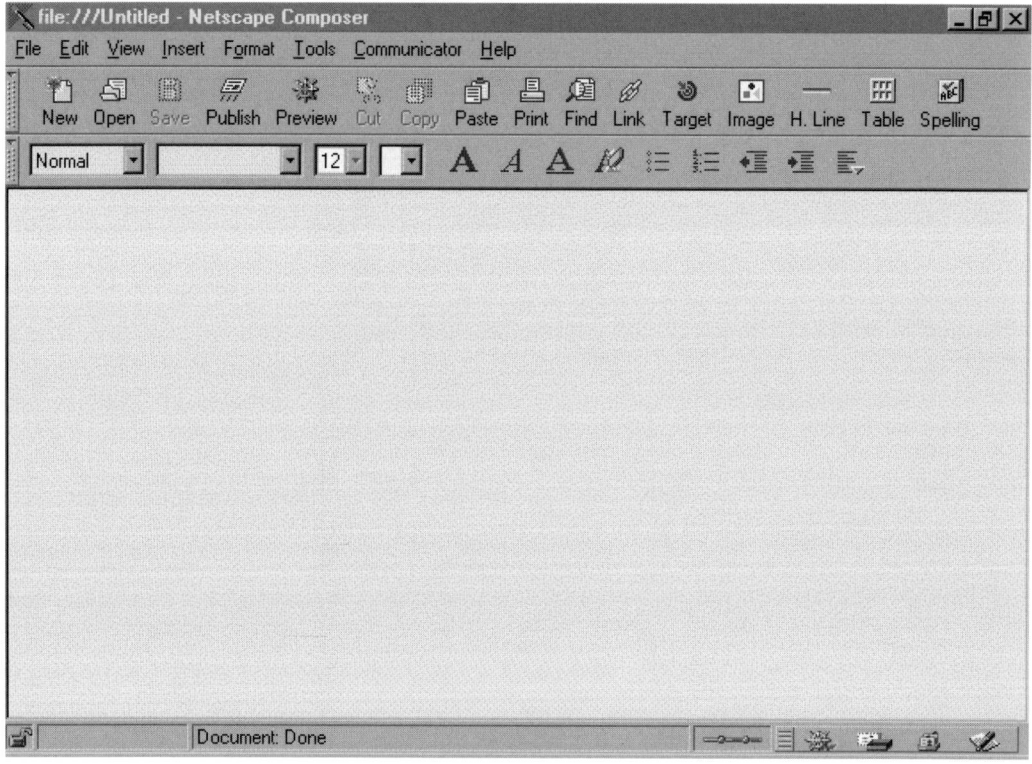

Talking points

Points to think about

1. Do you think that it is fair to use shareware over a continued period without sending any money to the author?

2. Would you be happy placing your online CV in an unrestricted access page on the internet? Would you prefer to restrict access either by building a password routine into your HTML page or by choosing not to register your page with any of the online search engines?

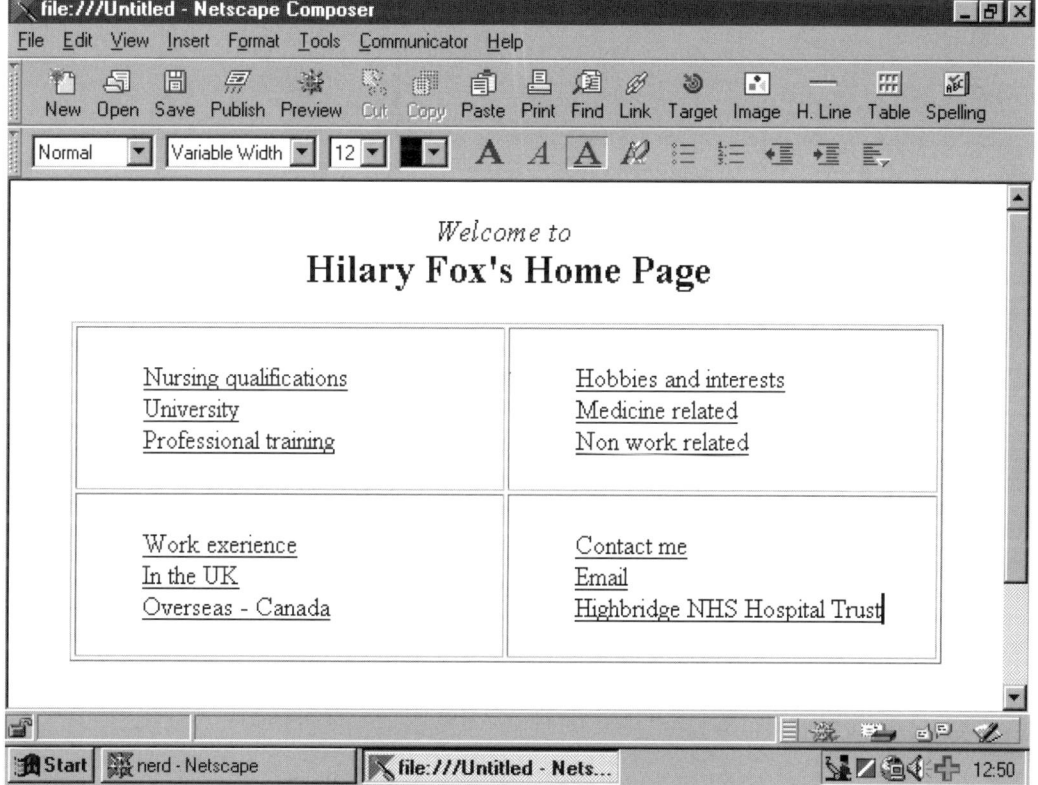

Fig. 30(b). Using Netscape to develop a home page using tables. The words underlined are links to related pages.

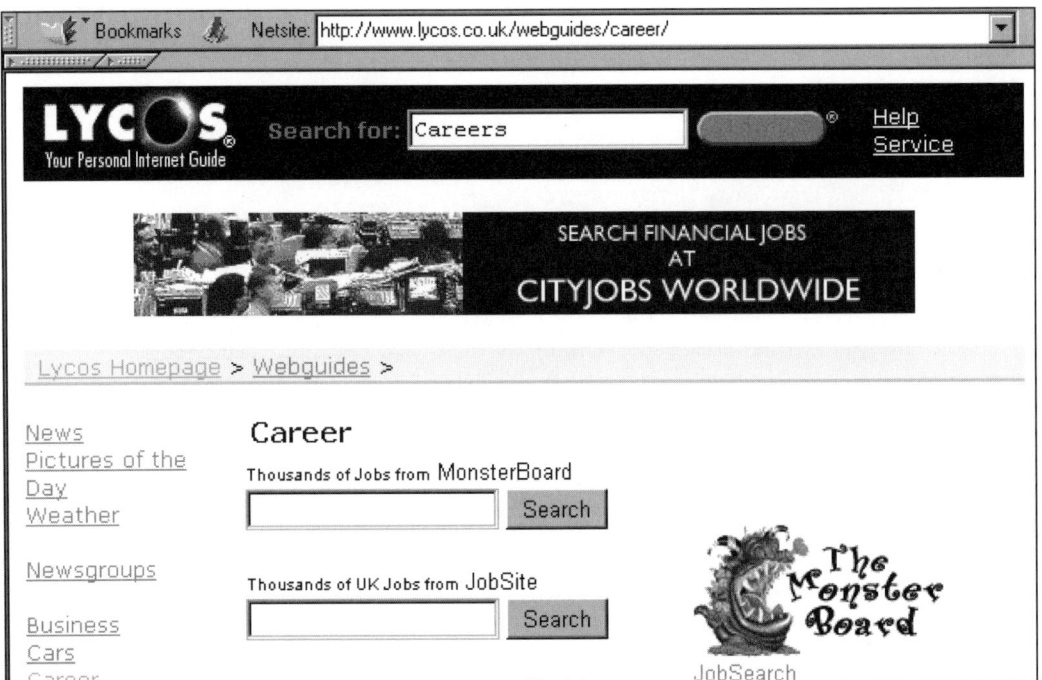

Three of the best-known search engines on the internet. They form excellent starting points for career searches: Lycos (*top*), Yahoo! (*centre*) and Infoseek (*bottom*).

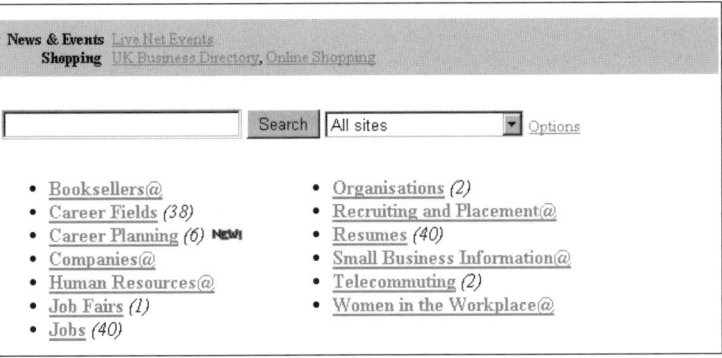

5 Choosing a career online

In this chapter we will explore:

▶ using online career resources
▶ accessing online university and college resources
▶ searching for postgraduate opportunities on the internet.

Using online careers services

When you start looking for a new job or a new career, it's often difficult to find a good starting point from where you can build a plan that will lead to the changes that you desire. One of the most difficult things is building confidence in your own ability, including the ability to seize the opportunities that are out there. There are many thousands of career based sites on the internet and the next few sites listed will provide a great starting point to help guide you on the road to a successful new challenge. So get on that surf board – your new career starts right here!

Great starting points

AGCAS
http://dialup1.csa.man.ac.uk/agcas
For a really professional career support site, visit the website of AGCAS, the Association of Graduate Careers Advisory Services. These pages offer some really top quality information. Founded in the late 1960s, AGCAS is concerned with career counselling in most of the higher education institutions in the UK. When you look through the AGCAS site you'll find lots of really useful hotspots which link to everything from computer-based guidance programs to the provision of statistics on UK graduates. A really great site for graduate employment.

Career Builder Network
http://www.careerbuilder.com
Although this site is every bit as American as mom's apple pie, it really is the most incredibly good starting point for building confidence. In particular, the hotspot entitled 'managing your career' is a real hive of useful information. From this site you can access a number of FAQs (frequently asked questions). These when expanded give high quality and detailed information on common career questions. This site also gives access to a fun little test called the Birkman Method which should help point you towards a particular career. Using this method you create a profile which, on completion, results in a summary of your 'interest colour' and 'style colour'. These colours then translate to a number of different jobs which are displayed and which can be expanded to reveal a more detailed explanation of what's involved in them. This might seem a little like trusting your career to a crystal ball reader – but it is fun – and it does reveal a number of different choices which may be useful. Give it a try (Figure 31).

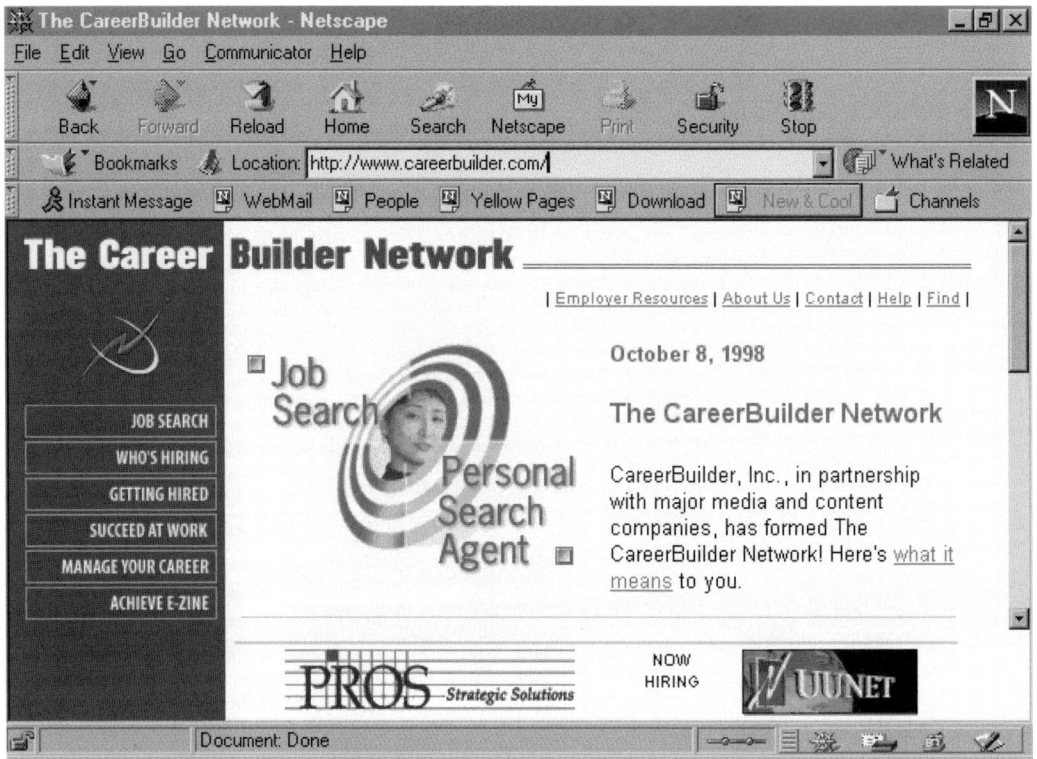

Fig. 31. The home page of the Career Builder web site.

CareerMosaic UK
http://www.careermosaic-uk.co.uk/
You'd best get used to CareerMosaic as you'll be visiting this site pretty regularly from now on. CareerMosiac is one of the most comprehensive resources of UK based jobs and careers available, and claims to be registering upwards of one million internet access calls every month. At the moment, rather than look at all the services provided, we'll concentrate on its excellent Career Resource Centre.

Fig. 32. CareerMosaic UK Career Resource Centre.

.... **Starting points**

Been a while since you've looked for a job?
Got a bit rusty?
Have you had a number of unsuccessful interviews?

If you've answered yes to any of the above, or if you just want to visit one of the most useful sites on the career hunting trail, then look no further. The Career Resource Centre provides information on CVs and covering letters, details of any new business trends, methods to access material on specific industries and how to carry out research on companies. Great information is hidden right there in the title of the research section which is 'research, research, research' – a subliminal message but a great bit of advice. Know as much as possible about the organisation you're applying to join! CareerMosaic will keep you busy for hours. An easy gold star award (Figure 32).

PlanIT – Continuing Education Gateway
http://www.ceg.org.uk/
This is a distinctively Scottish site but it is a great source of information for job seekers everywhere. You just can't help but be impressed by the content of this site. Operated by Glasgow City Council's Continuing Education Department, it offers a whole plethora of useful information.

▷ In particular the 'career' page is excellent, offering you access to an A-Z of prospective jobs. Each job gives you, in some detail, information relating to the nature of the work, the personal qualities required, core skills required, training, qualifications and adult entry requirements.

Fig. 33. Home page of the Continuing Education Gateway.

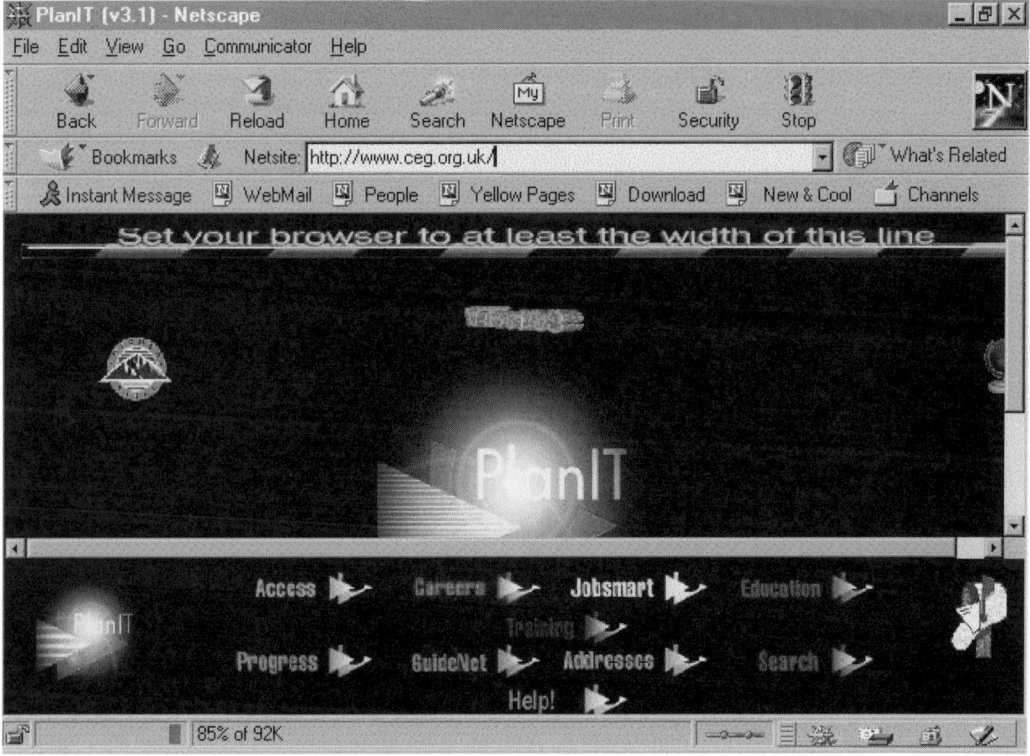

Careers services

▷ This site also groups job by industry. For example, entering the 'Emergency Services' section will return lots of information on all types of emergency service jobs and careers such as the fire, police and ambulance services.

This site is a treasure chest of useful information and a must for those just fishing, unsure of the actual path they plan on taking. Each description also gives further information and useful addresses which can provide a great starting point to jump in deeper. Of course, you can really never beat a one-to-one with an experienced career adviser, but if that's just not possible, or if you want to do some preparatory work first, then this site is a must. Another contender for a gold star (Figure 33).

Prospects Web
http://www.prospects.csu.ac.uk
Prospects Web offers a great starting point for graduates. You will find many useful services for the internet career hunter including:

1. A comprehensive UK and Eire database of job opportunities for graduates.

2. A database detailing postgraduate and research opportunities in the UK.

3. A section named Career Choice which gives expert advice to help you make the right career choices.

Fig. 34. The home page of Prospects Web, an essential bookmark for graduates.

Bookmarking interesting web sites

An area of particular interest in Prospects Web is the list of university careers services which is provided. By simply clicking on this hotspot you are transported to an A-Z listing of major universities and colleges, with each institution in turn having a hotspot to access its careers centres home pages – very useful indeed. Prospects Web also gives detail of the 'Mutual Aid Services to Graduates'. This allows graduates to call on the careers advice from a college or university other than the one from which they graduated. So, if you've just finished college or university and find yourself in a different town from where you studied, get down to the local higher education college or university and call on the expert service of a member of their trained career staff. See Figure 34.

Bookmarking your favourite sites

It would be impossible to list every source of useful career information on the internet. Indeed, if you access any of the above, they will lead you to hundreds more sites and places of interest. Whenever you come across an interesting website, remember to click to save the address:

▷ browsing with Internet Explorer – click *Add to Favorites*

▷ browsing with Netscape – click *Add Bookmark*.

However, several sites are worthy of a mention. They are all American but provide a great set of career-related resources which is relevant to all job seekers. Go have a look!

e.span
http://www.espan.com/
The e.span site offers an interesting little 'keep you up to date' tool called 'Article of the week'. This site simply gives you some good advice, in essay format, about subjects such as choosing a new career path and gaining confidence in applying for jobs and attending interviews. The articles change weekly and a history of previous articles is available. Great background reading.

Job Seekers Network
http://www.jobseekersnetwork.com
The JobSeekers Network provides some valuable help in CV writing and interviewing tips. This site also offers some fun stuff in its section entitled 'Salary Surveys'.

The Job Resource, Careers Advice
http://www.thejobresource.com/
A great site which offers well presented career help, particularly concerning the development of HTML CVs, and researching employers on the internet.

Central university and college resources

If you're about to dive into the world of further or higher education you'll

Further and higher education

be making one of your life's biggest decisions. It is vital that your decisions are the right ones. Whether studying full or part-time, the college experience is an exciting and fulfilling one, and one that you are likely never to regret. Not only academically, but socially through meeting new friends, further/higher education is sure to be an exciting and useful experience. Your knowledge will be expanded, and you'll grow immensely in confidence compared with when you were at school. The exercise of your mind will ensure that you remain receptive to change and development long after you've finished your course.

Just as is the case when looking for a new job or career, research is the key word when choosing a course and a college or university. Take your time; extensively research the internet resources described in this chapter, and involve friends and family in your decision.

Personal checklist for choosing further or higher education

1. Do you want full-time or part-time study?
2. Would you like to study away from home?
3. Can you afford the cost of study?
4. Would you rather do a vocational course or a strictly theoretical based course?
5. What is the main reason for choosing an academic course – is it to secure a good job, change career or purely for personal development?
6. Has the course chosen got a good reputation, have past students managed to secure jobs?
7. Have you got the correct skills and qualifications required for entry to your chosen course?
8. Are you committed to the hard work that will be needed for successful completion?

Useful internet sites for colleges and universities

The Careers Service
http://www.open.gov.uk/dfee/
The Careers Service is part of the Department for Education and Employment. It offers help to young people by detailing the availability of further education courses, training opportunities and local employment opportunities. Many Careers Offices also work with adults and here similar services are provided. This site offers a basic introduction to the careers service, and it should undoubtedly be useful to parents looking to ensure that their children are accessing the service to achieve the maximum benefit from it.

JANET: UK Universities and Higher Education Colleges
http://www.ja.net/janet-sites/university.html
JANET is the United Kingdom's academic and research network. It connects several hundred colleges, universities and research bodies

linking academic research and other information sources. This site gives A-Z access to all the JANET members, allowing you further access to educational institutions' home pages.

UCAS
http://www.ucas.ac.uk/ucc/index.html
UCAS stands for the Universities and Colleges Admission Service. It is the organisation that processes the vast majority of applications to UK higher education institutions. This makes it particularly good at informing you of course structure and qualifications required. This site has a fantastic search routine that is a real must for checking out courses. By simply choosing a subject area and its level of study, a region in the UK where you wish to study, and a decision on what qualification requirements you would like to see displayed (e.g. A-levels, Scottish Highers), UCAS will display for you a list of relevant courses and institutions. Further clicking on a chosen course reveals the grades required. Used in conjunction with other sites listed in this chapter this site will prove a real winner (Figure 35).

UK Academic Sites
http://src.doc.ic.ac.uk/uk-academic.html
Just as the title suggests, this site gives an extensive A-Z listing of college and university sites and professional bodies. This site is particularly interesting in that it breaks each institution down into the various schools in existence within it, allowing easy access to specific academic departments.

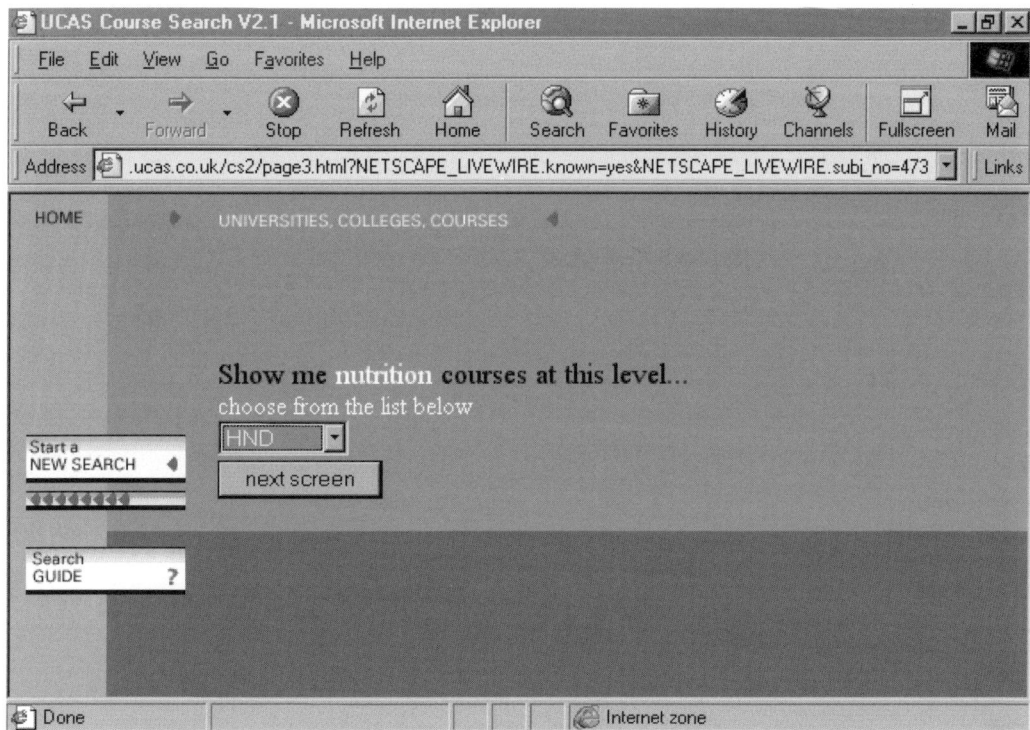

Fig. 35. UCAS is one of the best sources of information and links to universities, colleges and academic courses.

UK Academic Sites

University of Wolverhampton: UK college and university maps
http://www.wlv.ac.uk/ukinfo/uk.map.colls.html
Developed within the University of Wolverhampton's School of Information Technology in 1994, both these maps offer a fantastic visual resource to access UK colleges and universities. By simply pointing and clicking on a hotspot on a map of the UK, you reach the home pages of the institutions listed, allowing further access to courses and study facilities. This is a truly excellent site which offers you the chance to have a peep through the country's principal universities and colleges. You'll find details of departments, courses, student facilities, the names of key staff, and much more (Figure 36).

Yahoo!
http://www.yahoo.com
Yahoo! is probably better known to you as one of the most popular internet search engines which can be used to find general topics of interest. It is, however, worthwhile clicking on Yahoo!'s 'Education' section on its home page. From here you can choose to view a comprehensive list of college and university internet sites. Other search engines have similar sections which might prove useful in your pursuit of appropriate further or higher education.

Continuing and postgraduate education

Postgraduate education comes in many shapes and forms. It can be full-time, part-time, or carried out by distance learning. In this section

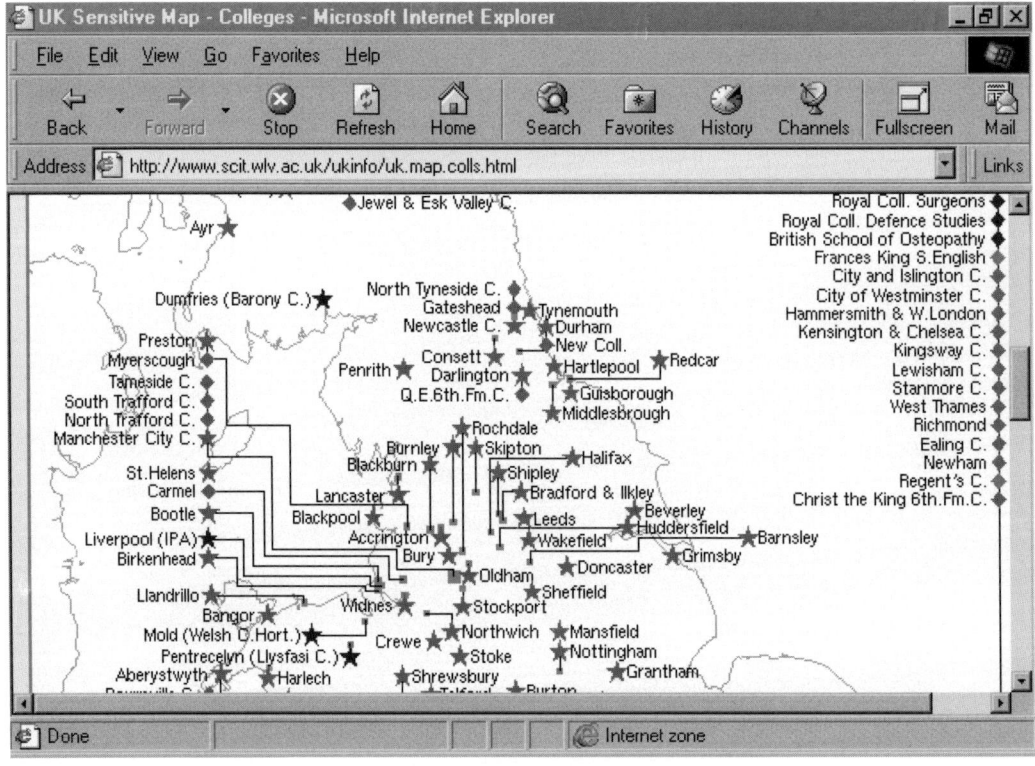

Fig. 36. UK colleges and university maps, a wonderful resource from the University of Wolverhampton.

Postgraduate education

some options will be given to help you make the right decision to further your education. But first, a practical checklist.

- Do you want to study full-time or part-time?
- Are you aware of the commitment that the course will take from your free time?
- Do you want to study with others as part of a taught qualification?
- Have you a burning research issue that only you can answer?
- Will your chosen course help your career?

Listed below are a number of useful sites and methods which can be used to identify an appropriate postgraduate course for you.

Individual universities and colleges

The likelihood is that you will probably be studying part-time for your postgraduate course. In this case local facilities are a must. Probably the simplest way to get started on the course hunt is to crank up your favourite search engine, key in the names of a few local colleges and universities and have a rummage around their web pages.

You'll find that most of these pages will have specific information on postgraduate courses as well as links to departmental and staff pages detailing specific research opportunities. Similarly, if it's an MBA you're after (and more and more people seem to be following this route) then key in 'MBA' and away you go.

- A point worthy of mention: if you're carrying out postgraduate study after completing a first degree or professional qualification then how about choosing a different institution for your postgraduate study? It could make your CV that little bit more interesting and ensure that your qualifications section doesn't just look like a blur of subjects studied in the one institution.

Association of Business Schools
http://www.leads.ac.uk/bes/abs/abshome.htm
The Association of Business Schools covers all the major business schools in UK universities and polytechnics. It provides various online statistics, reports and guidelines relating particularly to the Master of Business Administration (MBA) qualification offered by higher education institutions. If management education is your aim, and you want to ensure that you are studying both in an institution and on a course that's well respected, then this site is the place to have your questions answered.

The Open University
www.open.ac.uk
Welcome to the world experts in the provision of qualifications that are suited to all lifestyles. Use your browser to have a look at the online prospectus and pick up some useful hints. The Open University is also

The Open University online

at the forefront of providing distance learning via the internet. Therefore, if you're disabled in some way, or if you live in a remote part of the country, you can participate fully in a course, from start to finish, from your nearest PC. The opportunities found here are sure to be replicated by other institutions over the coming years.

Prospects Web
http://www.prospects.csu.ac.uk/
Look under the 'Postgraduate Opportunities' page and you'll find a wealth of useful information relating to postgraduate courses and research opportunities in higher education institutions in the UK.

Points to think about

1. Is there a danger that colleges and universities who do not offer courses across the internet could risk losing students to more sophisticated, innovative and forward-thinking institutions?

2. One of the main benefits of study is the opportunity to socially interact with your fellow students. Do you think that, with the rise in opportunities to study alone via the internet, a very important part of the enjoyment of completing a course of study will be lost?

6 Finding out about jobs online

In this chapter we will explore:

▶ how to discover the skills and qualifications needed for specific careers
▶ how to use the full range of services provided by CareerMosaic
▶ the benefits of using email to keep up to date with jobs available.

Looking at occupational profiles online

Remember that last car you bought, or that new PC that you're using right now to access the internet? Yes, you spent hours reading up on the features, the price, how well it was likely to perform, what was included in the price. Well, if it's good enough for a purchase that's likely to last only a few years it's sure good enough for a decision that could last a lifetime.

Choosing a new job or career is traumatic, difficult and not without some stress. In the past your best hope of finding out about the 'real' aspects of a job or career was to ask someone who was currently doing that job or to visit your local careers office or reference library and look up a book that might have been a couple of years out of date.

No more. Occupational profiles on the internet can really help you. By carefully surfing through career sites you can find out the requirements of a whole host of jobs allowing you to determine what qualifications and skills are needed and what the likely benefits of the job are. In short, they can help you determine if the job's the right choice for you. These sites will also prove invaluable when attending interviews, ensuring that you show a real understanding of the job for which you are applying. Take a look at the following sites:

AGCAS Occupational Profiles
http://www.sys.uea.ac.uk/Miscellaneous/Careers/agcas/
AGCAS is the Association of Graduate Careers Advisory Services, and this site is set up particularly for graduates. However, if you are not a graduate, don't be put off by this. The information provided is truly comprehensive and has relevance for most job seekers who just want to know more. The database organises jobs by industries, and about thirty industry types are covered. By simply choosing the required industry you are presented with a range of jobs available. Then, simply click on the job or career that interests you and wait for the display of real information-bursting pages of detail. Each of the AGCAS occupational profiles follows a standard pattern and gives around four pages of information covering qualifications, gender equality, opportunity for freelance work, salary, any age restrictions and much more. At the bottom of each profile is a list of other jobs that are similar to the one

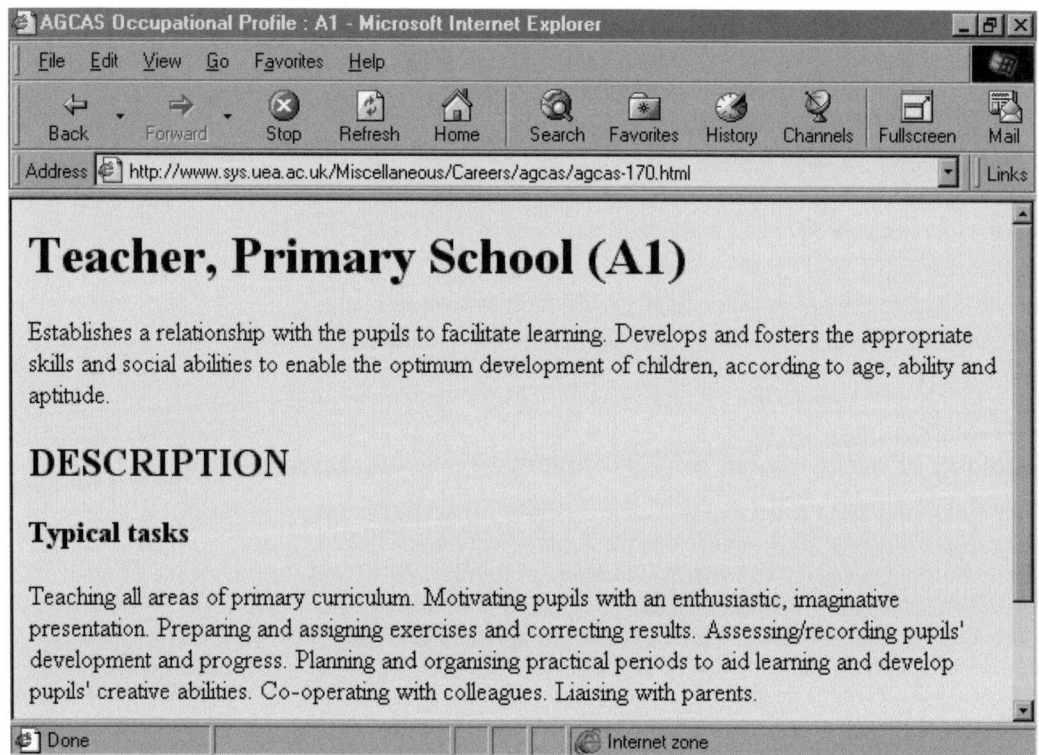

Fig. 37. An example of online job profiles which can be viewed on the excellent AGCAS page.

being profiled, allowing you easy access to the occupational information relating to these job areas. Another site worthy of a gold star (Figure 37).

▷ *Example* – David is in his final year at school and is unsure of what he would like to do with his life. David thinks that he might like to join the police force, as police work, particularly the work of a detective, interests him. By search through the AGCAS occupational profiles David not only has a fuller understanding of the duties of a detective, but also of the qualifications and skills required to be considered suitable for this career.

Ivanhoe Career Guides
http://www.ivanhoe.co.uk
Ivanhoe offers students, graduates and professionals, a source of information relating to career choice in the UK. Although restricted to ten main professional areas, Ivanhoe is supported by the UK's leading professional bodies, so up to date information is always assured. Ivanhoe guides are split into areas such as the information systems professions through to the legal and engineering professions. By choosing a particular profession, a comprehensive guide is made available which covers the industry, education and training, careers in the industry, professional bodies and the industry's leading employers.

CareerMosaic

CareerMosaic – indepth help online

CareerMosaic UK
http://www.careermosaic-uk.co.uk/
Time for a return visit to CareerMosaic. This is one of the most comprehensive online career resource services available through the internet. Part of a worldwide organisation, CareerMosaic UK provides a compendium of jobs and resources available within the UK. The site is split into six main areas namely, JOBS, Employers, CMCV, Career Resource Center, University Update and International Gateway.

JOBS at CareerMosaic
http://www.careermosaic-uk.co.uk/usenet.htm
This is a comprehensive UK-based job vacancy database. An excellent job search facility allows you to filter your job search geographically, by town, by postcode and even by restricting it to a particular company. This search facility also allows you to access jobs available on newsgroups, a topic that will be expanded in a later chapter (Figure 38).

Employers at CareerMosaic
http://www.careermosaic.co.uk/cm12.htm
Continuing the general up-beat feel of the CareerMosaic site, 'Employers Showcase' gives you a comprehensive employer-profiling service for many of the major British companies as well as giving details of their current vacancies. According to the people down at CareerMosaic, the companies listed are amongst the most progressive

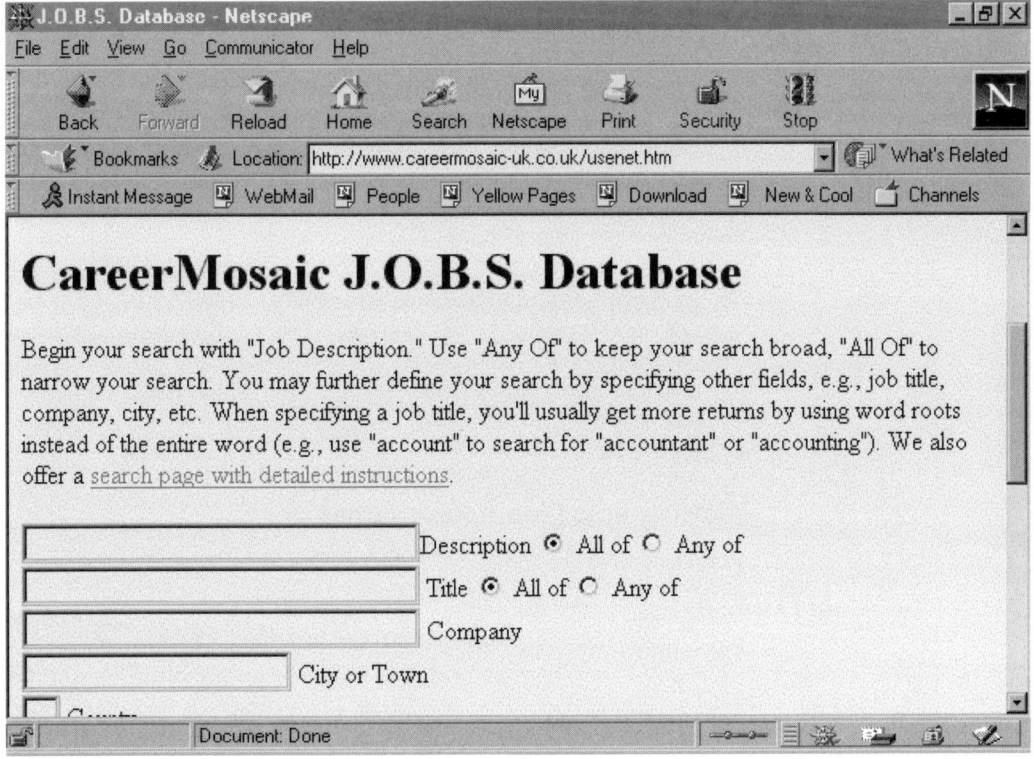

Fig. 38. CareerMosaic, one of the most comprehensive careers resources on the internet.

Email job opportunities

in the country and all have a commitment to internet employment. Why not look these companies up, and contact them direct yourself – maybe using some innovative way to do so – then see if they live up to their CareerMosaic reputation?

Career Resource Center and CMCV
http://www.careermosaic-uk.co.uk/crc.htm
You'll already have visited these sites in Chapter Three of this book. Choose the Career Resource Center to post your CV for employers to view. A very useful utility offered to employers, and one that is sure to benefit those registering their CV with CareerMosaic, is the 'full-text' search option. This means that employers can search for specific words, and, if these words appear anywhere within your CV, then your details will be returned as a suitable match for their enquiry. There also exists in this area of CareerMosaic the ability to search through the tens of thousands of CVs already registered. Why not use this option to look through the best of the rest and get some useful tips that can then be used when creating your own CV?

University Update
http://www.careermosaic-uk.co.uk/ccc1.htm
This site gives a wealth of informational links to major resources for universities and colleges in the UK. Apart from useful college and university maps and alphabetic listings, there are also various excellent links to graduate recruitment and advisory resources. If you fancy heading off and studying at a university within Central Europe or the USA then there's a great link to a useful page of worldwide university and college internet pages.

International Gateway
http://www.careermosaic.com/cm/gateway/
So, being in job hunting and career changing mode has given you the appetite to wander. Whether it's computing in Sydney, or accounting in Hong Kong these links will guide you to the best jobs available on the international market (Figure 39).

▷ *Example* – Through the persistent use of CareerMosaic, Eilish has managed to secure a job interview. Eilish is desperate to make a good impression and would like to find out any tips that might help her during the actual interview. By reference to CareerMosaic's Employer page and Career Resource Center, Eilish now feels that she is better prepared to face the interview.

Getting email job opportunities daily

As previously mentioned, electronic mail is the undoubted killer application on the internet. More and more companies are accepting this as a reality, and more and more correspondence is being conducted across the internet each day with the help of email.

So why not harness this opportunity to help you get that elusive job?

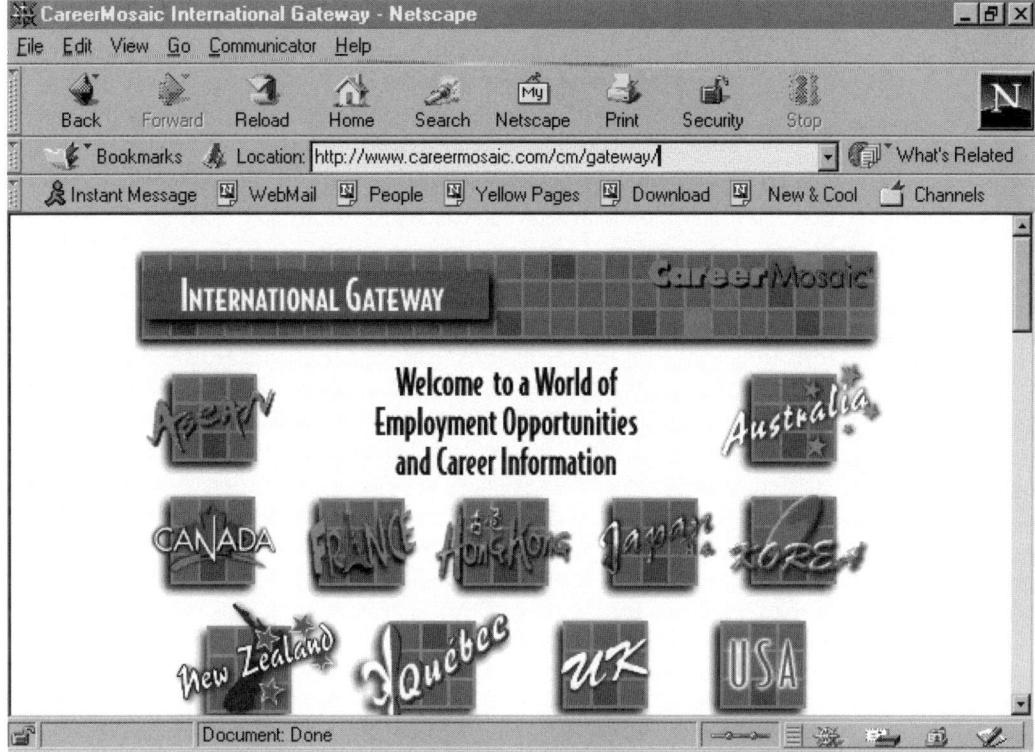

Fig. 39. The international gateway page at CareerMosaic.

How do you go about doing this? Well, it's very easy. There are two main methods of making email work for you.

1. Firstly you could send a general email with your CV included as an attachment, and maybe with the address of your home page in the main body of the message, to a number of companies asking them to let you know if there are any opportunities available which match your skill set.

2. Secondly, more and more large organisations and employment agencies on the internet have automated email services where, on entry of your skills, salary requirements etc., a daily list of available jobs will automatically be sent to your email address. You can then look through these specific jobs at your leisure ensuring that you never miss any opportunities.

The main benefits of receiving job details by email are:

▷ daily update of the job market

▷ easy way to ensure that your job search is comprehensive

▷ great for those already in work but who want to keep an eye on the job market ready for their next career move

▷ speedy, instant reply to available opportunities.

Questions

Your questions answered

What are occupational profiles?

Occupational profiles are details of the full requirements for a particular job as well as the duties required to be undertaken and the opportunities available within that job.

How might you find out about a particular employer's business via the internet?

Most job-related agencies provide detailed profiles of major companies advertising on their site. By simply clicking through these sites you can usually access some detailed information relating to the activities of prospective employers.

Points to think about

1. Receiving daily job details via your email account is undoubtedly a very useful and easy to use option. Do you think that this method of job seeking can have any downsides?

2. How do you think occupational profiles can help you prepare for a face to face interview?

7 Exploring employers online

In this chapter we will explore:

▶ *searching through company profiles*
▶ *accessing national and regional newspapers online*
▶ *signing up with employment agencies*
▶ *opportunities for IS/IT specialists on the internet.*

Searching company profiles online

When you're setting off down the road for that elusive interview you will make sure you're smart, well groomed and ready to go get that job. But what do you know about the company you're applying to work for?

Enter **company profiles**. You'd be amazed the amount of times interviewers ask the question, 'And what do you know about the company' – only to be told 'Well, not really very much.'

With access to the millions of online resources available on the internet this should never happen to you.

Without paying a subscription, access to detailed company profiles is not always easy to obtain on the internet, but most of the job agencies that you'll look in on will at least publish some information about the companies for whom they recruit. Look out for hyperlinks to 'company information' or 'profiles'. Keep ferreting around, and you'll find plenty to keep you productively occupied.

> *Tip* – remember to bookmark any useful sites as you go along.

Newspapers online

All of the major national newspapers now offer online services, mainly dealing with the reporting of news and magazine articles. However, more and more of these sites also give access to classified adverts such as job vacancies and appointment pages. Save yourself some money rushing out to buy those dailies just for the job vacancies – surf them online instead. It's easier and it's quicker. Two good places to start looking are The Biz, and JobHunter.

The Biz
www.thebiz.co.uk
Rather than list every newspaper available, point your browser towards this address, where you can get a list of the home pages of the main ones.

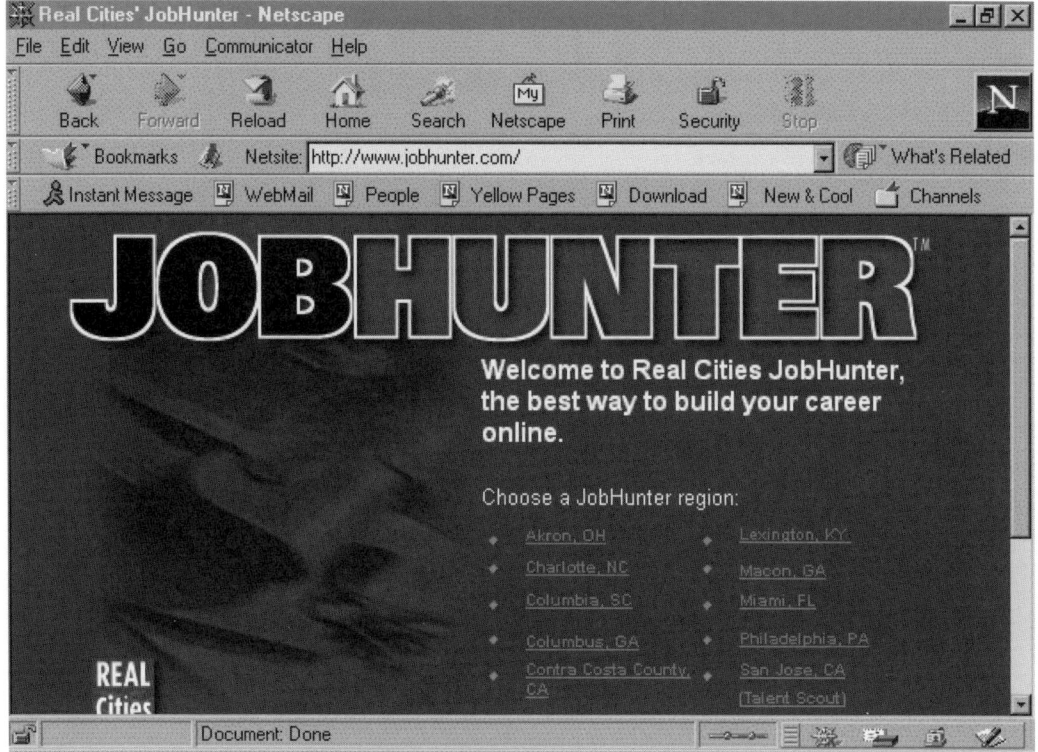

Fig. 40. The home page of Jobhunter, another great careers resource.

JobHunter
http://www.jobhunter.com
JobHunter lists all the jobs available through a list of hundreds of local and regional newspaper vacancies updated daily giving you the very latest in jobs from your area. The main benefit of this service is that you may get access to a job before it's advertised nationally. Also, if you're maybe wanting to work part-time or you are returning to work after a period of absence, there is a greater chance that the vacancy you're looking for will be found here. JobHunter has a great search routine that lets you home in on the area where you'd like to work, provides a list of jobs available in that area, and gives details of individual job adverts (Figure 40).

Signing up with employment agencies

Before you actually commit yourself to a particular online employment agency, do make sure that the one you choose will fully meet your requirements. Employment agencies are there to provide a service. That means that the users should call the shots. Decide for yourself, but be wary of any agency that requires a joining fee from you. You are their commodity. Their success in winning fees from employers depends on you and all the other candidates. Why should you have to pay for the privilege of making them money? Employers pay a fee for access to online agencies, so you shouldn't have to.

How do you ensure that a particular agency is reputable? Well it's difficult, but here is a checklist to help you along:

1. Check the number of jobs the agency has available each day – the

Employment agencies online

more jobs available the more they are being used by employers.

2. Does the agency specialise in a particular industry or work type, for example permanent or contract work?

3. Check to see if agency home pages have won any prizes from industry bodies or magazines for their services.

4. Look for any testimonials from successful job seekers.

5. Check out the names of the companies using the agency – if you find the big boys then you can be pretty sure that the agency is doing its job well and has respect from big business.

The following sites are amongst the best on the internet at present. Have a look at their home pages and make up your own mind.

JobSite
http://www.jobsite.co.uk
JobSite offers a very intuitive user interface and easy to understand instructions. JobSite allows you to look through featured jobs, or you can choose to have daily job details emailed directly to you. When you find the job you're looking for a very clear display gives you all the detail that you need relating to that job. JobSite offers jobs in IT and computing, science and engineering, commercial, management and professional, healthcare, and education and professional (Figure 41).

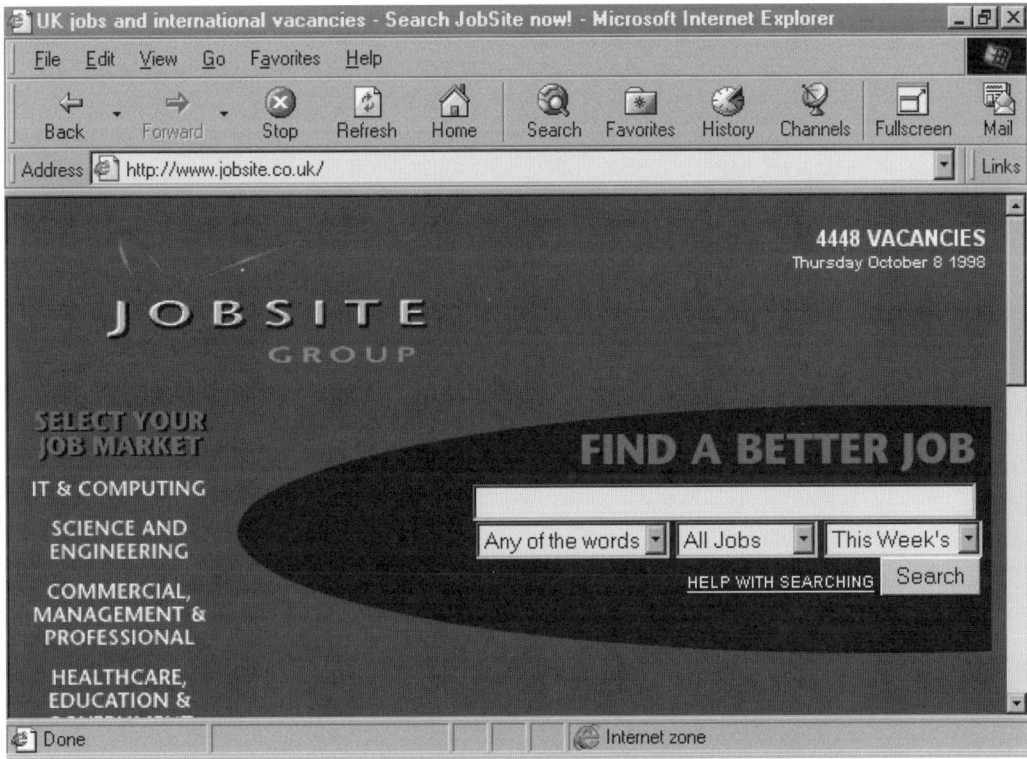

Fig. 41. The home page of JobSite, an essential stopping-off point if you are looking for jobs in computing.

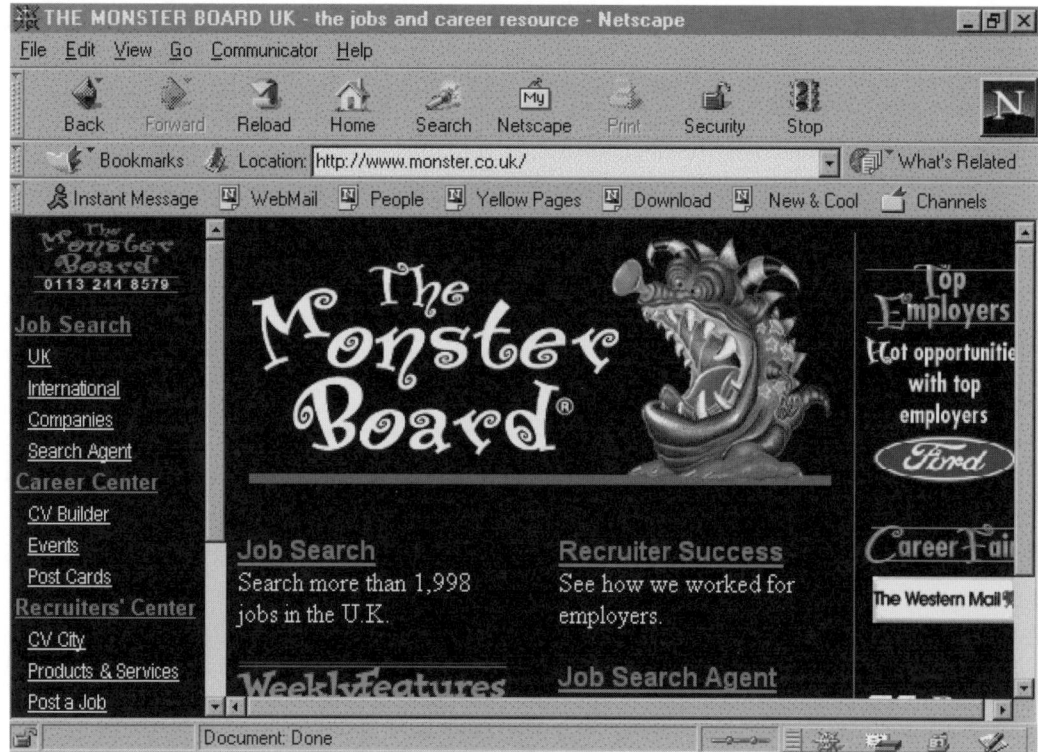

Fig. 42. The very distinctive home page of Monster Board, your gateway to jobs and careers of every kind.

Monster Board UK
http://www.monster.co.uk
Monster Board provides almost 2,000 jobs online each day. The job search routine is effective and very easy to understand. Monster Board is very visual; each of the functions available is supported by a monstrous little character. Let 'Thwacker' help you search through the vacancy database or let 'Skeeter' guide you through resources relating to each employer's business (Figure 42).

Top Jobs on the Net
http://www.topjobs.co.uk
Top Jobs on the Net provides instant access to top management, professional and technical jobs online. If you want to know how good this site is, visit Company Showcase and just look at the big names! If you are after a top job then look no further.

Reed Online Employment
http://www.reed.co.uk
Reed is one of those sites that's been designed with job seekers in mind. By simply entering the area you wish to work in, and the salary band and town, you'll quickly be taken to the jobs available. This site also offers various features which change regularly. These cover such areas as jobs for students, how to get promotion and details on government employment policy. Reed have quite a nice option that means that when you find a job that you like, they attempt to hook you into their service, by offering you a sign-up option after the job detail is presented. Sneaky but effective!

Job sites on the internet

Taps.com
http://www.taps.co.uk
Once again, have a look at the 'Marketplace' and just see how major employers feel about this site. Taps.com is supported by some major players such as ASDA, ICL, Volvo and the BBC. This support gives you an idea of the usefulness of this site to the serious job hunter (Figure 43).

Other pages of interest

The following URLs also lead to some interesting pages:

WorkWeb
http://www.workweb.co.uk

PeopleBank
http://www.peoplebank.com

NetJobs
http://www.netjobs.co.uk

Jobfinder
http://www.jobfinder.com

100.hot
http://www.100hot.com
Although it's American, have a look at this one. You'll find the top 100 internet sites relating to around 70 different subject areas. Look under 'Job' and see the top career and jobs sites on the internet.

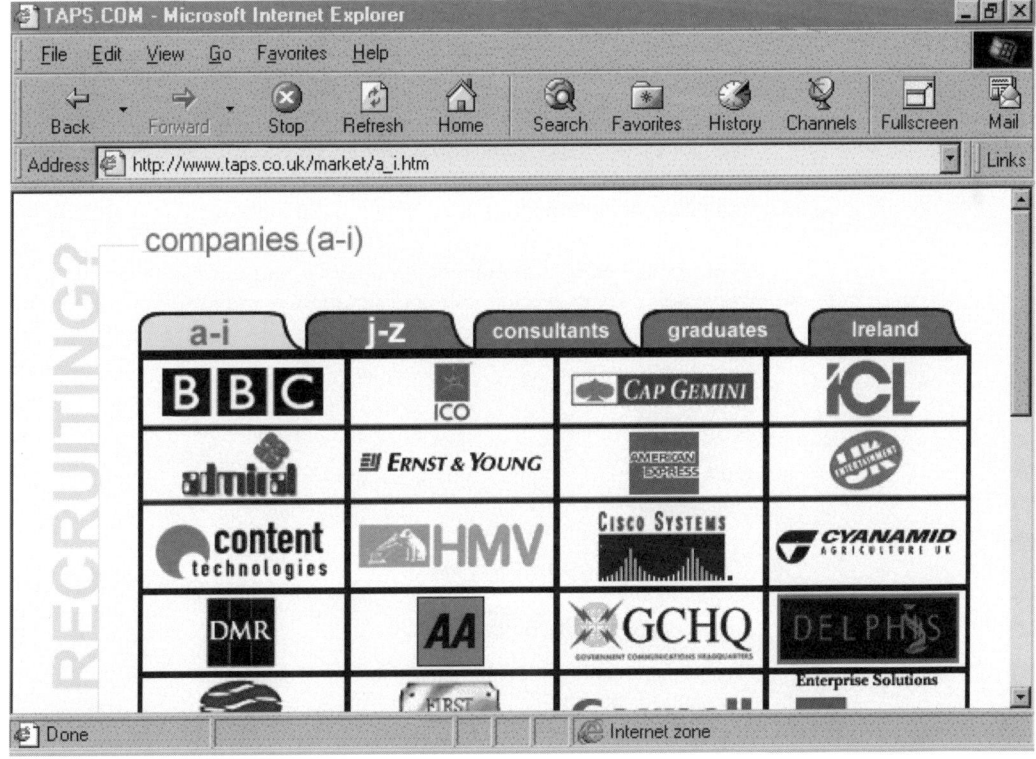

Fig. 43. The home page of TAPS. The letters stand for 'The Appointments Section'.

Jobs in IT

Getting IT jobs on the internet

Since the internet is above all associated with the computer boffin, the amount of jobs available for those wishing to pursue a career in information technology is plentiful. Indeed, there are thousands and thousands of jobs available. For IT people the internet is sure to become one of the principal methods of getting work in the very near future.

Apart from all the major employers, a number of online recruitment agencies have been set up particularly with IT jobs in mind. If you're a hi-tech dude, the following pages should be of interest to you.

JobServe
http://www.jobserve.com
JobServe really is about the best online IT job service on the internet, and it shows. The site really is wonderful and is very easy to use. The people down at JobServe know why you visit their site – to get a job. So the first thing that hits you on the JobServe home page is the search utility. Put in some details of the kind of job you're looking for, as well as your preferred locations, and hey presto a list of appropriate jobs is displayed – brilliant.

Apart from the JobServe database, there's an email facility that will send you details each day of jobs matching your skills. And, just to ensure that you get access to the most up-to-date jobs available, JobServe has an 'instants' page, which is updated literally by the minute – have a browse and see what's available! (Figure 44). JobServe is very easy to use. Simply email:

subscribe@jobserve.com

and details will be sent back to you by return. Then, just sit back and wait for those hi-tech jobs to just roll into your electronic postbox! If you can't find what you want with JobServe – and this will be unlikely – there are many other agencies offering IS/IT jobs.

You could also try contacting the home pages of all the major IT companies such as Microsoft and Borland by simply surfing straight to their home pages. The following sites might be worth a peek:

Microsoft Jobs
http://www.microsoft.com/jobs/

Volt UK
http://www.volt.com

Your questions answered

What is an online company profile?

An online company profile is an internet page that gives extensive company information relating to its business activity, geography, culture and people.

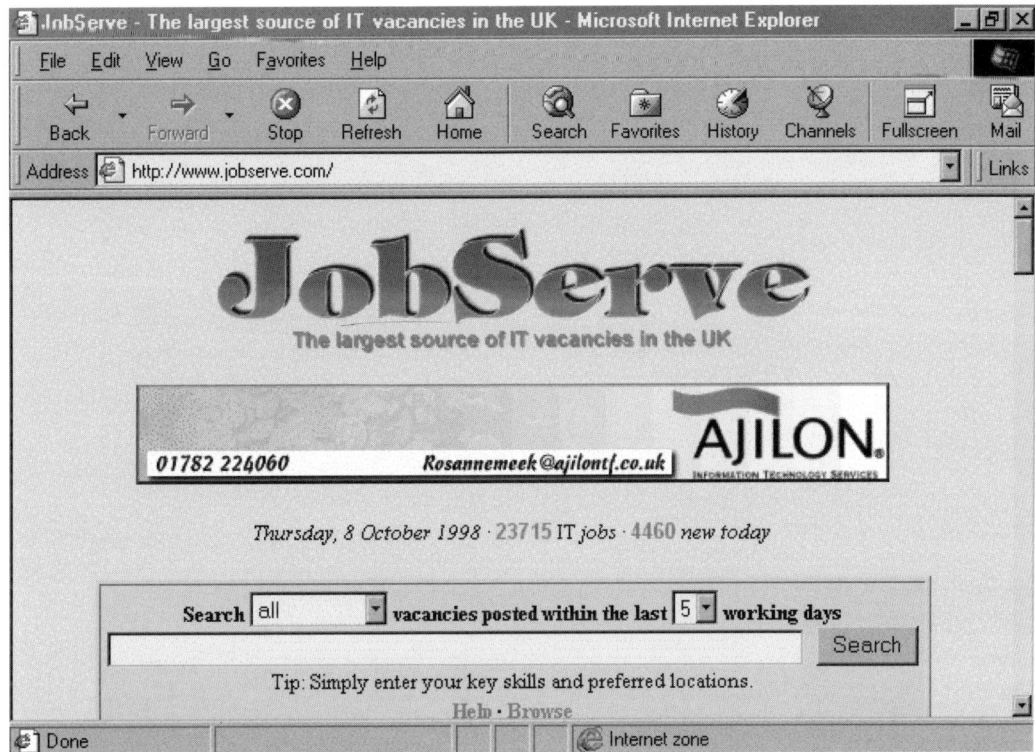

Fig. 44. The home page of JobServe, possibly the best IT jobs service on the internet.

Are there any charges for using the facilities of an online employment agency?

Some online recruitment agencies offer their services for free. Some agencies however have a charge for certain services provided.

▷ *Example 1* – Paul is currently employed in administration. As he is looking to relocate from London to the Lake District, Paul wants to know, on a daily basis, any job opportunities that might become available in Cumbria. Paul has decided to sign up with three employment agencies who allow geographical filters to be placed on job requests and who will send him appropriate vacancies daily via email.

▷ *Example 2* – Cyril has recently studied at night school for a certificate in computer programming. Adding this new qualification to his degree, he has decided he would like to work full-time as a software developer. Cyril has signed up with JobServe and has already found four jobs in his chosen locale that he feels qualified to apply for.

Points to think about

If you're about to go for an interview and you can't find any profiles on the internet do you think it's acceptable to email the company direct and ask for further information?

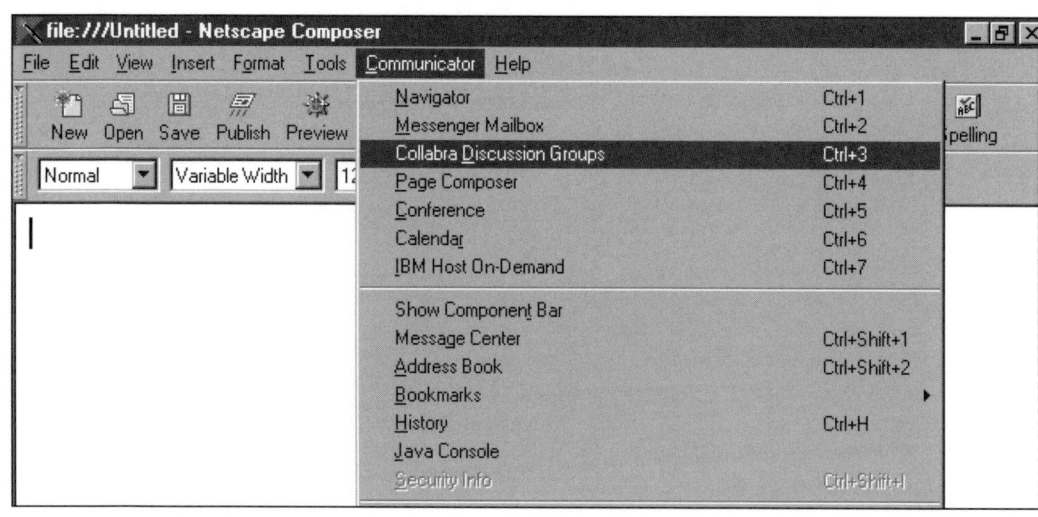

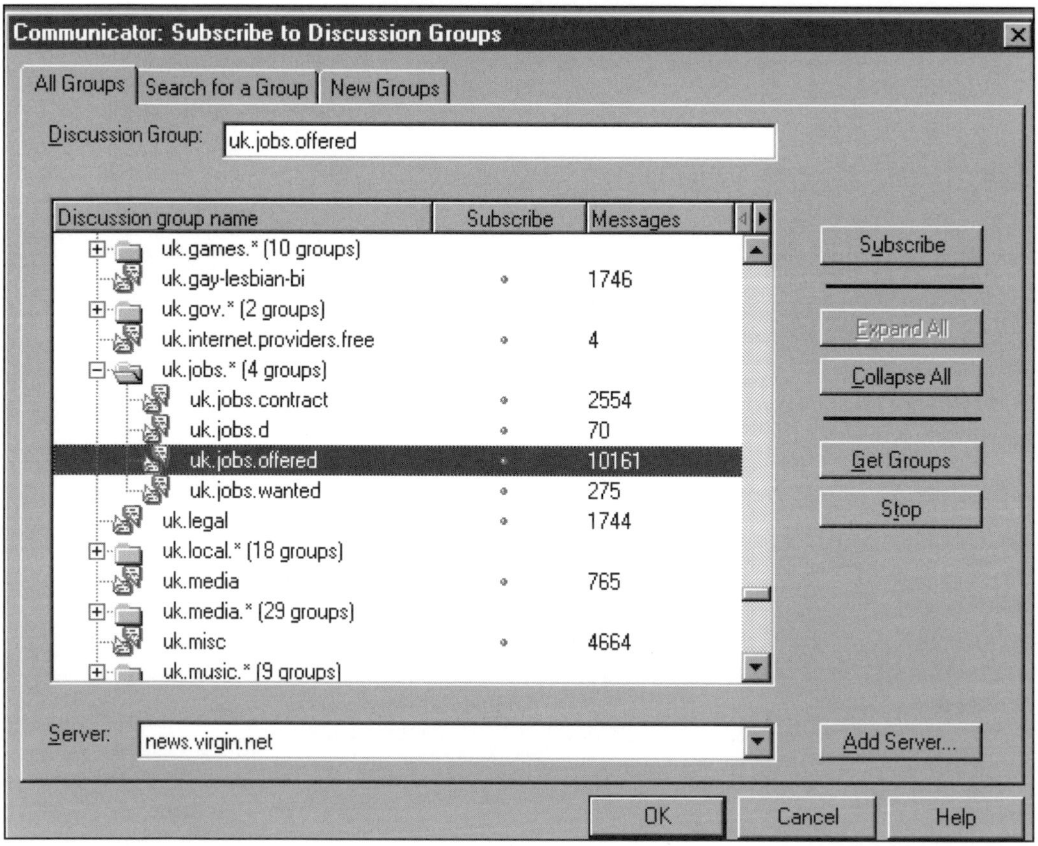

Fig. 45. Accessing newsgroups using the Netscape browser. Click *Communicator*, then *Collabra Discussion Groups* (top picture). Then select the newsgroup you wish to subscribe to.

8 Newsgroups for job seekers

In this chapter we will explore:

▶ *newsgroups*
▶ *using newsgroups effectively*
▶ *using newsgroups to secure a new job.*

....

If you've never heard of newsgroups then there's not much to worry about. As a serious job seeker looking to the internet for further opportunity you will have already visited the most richly varied source of jobs, namely those located on the world wide web (WWW).

At the start of this book we said that, to keep things simple, the words internet, net, and world wide web all meant more or less the same thing. Well, to be more exact, what you've actually been doing in the last few chapters is surfing the 'web' – the most user-friendly aspect of the internet. Newsgroups, however, are another aspect of the wider internet, and another rich source of information it will pay you to know about. The newsgroups are sometimes collectively referred to as **Usenet**.

What is a newsgroup?

A newsgroup is a kind of freely available electronic **bulletin board** on the internet. On this 'board' individuals from anywhere in the world can post all kinds of messages. **Posting to newsgroups** is very like sending email.

▷ *Note* – Newsgroups are quite separate from 'news' in the sense of commercially produced newspaper or television news. You do not have to pay anything to read or post news in newsgroups.

Newsgroup messages relate to specific subjects of interest, both personal and business. There are upwards of 30,000 active newsgroups on the internet today, each relating to a specific topic of interest. Every conceivable subject is catered for, from the very wackiest to the most intellectually serious. Newsgroups offer a fantastic opportunity for internet users to engage in public debate. Each one deals with a specific topic which is identified in the newsgroup's name. The number of newsgroups is growing all the time, and in many foreign languages from Chinese to Russian, as well as English.

Newsgroup names

Newsgroup names follow a standard convention. They are organised into categories, and each category into a hierarchy of activity. Each part of the newsgroup name is separated by a full stop. Here, for example, is the name of a job-related newsgroup which is full of messages about jobs on offer in the United Kingdom:

uk.jobs.offered

Newsgroup names

The following hierarchy of names illustrates the most common newsgroup categories:

alt	alternative interests
uk	UK interests
us	US interests
comp	computers
rec	recreation, sports etc.
soc	social issues
sci	science issues
talk	chat
biz	business.

The newsgroups are not quite as user-friendly as the all singing and all dancing web pages that you'll have become used to when surfing on the internet. When you're looking through internet job-related pages, it's usually easy to look at the contents of the jobs on offer, because of the sophisticated design used to attract visitors to that particular web site.

In the newsgroups, the information and presentation is much more basic, much as with email. The title of the newsgroup gives you some idea of its content, but there's not much else to give the game away – no colourful pages for example. This means that you have to read some of the messages to see what the newsgroup is all about (Figure 46).

Fig. 46. Using Outlook Express to view messages in the newsgroup uk.jobs.offered.

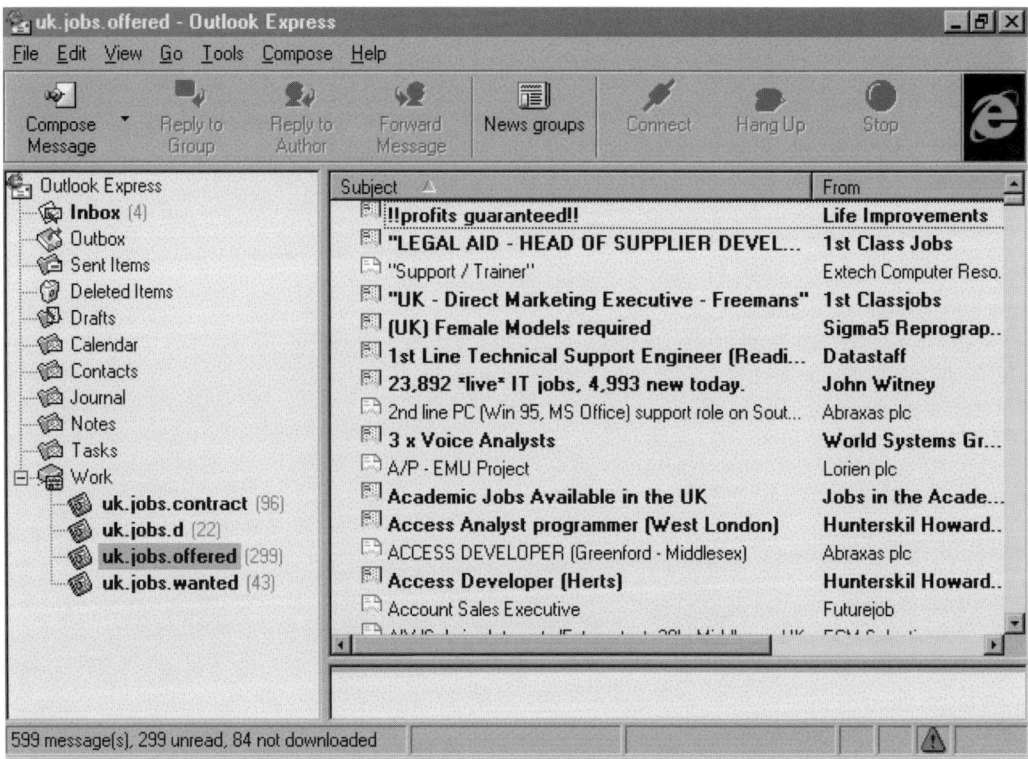

Accessing newsgroups

All of the newsgroups vary in how they operate. Some concentrate on discussion, encouraging members to openly debate and discuss topical issues relating to the newgroup's purpose. Others encourage question and answer type debate and provide mutual member support. The latter type of newsgroups often deal with hardware and software matters, enabling members to swap technical information and problem solving tips.

Accessing the newsgroups

Before you can access newsgroups you must ensure that your ISP supports them. Nowadays they virtually all do, and it should be easy for you to start exploring the newsgroups available.

This leads to another important point. Whilst newsgroups are pretty much world-wide it will be very much up to your ISP to decide which newgroups they offer you. There is no guarantee that all the newsgroups offered by one ISP will be offered by another. However, all the main newsgroups relating to employment and academic opportunities should be available from whichever internet service provider you happen to use.

Free speech and censorship

You're sure to have heard about some of the nastier sides of the internet relating to illegal pornography, drug information and terrorist activity such as bomb making. Whilst each individual has the right to decide what material they access – a basic human right that must surely be upheld – it's worth mentioning the dangers of some newsgroups that are available.

Unfortunately, some of the newsgroups are rather infamous places where nasty stuff goes on. Through usage of the world wide web you may have came across pages offering items of a violent or sexual nature. Many such web sites today require access codes and passwords to see the material stored in them, offering some form of security for internet users with young children. However, in the newsgroups this form of security is generally non-existent, and unsavoury discussion areas and the opportunity to view dubious material is much easier to access. Please watch out – especially if children are familiar with access methods for your computer.

Filtering unwanted material

America Online and some other service providers offer **parental controls**. These enable you to be your own censor, and prevent access to such web sites and newsgroups. For example, you can instruct the computer not to access any web site or newsgroup that contains certain words; you can often decide these words yourself, and protect your decisions with a password, or you can let the ISP make the decisions for you automatically.

Using your browser to access newsgroups

Using your browser to access newsgroups

If you've signed up with any of the service providers such as AOL, CompuServe, Btinternet, Demon or Virgin Net, then look no further. All provide instant access to newsgroups. Using the technical phrase, they act as your **news host** or **news server**. Look through their main menu and access them from there (Figure 47). You need to find the right key word to click such as:

▷ newsgroups
▷ community
▷ discussion
▷ discussion groups
▷ usenet
▷ bulletin boards
▷ internet.

If by any chance your ISP does not offer access to newsgroups, then your browser (Internet Explorer or Netscape Navigator) can provide access to free **open news servers** all over the internet. To find one, just use a search engine and type 'open news servers'. Pick one that takes your fancy, then, in your browser, type the name of the news server you have selected into your browser preferences. Here is an example of one which offers a staggering 56,000 newsgroups:

news.ausmail.com

Fig. 47. Preparing to view newsgroups using AOL.

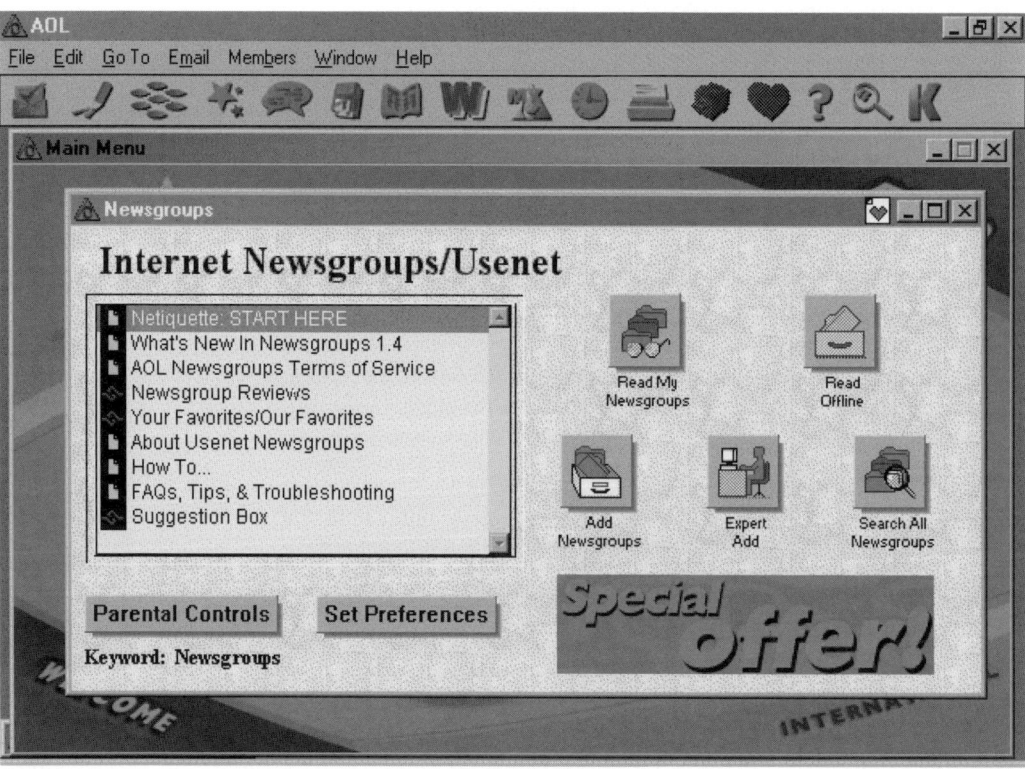

Joining a newsgroup

Other 'newsreaders' software

If you fancy a look at specific newsgroup readers then download the software available from the following sites and crank them up – see what you think! They will give you all kinds of optional control buttons and preference settings:

ForteAgent/Free Agent
http://www.forteinc.com/forte/agent/agent.htm

Nuntius
http://www.guru.med.cornell.edu/~aaron/nuntius/nuntius.html

Remember, if you use any of the software offered above for an extended period, usually after 90 days, then you have a moral duty to recompense the author of the software. This is known as **shareware**, a concept in which you 'try before you buy'. The usual suggested fee is between £10 and £30 (very often in US dollars).

Joining a newsgroup

To join or **subscribe** to a newsgroup is very simple. There are no membership fees. You can visit instantly and as often as you like. You need to subscribe (just a click of the mouse) in order to read the messages. You can also just as instantly leave or **unsubscribe** to the newsgroup – or rejoin it – whenever you choose, just by clicking with your mouse.

Accessing newsgroups with Internet Explorer

When using Internet Explorer, you access the newsgroups by choosing the *Newsgroups* option from the *Tools* menu. Then choose to open *All groups*. You will then be presented with a continuous list of all newsgroups provided by your ISP (Figure 48).

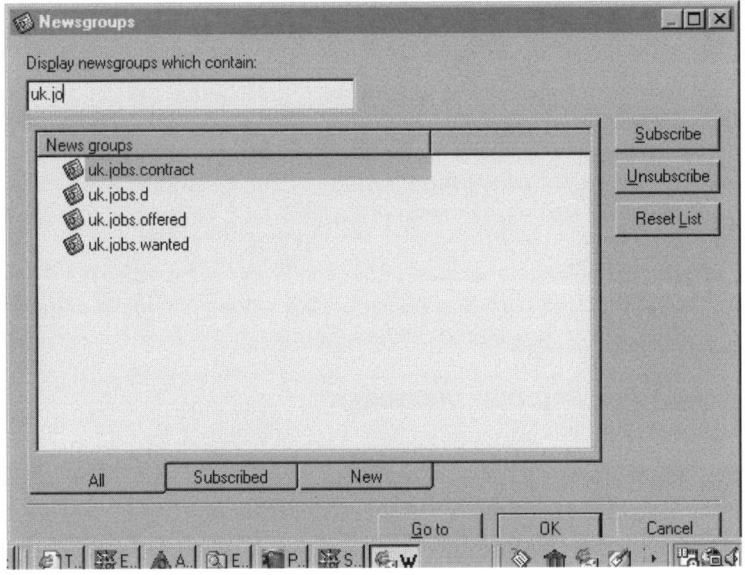

Fig. 48. Preparing to access the newsgroup uk.jobs.contract using the Internet Explorer browser.

Accessing newsgroups via your browser

You then simply key in a suitable word, such as 'jobs', choose the particular newsgroup that you'd like to access and then choose *Goto*. This lets you have a look at the messages stored in the particular newsgroup accessed (Figure 49).

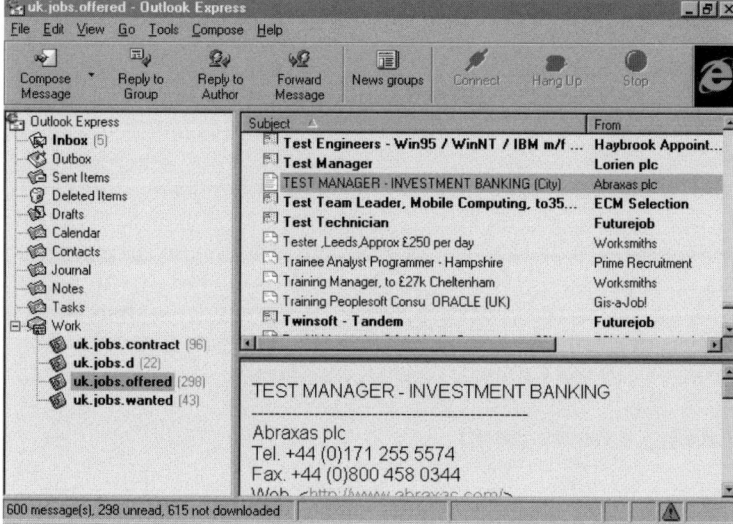

Fig. 49. Viewing messages in the newsgroup uk.jobs.offered using Outlook Express.

After visiting, if you like what you see, then simply mouse-click on the *Subscribe* icon to join this newsgroup. You can also unsubscribe in this area by mouse-clicking on the appropriate icon.

Accessing newsgroups with Netscape Navigator

In Netscape Navigator joining newsgroups is just as easy. From the *Options* menu choose *Show All Newsgroups*. This will download all available newsgroups from your ISP. The first time you do this, it could take five or ten minutes, because there could be 20,000 to 30,000 of them. But you won't need to do this again, even after you have switched off your computer. The list will be saved on your hard drive.

To view the messages held in a particular newsgroup simply click on the folder of the newsgroup in the left panel; this will reveal the headers of the messages available. Then click on any one of these headers shown in the right panel; the message will then be displayed in the bottom window of your screen.

Subscribing couldn't be simpler, either. Once you've found somewhere to hang your hat just tick the box next to the newsgroup folder name in the left hand window of your screen. Simple.

Reading newsgroup messages

Once you've subscribed to a newsgroup you'll want to ensure that you get as much useful information out of your 'membership' and participation as possible. Each newsgroup to which you have subscribed could have hundreds – even thousands – of messages

Newsgroup netiquette

posted daily. Some of the biggest newsgroups on the internet are to do with jobs. To read all of these messages on-line would run up huge telephone charges and ISP charges. The best way to read newsgroup messages is therefore offline.

Reading messages offline with Internet Explorer

Choose the *Read News* menu item from the menu that appears after mouse-clicking on the *Mail* icon. Then choose *Download This Newsgroup*. Next, choose to download one of the following:

> all newsgroup messages
> only newly posted messages
> only message headers.

Downloading complete messages can take up lots of room on your PC, so beware. Better to download **header** detail only. You can always go back for the **body** of the message if the details take your fancy. You can also choose to mark specific messages online and simply download these messages.

Reading offline with Netscape Navigator

Newsgroups to which you are subscribed automatically download message headers each time you go online.

Writing a newsgroup message

Once again, this is easy stuff. In both Internet Explorer and Netscape Navigator you just highlight the message to which you wish to reply. Then you choose to

▷ reply privately to the author of the message, or
▷ post your message publicly, to be seen by all members of the newsgroup.

Then, simply click on the *send* icon or menu button. And that's it.

When reading messages, especially in the job-related pages, you will often see hyperlinks in the messages. These hyperlinks exist to send you at a click of your mouse towards web pages, as well as to let you send a reply to the message sender. This method of reply can often save time – something that's crucial in getting that all important job or career change.

Observing newsgroup netiquette

There are some simple rules to be followed. Remember email? Well, newsgroup etiquette is just as important. Newsgroup members are there for a purpose, because they have an interest in a particular subject or issue. In your case the newsgroups you join will have members interested in jobs and careers. Therefore, any inappropriate use of the

Newsgroups for job seekers

newsgroup will be met with some wrath by other members – remember the time it takes to read and understand newsgroup messages? Make sure you become a responsible newsgroup member.

A checklist for good newsgroup membership

1. Watch out for **flames**. Flames are more or less hostile or angry messages sent by other newsgroup members when you breach the rules of the newsgroup. This breach of rules could be something as simple as posting a message that isn't related exactly, for example, to a job advert. **Flame wars** can erupt when someone replies to a flame and heated exchanges occur. This could be alarming if directed at you.

2. Feel free to **lurk**. Lurking means looking about the newsgroup, and having a peep at the messages. Lurking is fine, but once you have the confidence then active and sustained participation is better.

3. Avoid **spamming** (see Chapter Two).

4. **FAQs** should be read – especially if you're a new member. Other members post these messages to save the same, often straightforward question, being asked over and over again by newbies.

5. Use plain English in your messages – have a look at some existing newsgroup messages and gauge the tone.

6. Avoid the USE OF CAPITALS – it's considered rude and generally denotes SHOUTING.

7. When replying to messages, take out any unwanted text in the original message – this will make the message go quicker and reduce storage space on the news server.

Useful newsgroups for job seekers

As a serious job or career seeker you'll likely want to have a look at the most relevant newsgroups that are likely to interest you. The following table outlines the main newsgroups that are worth a look. However, remember that there are thousands of newsgroups on the internet with millions of members. Have a lurk around and see if there are any job-related sites that take your fancy. Then subscribe and contribute!

uk.jobs.offered
This newsgroup contains loads of daily job offers mainly posted by recruitment consultants. Whilst IT jobs are the main category represented here, there are a number of sales and other jobs posted. Good contacts for local job agencies could also be useful to the general job seeker.

Examples

uk.jobs.wanted
You'll find a real rag-bag full of jobs related stuff in this newsgroup. In the main it's people looking for work – so grasp the opportunity and post your online CV. There are also some jobs on offer as well as links to other employment newsgroups and worldwide web pages.

uk.jobs.contract
If you fancy earning big bucks with little responsibility but no security then contract work is for you. Again the job details posted in this newsgroup are mainly IT related, but have a good look around as there are jobs relating to other industries.

alt.jobs.overseas
This is an international newsgroup offering lots of vacancies and covering lots of industries. All the jobs available are overseas.

▷ *Example 1* – Martin has been an avid internet job seeker for nearly three months. As he has not yet managed to find a job that's suitable for his present circumstances Martin is looking to find new sources of opportunity. Since finding out about the benefits of newsgroups from a friend, Martin has now contacted a recruitment consultant in the USA through the newsgroup 'alt.jobs.overseas'. They have subsequently exchanged emails, and Martin has arranged to meet a UK based representative of the company for an interview in the next few weeks.

▷ *Example 2* – Philippa lives in Denmark and is soon to return to the UK when her current work contract ends. Before returning home, Philippa has decided to take preparatory steps to help secure a new job. By posting details of her home page on the newsgroup 'uk.jobs.wanted' Philippa has ensured that prospective employers have an early opportunity of viewing her CV online.

Points to think about

1. Do you think the advance in design and the increase in usage of the user-friendly world wide web page, is likely to reduce the need for job-seekers to use newsgroups?

2. In your opinion should stronger measures be put in place to censor material available on the internet? Should we learn to take more responsibility for our own actions?

Your questions answered

What is a newsgroup?
A newsgroup is a collection of messages posted to a central computer by individuals and companies relating to a particular theme. There are thousands of newsgroups available covering every conceivable business and personal topic.

Hot tip

Check out the really comprehensive list of job-related news-groups which appears at the end of the book.

It's OK to lurk

What does the term 'lurking' refer to?

Lurking is the term used to describe the activity of scanning through newsgroups and reading the messages posted there before deciding to subscribe to that newsgroup.

Right: Posting a message to the newsgroup uk.jobs.offered using the Netscape browser.

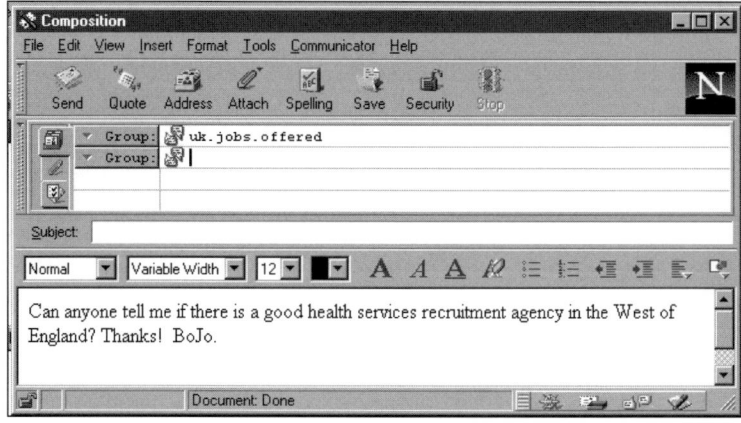

Below: A lurker posts their first message in a newsgroup.

9 Checklists for getting that job

In this chapter we will explore:

▶ completing a job application form correctly
▶ preparing effectively for an interview
▶ performing well at interview.

Well, you've done all the hi-tech groundwork. You've written your online CV, set up your HTML home page, checked out job and company profiles and signed up with some of the big on-line employment agencies. And, if everything goes according to plan, the next stage is to leave that PC behind and get down to the more tedious side of the job-seeking process, filling in the forms and attending interviews.

It doesn't matter how comprehensive your online search has been, everything will be of no avail unless you master the techniques needed to impress prospective employers. It's time to get back to basics.

Completing an application form

The application form gives you the ideal opportunity to write the script of the interview. Remember all those interviews that you've previously attended? What did the interviewer refer to? In the majority of cases it's sure to have been the application form. And here lies your greatest opportunity.

It was you who completed this document therefore it's you who are the world's expert on its content. So, ask yourself, can you really afford to miss this great opportunity to influence your future? The answer is of course, no. If your application form is completed incorrectly or shabbily your chance of securing an interview for the job is greatly reduced.

Checklist for completing application forms

1. Ensure that you've got a copy of the job description before you begin completing the application form.
2. Be positive in your views.
3. Don't lie.
4. Before completing the form read it over a couple of times. Ensure that you take a photocopy to practise with.
5. Allow yourself plenty of time to complete the application form.
6. Look out for any special instructions that the company might require for completion of application forms such as the use of black ink or the requirement to complete the form in capital letters.

Composing a covering letter

> 7. In the 'additional information' section ensure that you fill in as much information as possible, ensure that the information that you provide is suited to the requirements of the job – show willingness and enthusiasm in your writing!
>
> 8. Remember to photocopy the completed application form before sending it off to the company, you can then use this to remind you of what you've written if your quest to secure an interview is successful.

Preparing a letter to accompany the application form

It's common courtesy to send a covering letter with your completed application form. This letter should be brief and include the following sections.

Introduction
Outline the exact details of the job for which you are applying, including any references that you may have come across on internet pages.

Your enthusiasm for the job
Make this a short paragraph setting out your enthusiasm for securing the job. Remember, this letter will be sitting with your prospective employer at the interview stage. Remind him or her of your motivation to win employment and – very important – the benefits you can offer to the organisation.

Your skills
This section should not be a carbon copy of your CV, or of the details listed on your application form. It should be an innovative expression of how your particular skills are suited for the job. Maybe the job involves working with the Chinese community and you have studied Cantonese as part of an evening college course. Don't just state 'studied Cantonese for 16 weeks' but rather expand a little and maybe say 'after completing a beginner's course in Cantonese I practised the language by talking with staff in my friend's parents' Chinese restaurant.' Bring your skills to life.

Availability for interview
One of the golden rules to follow when completing job application forms is: be flexible. Remember, your prospective employer will be very busy and any difficulties made by job applicants as to dates and times of interview could be viewed in a dim light. Instead, show your prospective employer that you are willing; be positive in making yourself available for interview whenever required.

▷ *Example 1* – Through the services of an online employment agency, Will has managed to find details of an analyst/programmer job that he finds interesting. Will has contacted the company offering the job, and has been sent an application form. As the form is quite

Approaching an interview

difficult to understand and requires a detailed account of his qualifications and career to date, Will has decided to photocopy the form, complete a trial run, and then photocopy the completed form before sending it off to the organisation.

Preparing for interview

If all has gone well, you'll have received notification that you have been placed on a short list for the job being applied for, and you'll have been called for interview. Now it's time to get down to the real hard work. Remember, on average you probably have a one in eight chance of getting that job! The stakes are high, and it's down to you.

Interview preparation checklist

1. Make sure you know the date, time and venue of the interview.
2. Record this information in your electronic organiser or diary.
3. Make sure that you know plenty of information about the company, its ethos, the number of employees it has, the activities it undertakes, any likely expansions, any legislative or competitive threats – if you can't find any information on the internet then it's perfectly acceptable to send an email or call and ask for annual reports or product brochures to be forwarded through the post to you.
4. Prepare a list of questions that may be asked at interview. Develop and practise some convincing answers.
5. Prepare answers for the three 'killer' questions that devastate so many applicants:

    'Tell us about yourself.'
    'Why should we choose you?'
    'What can you bring to the company?'

6. These questions have been asked a million times and yet they are often met with a blank look and a wall of embarrassing silence.
7. Concentrate and focus on the objective of the interview – securing that job.

If possible, visit the company's premises – take mental notes of the place, the cars and the people coming and going – soak up the environment.

Attending the interview

Enter stage left! This is it, your big chance to shine. You've been called for interview, you've completed all your research and practised your answers to all those difficult questions, so why should you be worried? Be positive, look forward to the actual interview, and relax.

Interview checklist

A great tool for relaxing is to picture those who are interviewing you in normal circumstances, away from work. Imagine them washing the car, visiting the local supermarket or taking part in a game of sport. At work, however, they are the next hurdle to overcome in your career. They can help decide whether you can afford that new car, buy that new house or go on that extra foreign holiday, so they are very important. Treat them with respect. But remember, too, that like you they are human.

Another useful relaxant is to have a packet of mints in your pocket. Just before you enter the interview venue pop a mint into your mouth. Not only will you feel more relaxed but any nasty breath smells, often caused by nervous dryness of the mouth, will be eradicated.

Interview attendance checklist

1. Remember to dress appropriately. Nine times out of ten, formal wear is the order of the day. Unless you have been specifically told, never attend an interview wearing informal clothing.

2. When you arrive at the venue for the interview take time to look around. This means planning to arrive early. An extra benefit of early arrival is that you can see what the other candidates look like – can you beat them?

3. In the reception area have a look at the walls and the furniture. What do they tell you? This could be the outward face of the company. Also, if organisations have achieved any awards or prizes they are sure to display them in reception for all to see. Look out for certificates for quality awards such as ISO9002, or Investors in People certificates. These type of awards can tell you a lot about an organisation. Look out for recent copies of the company newsletter, again, a useful barometer of the ethos and culture of the organisation.

4. Introduce yourself in a bright and friendly manner. Extend your hand to shake hands with the interview panel – do not sit until you are invited to do so.

5. Try and temper your body language. Don't fold your arms, twitch or move about unnecessarily portraying nerves to your interviewers.

6. Put yourself in the shoes of the interviewers. What are they looking for? What specific requirements do they have of a prospective employee?

After the interview

7. Listen carefully to questions posed and take your time to answer each question – do not be tempted to ramble into unrelated detail.

8. If you are being interviewed by a panel of interviewers ensure that you maintain appropriate eye-contact with the complete panel – scan the panel with your eyes as you answer, ensuring that you give equal precedence to all members.

9. Avoid looking towards the floor.

10. Carry with you to the interview any proof of projects that you have worked on and which you are particularly proud of – at an opportune moment ask if you can hand these items around and show the panel of the quality of your work.

11. At the end of the interview always ask at least two pertinent questions relating to the organisation and job for which you are applying.

12. Remember to ask the interviewers when you are likely to hear the result of the interview.

13. Thank the interviewers before you leave.

14. Smile, smile, smile throughout the interview.

▷ *Example 2* – Irene is attending an interview for the position of secretary in a large public sector organisation. Irene has arrived nearly 20 minutes before the interview start time. On arrival in the organisation's reception, Irene is busy soaking up information from the company's brochures and newsletter, which reveal that the company is a great supporter of charity. She makes a mental note to remind her interviewers that she recently took part in a 10 kilometre fun run for her local hospice.

What to do after the interview

Immediately after the interview jot down details of how you feel you performed. What were your strengths, what did you do wrong – and remember to write down, for future reference, any unusual questions that you were surprised to be asked.

Then wait...

Sometimes employers will ask candidates to wait around the interview venue and call back the successful candidate. However, this is becoming less and less popular. Most employers arrange to call the successful candidate the same day or the day after the interview, whilst some employers may choose to wait until the successful candidate has accepted the position before contacting those who were unsuccessful.

Points to think about

▷ If you've secured the job then well done – no more advice for you – you've passed all the hurdles – good luck, work hard and success will be yours.

▷ If you're unlucky enough not to get accepted then take it as an opportunity to revise your method of preparation and attendance at interview. Don't worry if the letter that you receive is short and to the point – it is very difficult to tell someone that they have been unsuccessful. It is perfectly acceptable to ask the interview panel the reasons why you were unsuccessful. Whilst many employers would be unhappy to discuss the reasons for your failure by phone, a written reply is often forthcoming.

Even if you have not been successful, use the interview as a learning phase and a building block to getting that successful job. Perseverance and good technique will almost certainly result in you getting the job that you want.

Your questions answered

Why should you plan for attending an interview?
Proper planning will ensure that you are prepared to effectively participate in the actual interview and should help you secure the job for which you are applying.

What is body language?
Body language is the non-verbal messages sent out by the movements of body and eyes. Body language, when analysed, can reveal as much about a person as that which they say through speech.

Points to think about

1. A job interview typically lasts around 30 to 45 minutes. Do you think that an employer can really determine your suitability for a job in this time? If not, is there a better way of choosing employees?

2. The process of preparing for a job interview is often laced with anxiety and needless stress. Do you think that it would be acceptable to call your prospective interviewer to discuss the requirements and functions of the job for which you are applying?

10 Top job sites and careers services on the internet

Whether it's information or sources of opportunity about a new job, new career, full-time college or university course or a return to study or work after a period of absence, the following sites are some of the best around.

1st Impressions
http://www.1st-Imp.com
Launched in 1996, this is a well presented résumé-writing and career management resource. 1st Impressions has provided services to clients located all over the United States as well as in 31 other countries including the UK. This professionally developed site has many additional features including information about immigration to the USA, employment news feeds, bookshop, reading room, disabilities corner, job corner, updates on US job fairs and other resources.

100hot.com
http://www.100hot.com/
This page details the 100 best sites on the internet across a number of business- and hobby-related categories. Keep an eye on the Job section to find the best world-wide internet sites worthy of a visit.

Accountancy Magazine
http://www.accountancymag.co.uk/jobindex.htm
This page presents a small selection from 50 pages of recruitment advertisements to be found each month in *Accountancy Magazine*. It includes links to related sites such as accountancy books, accountancy courses and conferences and accountancy enterprises.

Accounting Web
http://www.accountingweb.co.uk/
This is an impressive Bristol-based information resource for accountants, presented in a magazine-style format. It contains many useful links. The site offers news, lists of accountancy firms, links, databases, discussion, a directory, suppliers, a press zone, library, jobs, search, and help. You can gain direct access to some 1.4 million live company reports from Companies House and other sources as compiled by the UK financial publisher ICC. There are no set-up or monthly charges, and it is free to search. Its jobs section contains handy links to a collection of top online recruitment sites for accountants and finance professionals. You are invited to subscribe.

Top job sites and careers services

AGCAS Occupational Profiles
http://www.prospects.csu.ac.uk/student/
Every year higher education careers advisers write, edit and up-date detailed profiles of graduate occupations. These form the AGCAS Occupational Database. You can access these job profiles here by selecting a work area of interest. These include education, social and pastoral care, health care, law enforcement and protection, hotel, catering and accommodation services, plus leisure and recreation services. There is also advertising, promotion and marketing, buying, selling and retailing, insurance and pensions, finance, legal services, employment and labour, information technology and management services, administration, transport and distribution, property and construction, physical resources and the environment, animal and plant resources, manufacturing and processing, engineering, scientific services, information services, creative arts, design and crafts, publishing, media and performing arts.

AltaVista Careers
http://jump.altavista.com/career
AltaVista is one of the internet's best-known search engines. You can use this page to search every major job site on the web simultaneously. As a test we input the word 'optometrist' which produced no less than 322 vacancies worldwide. 'Beautician' produced 45, 'illustrator' produced over 10,000, and 'oceanographer' produced 218. You would of course narrow the field considerably by including 'UK' in your search. Remember to bookmark this page. AltaVista's home page address is: http://www.altavista.com/

The Biz
http://www.thebiz.co.uk
The Biz (Business Information Zone) is a great site for finding out information about British industry and companies. Split into ten industry categories, the Biz gives you a wealth of information for each industry with information such as the names of professional bodies and details relating to major companies and employers in each sector. This site also contains a nice little entry called Biz Buzz which is billed as the world's first alternative interactive business magazine and which provides some entertaining and informative business-related articles.

Bridges
http://tour.bridges.com/
This North American service offers a comprehensive library of career related articles packaged as a daily magazine. It delivers independently researched job profiles, labour market analysis, and career development tools to over 1,500 schools every day. Over 2.5 million 'hits' are recorded annually on its national and regional services. It offers tools for individual and classroom career exploration, decision-making units for students, motivation, ability and personality assessments linked to career profiles and college search tools. Using its Career Research Tool you can enter personality traits, skills, interests and values, and get back a list of suggested careers. This is one of a number of nicely presented features which would be of value to a UK user.

Top job sites and careers services

Bristol University Careers Service
http://www.bris.ac.uk/Depts/CAS/
This includes a very useful list of employers' web sites, an excellent reference for UK job seekers. This list features many well known leading British companies, from Abbey National and Anglian Water to Voluntary Service Overseas and Zeneca, and the links take you straight to their home pages. Presented A to Z, the list contains helpful annotations to show those company web sites which contain careers information, and those which contain actual job vacancy sections.

CanDo Disability Careers Network
http://cando.lancs.ac.uk/
CanDo is the British careers site for disabled students and graduates. The CanDo site offers some great resources for disabled people who are thinking of going to university or looking for employment. This site covers a number of useful topics for disabled people and it provides a very straightforward and easy to use search routine. If you choose to access the additional services provided by CanDo you are required to register. However, this is easy to do and worthwhile as it enables unrestricted access to the site.

Career Guide
http://www.career-guide.com
Career Guide hosts the online sites for its three publications which assist graduates, MBAs and alumni in making the right career moves. They are the *Top Graduate Career Guide, Top Technical Career Guide* and *MBA Career Guide*. The site features a business schools review, where you can search for business schools world wide. You can register your CV and make a selection from top recruiters world wide. Your CV will be forwarded electronically. The company has offices in Regents Park, London. It runs separate annual careers forums in London for both graduates and MBAs. The Graduate Forum is targeted at Europe's top young professionals and is dedicated to recruitment for major consultancies, banks and corporations; the MBA event is dedicated to the recruitment of MBA students and alumni from European and US business schools. Participating organisations include ASDA, Barclays Capital, Bertelsmann, Chase Manhattan, Diageo, IBM, Johnson & Johnson, KPMG, NatWest, Pearl Assurance, Roland Berger, Siemens, SmithKline Beecham, Thorn Group, and many others.

Career Lab – 200 readymade letters
http://www.careerlab.com/
Based in Englewood, USA, Career Lab describes itself as a friendly, service-oriented consulting firm providing career management advice for senior executives and top professionals, as well as career, outplacement, and human resources consulting for companies world wide. Travellers from more than 100 countries have visited this web site, which apparently receives about 400,000 hits per week. A feature of the site is its collection of well over 200 ready made letters, a boon to employees and job seekers everywhere. They show you how to clarify your career direction, find a part-time job, or manage being caught

Top job sites and careers services

without a résumé. They show you how to enlist help from friends, business acquaintances, recruiters and employment agencies. Still more letters show you how to answer *wanted* ads like a professional, how to win good references, write sales letters, and uncover hidden job markets. Others say 'thank you', request help from consultants (or show you how to become one), build good relationships, promote yourself in the media, stop yourself getting fired, negotiate a pay rise, and more. You can easily adapt these letters to your own situation. They receive more than 20,000 hits each week – and it's easy to see why. Career Lab is part of Lincolnshire International, a human resources consulting firm which also has UK offices.

CareerMosaic
http://www.careermosaic-uk.co.uk

CareerMosaic's UK pages give an absolute compendium of information for job seekers. Whether you want to work in the UK or abroad, learn how to write the perfect CV or look through UK college and university courses, then CareerMosaic is a must for you. If you are out to land a job with some of the big boys then a visit to 'Employers Showcase' is the place to head on this site.

Career Resource Center
http://www.careers.org

Career Resource Center claims to be the internet's most complete and extensive index of career-related web sites. It contains more than over 11,000 links to jobs posted by employers, posted in newspapers and to internet newsgroups. The site's career resources include bibliographies, publications, software lists, resource evaluations, and event calendars. Resources are cross-referenced both geographically and alphabetically. Its learning section offers links to colleges and libraries, while its career reference page provides links to US state employment offices, as well as links to a variety of other helpful services. The Career Services leads you to employment agencies and out-placement firms. If you get tired of job-hunting, check out the *After Hours* page for links to travel and recreation, hobby, leisure and other 'fun' sites. Though the service is US based, its extensive and well categorised links make this an essential resource for job seekers everywhere.

Career Solutions
http://www.careersolutions.co.uk/

This is the UK web site of Sandy McMillan and two colleagues, Jenny Summerfield and Craig Watson. The first two belong to the Institute of Personnel & Development. The site offers free advice on a broad range of career-related topics, useful books and software to buy, and access to friendly and confidential help. There is a clear site map to guide you around.

Career Talk
http://www.careertalk.com

This is a syndicated column offering advice on all kinds of career-related topics including job search, salary negotiation, profiling a company,

Top job sites and careers services

attending behavioural interview, changing careers, the art of asking questions, writing a net résumé, résumé tips, compensation and benefits, accessing the hidden job market, pre-interview quizzes and more. The web site is a project of Seaton Corporation, an American HR company involved in interview training, selection and outplacement.

Career Zone UK
http://www.careerzone-uk.com/
Career Zone UK offers free, impartial advice and information on all aspects of career, employment, education and training advice in the UK. Its pages provide plenty of advice and information for all-comers. It contains over 300 categorised links to careers-related sites. It employs consultants and counsellors who are trained to a minimum of the Diploma in Careers Guidance, NVQ level 4 or equivalent to answer queries. If you have careers, recruitment, employment, education or education articles or information you'd like to see published then you are invited to contact the editor. This useful-looking site appeared not to have been recently updated, but its handy and extensive links to British professional and official bodies alone would make it worth a visit.

Careers Services National Association
http://www.careers-uk.com
CSNA is an association of all the English careers service organisations which provide statutory careers guidance services under contract to the UK Government. The Association helps to retain a national identity for the Careers Service and a voice for its members. This web site contains a directory of all organisations in the UK which provide careers guidance under contract to the Department for Education and Employment. The organisations also offer a range of associated services for employers and job seekers. You can also access the web sites of other major providers of careers-related information and advice, largely in the public sector, and find out more about the work of the Association.

Cascaid Careers Software
http://www.cascaid.co.uk/
Cascaid is part of Loughborough University, and is dedicated to education and business working together. It develops careers software and support materials to help individuals, whatever their age or ability, and to support the work of professionals in education, careers guidance and counselling. Its products include Kudos, a user friendly computer program designed to give students career ideas and information, and Adult Directions, a complete package for adults of all ages and abilities combining self assessment, guidance and information. There is also Career Quest, a questionnaire processed to give students a personalised print-out of career ideas and information; and CareerScape, a user friendly database with details of over 690 careers and related articles on education, employment and training.

Top job sites and careers services

Computer & Communication Companies
http://www.cmpcmm.com/cc/
A project of Webstart Communications, this site will give you all the links you could possibly want to employers in the IT field. The home page plunges straight into main classifications, with more than 10,000 links available to you. These include new entries, companies, media, organisations, programmes and projects, usenet news groups and FAQs, standards, countries and states, cross references to other lists of computer or communication related URLs, and a compendium of general pages.

Construction Site
http://www.CareersNet.co.uk
Produced for EMAP, this web site specialises in careers information for the British construction industry – including architects, engineers, surveyors, contractors, builders, and geotechnical engineers. The site is supported by a range of leading magazines and exhibitions serving the construction industry. These include *The Architects' Journal, Architectural Review, Construction News, Civil Engineering International, Ground Engineering* and *New Civil Engineer.* The site leads you job vacancies, a CV service, courses, development, profiles, what's new, a newsletter, and information on recruiters. You can search for temporary and permanent jobs in specific UK locations, or overseas by continent. If you are a job seeker, the screen will guide you through a CV building process. Your CV will then be available to active recruiters. You can prevent your current employer from viewing your CV.

Cornwall and Devon Careers Service
http://www.careers-cd.org.uk/
This is a nicely produced site with an excellent collection of UK links that would be helpful to any job hunter in the UK, as well as to local applicants.

Cymru Prosper Wales
http://prosper.swan.ac.uk
Here is a database of Welsh employers' details and current vacancies. It is run by the Higher Education Careers Service in Wales. There are only a handful of job vacancies, and rather more details of short-term graduate placement schemes.

Datagold
http://www.datagold.com/
Datagold allows you to search more than 35,000 UK business web sites here, and in the Datagold Channels you will find over 130,000 UK companies listed. You will find listings of UK companies, which you can then search by location. Titles include a training directory, accountants directory, recruitment directory, a marketing directory which includes PR and market research, management consultants directory, an export directory and internet service provider directory. The site says it now has over twice as many UK sites indexed as its closest competitor, and challenges you to compare results with Yahoo! UK and Yellow Web. If

---

ONLINE DATABASES

UK Directories
Advertising Companies
Design Companies
Exhibition Companies
Marketing Consultants
Market Research
PR Companies

Search Engines
Infertility
UK Motorsport

Also available on
CD-ROM.

Top job sites and careers services

you want to check out your prospective employer, this site is a definite must, but you are more likely to find a postal address and phone number than a web link.

Disgruntled
http://www.disgruntled.com
This site offers some great tips for CV building and the process of interviews. Disgruntled is a first class, free online business magazine. It has as its opening quote (allegedly attributed to Ronald Regan) 'They say hard work never hurt anybody, but I figure why take the chance.' This gives you an idea of the irreverent content of the magazine. Great fun!

E-CV
http://www.e-cv.com
This is an electronic CV forwarding service, with offices in the USA and Canada. It offers an economical way to deliver your information to recruitment managers worldwide. For example, its North American Premium Plan – its most popular – delivers your cover letter and résumé to 1,000 top North American employers and recruiters for $120 US. Another option is the UK Tech Plan for the technology career professional wanting a job in the United Kingdom. This list includes 2,000 of the top technology employers and recruiters in the UK. It also has some specialist Asian lists. It invites you to compare its service with traditional mail-based CV forwarding services that charge from $2.25 per CV plus postage. It says it now has 20,000 companies and professional recruiters registered in its databases. The company can customise delivery of your CV to specific industry segments or geographical locations.

E Jobs
http://www.ejobs.org
This is a handy source of information on environmental jobs and careers, developed by an American environmental analyst, David R. Brierley. E Jobs links to environmental opportunities mainly in the USA and Canada. It includes careers such as environmental engineers, nature and wetlands scientists, GIS, technicians, chemists, geologists, geotechnical experts, policy and law, wildlife conservation, land use planning, and education.

Earthworks
http://ourworld.compuserve.com/homepages/eworks/
Don't worry about the long URL – this is a good place to come if you are seeking job opportunities as a geoscientist, petroleum geoscientist or engineer, hydrogeologist, engineering geologist, remote sensing professional, oceanographer, or an environmental scientist in academia, the upstream oil and gas sector and the mining industry. The very numerous job descriptions are extremely detailed. This well-classified amateur site is said to be updated several times per day.

Electronic Recruiting News
http://www.interbiznet.com/
ERN says it is dedicated to defining excellence in electronic recruiting.

Top job sites and careers services

Its huge site contains more than 5,000 pages of free information that chronicles the evolution of key web recruitment resources, identifies new trends and prods the losers to improve. It publishes and archives three online *dailies* that cover facets of electronic recruiting: *Recruiting Itself*, *Job Hunters* and *Marketing*. You can register for a free subscription to its print edition. It delivers seminars and speeches on the subject all over the USA. Its says that its subscription web site helps support the continuing education of some of this new industry's most successful recruiters.

Electronic Yellow Pages
http://www.eyp.co.uk

Do you want to identify leading employers in a particular industry or occupational field? Do you want to check out the home pages of a prospective employer before you go to interview, or accept a job offer? Then 'Yell' is a great place to start, and as you would expect it is very well classified. You can do a yellow pages search by business type, location, or company name, or a general UK web search. If you get a lot of results, you can sort them A to Z. The results are likely to come up in big type, and so your browser may only display few per page, meaning a long trawl through each letter of the alphabet. Some of the company names include a web site link, so you can check out their corporate profile. Some also have street location maps, so you have no reason to get lost on your way to the interview. Electronic Yellow Pages was first trialled in 1987, and launched nationally in 1990. It is a project of British Telecom. This would be an excellent bookmark both for job hunters and all kinds of other purposes.

Employment Index
http://www.employmentindex.com

This site provides employment search information and job help. It is designed for career seekers, recruiters, employers, job hunters and employment professionals alike. The search categories below mirror *Yellow Pages'* indexes. Its Employment Search Categories will find you job-help information easily and quickly. These include employee assistance, employee benefit consultants, permanent employment, employee leasing, large employers, temporary employment, executive search & recruitment, training, government jobs, federal jobs, job listers (100+), retained executive search, college & university jobs, HR consulting, help wanted and job listings, résumés, employment screening, and employment outsourcing. You make use of more than 60 large general search engines and meta search engines on the site for other searches. Even though there is no general search facility, the quantity and range of specific search categories make this site unmissable.

Employment Links for the Biomedical Scientist
http://www.his.com/~graeme/employ.html

These are often trying times for PhDs searching for suitable employment, a problem that is not confined to the biomedical sciences or to the United States. The internet offers a particularly useful medium for

Top job sites and careers services

exchange of employment-related information. However, sifting through this large and ever-increasing volume of information can be a time-consuming task for the job seeker with specialised career options. This set of links is being compiled by a fellow scientist to help colleagues in the biomedical and other sciences who may be exploring the internet for online employment information. The resources are US based, but they do include quite a lot of specialised international links. This valuable amateur site is a must for all biomedics.

Employment Newgroups Listing
http://www.ipa.com/newsgroups.html
This is an extensive list of links to employment-related newsgroups in the United Kingdom, Australia, Bermuda, Canada, Denmark, and the United States. There are over 100 newsgroup sites to search. Many internet service providers do not support all newsgroups, partly because there are now so many of them (50,000 plus), so if you have a problem reaching a particular group, contact your provider. If you still have difficulty, you can easily access all newsgroups on the internet by finding an 'open news server'. There are lots of these, many of them free, and you can find one very easily by typing 'open news servers' into Yahoo! or your other favourite search engine. If you find a new employment-related newsgroup you are invited to let this site know. IPA Members can use QuickPost and QuickSearch in the members' area to quickly post job openings or search résumé databases. Never visited the newsgroups before? – never fear, all human life is there!

Employment Service
http://www.employmentservice.gov.uk/
The Employment Service is an agency of the Department for Education and Employment. This site shows how it operates and works with its clients, employers and partners. You will also be able to find the address of your nearest jobcentre. The site attempts to answer the questions, what will the future be like, what are we here to do, who will our customers be, and where will our priorities lie? You can find details of the Welfare to Work Scheme, Jobseekers' Allowance and the Jobseekers' Charter, and read the site in Welsh as well as English. The site's links are confined to other state-managed organisations.

Excite Search Engine
http://www.excite.com
Mainly known as one of the internet's most widely used and available search engines, Excite offers excellent opportunities for careers and education. Some excellent information provided related to the process of developing an effective CV.

Executive Grapevine
http://www2.d-net.com/executive.grapevine/
Here is another long URL, but worth the trouble. Executive Grapevine is an established publisher of range of highly priced but comprehensive employment directories. Here you can search its database of over 5,400 companies, which includes its International Database of

Top job sites and careers services

Executive Recruiters. The company is based in London Colney, Hertfordshire.

Federation of Recruitment and Employment Services
http://www.fres.co.uk/

London-based FRES is the professional association for recruitment agencies in Britain. It aims to be the voice of the recruitment industry, a guardian of professional standards, and an essential service to members. The site offers a few helpful hints and useful checklists for job seekers, plus a dedicated job seeker line giving information on how to obtain a list of member consultancies specialising in your area – call 0800 320 588. The site however is mainly intended to assist existing and prospective member firms, rather than job applicants.

Galaxy
http://www.einet.net/index.html

Galaxy is one of the top ten internet search engines. The Galaxy Directory focuses very much on information sectors such as commerce, industry, the professions, government, law, reference and science, and is very strong in these areas. Galaxy is an excellent resource if you want to track down prospective employers in fairly specific occupational fields. It does not have a specific UK section as do some of the others like **Infoseek** and **Yahoo!**.

GET: The Directory of Graduate Recruiters
http://www.get.co.uk/

GET: The Directory of Graduate Recruiters is an annual publication of the careers information publishers, Hobsons, who are based in Cambridge. This is its online version. There are links to careers services, search, current vacancies, professional bodies, distance learning, and more. You can access details of UK professional bodies, including their web pages, by choosing a general career area in the drop-down box. The site also has a useful international jobs information service, with links to Europe, China, Latin America, Poland, and south east Asia. There is additional information for postgraduates and MBAs. You can of course search for UK jobs. As a test we tried Arts Administration, which produced 14 results, some of them employers with current vacancies, others with general information only. The site is naturally keen for you to register your full details, but it means you will receive free information, and employers will be able to contact you directly. You will need an up-to-date browser (level 4) to view the site successfully.

Gis-a-job
http://www.gisajob.com/

'Gis-a-job, mate!' Yes, that really is the name of this bright and breezy UK web site which now hosts more than 46,000 jobs with more than 1,100 agencies. Job seekers can enjoy free job searches, free jobs by email and free CV storage, and explore quite a detailed agency directory and company directory. The site takes you to the Recruitlink Exchange, a keyword searchable directory of recruitment agencies in the UK. You

---

Gis-a-Job ?

Gis-a-Job is the bandwidth friendly site for finding that job you've been looking for.

Why not submit your CV to us? Over **80%** of those who do, say they receive either an excellent or good response from agencies. **So please bookmark us now!**

Job Seekers

Submit CV | Update CV
Hot 100 Jobs
Top agencies | Specialists
Related Services

Top job sites and careers services

can check these directories out for current vacancies, and click straight to the companies' home pages for additional information. You can also get details of all the latest jobs advertised on this site filtered to your skills and sent to you direct by email. Agencies can place unlimited free job ads and access free CVs online. There are some helpful FAQs. Based in Bletchley, near Milton Keynes, Gis-a-Job says it is 100% independently owned, and not affiliated or connected with any other product or company in any way. It makes its money from its banner advertising and by keyword sponsorship.

Glasgow University Careers Service
http://www.gla.ac.uk/Otherdepts/Careers/
This is another rather long URL, but here you can find all kinds of useful careers information. The site includes career planning and advice, useful web sites, information on vacation and part-time work, industrial placements and internships, excellent links to overseas opportunities, postgraduate study and funding, links to graduate recruiters, stuff on graduate recruitment, and lots more.

Graduate Agency
http://www.graduate-agency.com/
This UK site advertises graduate opportunities on behalf of employers using both the internet and your local careers service. You are invited to spend 25 or 30 minutes of your time completing the quite detailed primary application form just once, to become eligible to apply for any of the vacancies it lists. If you have left university, or are on vacation and do not have access to the internet, they will still contact you by phone or snail mail if they feel a vacancy matches your personal career aspirations. You should receive an acknowledgement of receipt of your details. Shortly after the vacancy closing date your application will be electronically compared against the criteria supplied by the employer. Should you be unsuccessful first time round there will be plenty of other jobs which you can be considered for.

Graduate Fair, London
http://recruitnet.guardian.co.uk/gradfair2.htm
The Graduate Fair, London, is a specialist careers information and recruitment event, which brings together undergraduates, graduates and employers and professional bodies to discuss career opportunities. Examples of attending companies include BT, Barclays, EDS, Rover Group, the Royal Bank of Scotland, IBM, KPMG, Tesco, several government departments, and voluntary organisations. The event is sponsored by *The Guardian* newspaper. Entry to the fair is free. Presentations are given by employers, and experienced careers advisers from the Association of Graduate Careers Advisory Services attend to answer queries and give brief CV tips. Computer-assisted careers guidance programs can be seen which match your job preferences to job descriptions. The site includes details of how to get there, exhibitors, and a floor plan.

Top job sites and careers services

Gradunet
http://www.gradunet.co.uk/
Gradunet offers a career forum, discussion groups, jobs notice board, professions index, career profiles and UK graduate recruitment. You can check out around 100 leading UK employing companies here, and view their corporate home pages and graduate recruitment pages. Gradunet flags the firms that are currently recruiting.

Grapevine
http://www.grapevine.bris.ac.uk/
Grapevine is a not-for-profit internet service run by the Institute for Learning and Research Technology (ILRT) at the University of Bristol in collaboration with William Solesbury and Associates. It offers an online source of career development opportunities for social science researchers in all sectors. These include research posts, lectureships, studentships and project work. You can browse through jobs listings sorted by discipline or region or view a summary listing of all jobs. If you want to advertise a job or training opportunity, add a Likeminds entry or CV online, you will first need to register. The site includes an advertising tariff. Grapevine had its official launch in March 1998, and the number of vacancies so far appear to be limited.

GTI
http://www.gti.co.uk
This is the homepage of GTI Careers Journals. It contains in-depth career guidance and information for UK and Irish graduate careers, with full details of, and links to, some leading 230 employers. A feature of the site is its 101 Vocations section, which gives realistic and informative background to working in a wide range of graduate careers. The links on the site are very effectively organised enabling you to move swiftly along the information paths that appeal to you. The overall presentation is honest, down-to-earth and entertaining, and for the UK graduate job hunter the site is a must.

Heriot-Watt University Careers Service
http://www.hw.ac.uk/careers/
The main value of this site in this context is its handy, but not comprehensive, lists of general careers websites for the UK and overseas.

Hobsons
http://www.hobsons.co.uk
The Cambridge-based careers publishers Hobsons produce a whole range of helpful publications for school leavers and graduates, including **GET,** and a series of employment casebooks. Check out *Download,* for graduates looking for a career in information technology; this includes key facts and in-depth profiles of some of the UK's major IT recruiters. Also try *International Recruitment,* which contains details of organisations providing graduate career opportunities throughout the world, including training offered, degree subjects required, vacancies, salaries, and case studies of employees.

Top job sites and careers services

HotBot Jobs
http://www.hotbot.com/jobs
HotBot is another of the internet's top search engines. This is its jobs page, which links to Career Builder, and to lots of other careers pages and career gateway sites. Along with AltaVista, Infoseek, Galaxy, and Yahoo!, HotBot is probably an essential bookmark.

Impact Publications
http://www.impactpublications.com
Founded in 1982, US-based Impact Publications publishes and distributes over 60 career titles dealing with the career-planning process, self assessment, resumes, cover letters, networking, interviewing, salary negotiations, and general job-finding skills.

Infoseek
http://www.infoseek.co.uk
You mustn't miss Infoseek, one of the leading international search engines on the internet. This is its UK home page, where you will find links to work, advice, jobs, and agencies. These links lead you to masses of information about UK-based employment – vacancies, CV posting, recruitment agencies and consultancies (more than 80), careers gateway sites, training and lots more. Make sure you bookmark this page.

Inside Careers
www.insidecareers.co.uk
In this professionally developed site, Inside Careers (formerly Ivanhoe Career Guides) offers in-depth information about selected professions. These include actuaries, chartered accountants, patent attorneys, chartered surveyors, engineering, insurance, the IT profession, the legal profession, management consultants, and tax advisers. It discusses current professional issues, education and training, and gives details of key recruiters and course providers. This looks like a site worth following.

Institute for Employment Research
http://www.warwick.ac.uk/ier
This is an essentially academic site of the University of Warwick, which undertakes research on employment trends. The site includes the Electronic Training Village, a space dedicated to bringing together experts in vocational training to share information and generate synergistic problem solving.

Institute of Careers Guidance
http://www.icg-uk.org
The ICG is the largest and fastest growing membership organisation for UK careers professionals, open to anybody involved in giving careers advice or information. National membership totals about 4,000. Its aim is to define and promote the ethics, principles and practice of high quality careers guidance to all individuals as their right. It advises on careers guidance, education, training and employment. Its activities

Top job sites and careers services

include, courses, conferences, exhibitions, library and publication services, magazines such as *Portico, Careers Guidance Today* and *Frontline*, shared mailing facilities, membership services and local branch activities across the UK, the Youth Start and Stepping Stones projects.

Internet Recruiting
http://www.netcruiting.com/book
Subtitled 'A human resources guide to global sourcing', *Internet Recruiting* is a comprehensive manual on web-based recruiting published in 1998 and available from Amazon, and Simon and Schuster.

Internet SourceBook Career Center
http://www.internetsourcebook.com/jobs/index.html
In Chapter 8, we discussed issues surrounding the use of newsgroups, and in particular newsgroups that aid job seekers. The internet SourceBook Career Centre provides a very interesting source of newsgroup details for jobs in the USA, Canada, Central Europe and the United Kingdom. There's even newsgroups offering jobs in Russia and in Australia. This site allows you to access direct all of the newsgroups listed giving you a very easy method of reading newsgroups that may be of benefit to you.

Interview Network
http://www.pse-net.com/interview/interview.htm
This unique site features job interview tips, questions and answers, and over 2,800 sample interview questions. Included are 600+ interview questions and answer tips on over 40 professions and job functions, questions to ask the interviewer, and what to wear at your interview. The questions are organised under accounting interviews, behavioural questions, business interviews, college graduates, consulting interviews, general job interview questions, healthcare interviews, hypothetical questions, information technology interview, job interview tips and strategies, journalism interviews, librarian interviews, marketing interviews, military interviews, public service interviews, social services interviews, teaching interviews, telecommunications interviews. More job interview help is available with links to job function trends, issues, and terminology and 'tested to impress' ideas that have worked for many people.

JobFinder
http://www.infolive.ie/jobfinder/
JobFinder is an online job service for those looking to work in Ireland. This site is jam-packed with information covering all aspects of IT and computing jobs, sales and marketing jobs and engineering and technical job vacancies. An interesting little service called JobAlert allows you to set up a personal space in JobFinder where daily updates are included that meet your skills and educational qualifications.

Top job sites and careers services

Job Hunt
http://www.job-hunt.org/
This is a valuable meta list of online job search resources and services. Its purpose is to provide a listing of useful internet accessible job-search resources and services. They don't try to include every job listing on the internet here. Only those services that are relatively stable and appear to be useful or relevant to a broad range of job types and geographical locations are listed. A single page of all of the links to job-related resources is purposefully kept in order to make searching the list easier. The JobHunt page began in December 1993 as a personal hot-list of about 20 or so links to job-related resources on the internet. Now, it gets between 5,000 and 12,000 hits daily. The total number of links on the page exceeds 700. The site is quite functional, but has won several awards for its informational value. It is an essential bookmark for the UK job hunter.

Job Search (UK)
http://www.jobsearch.co.uk/
This is a Brighton-based web site. It says that it maintains multiple sets of recruitment data, its own database as well as that of agencies whose web sites link directly to Job Search. You can search its vacancy and candidate databases free, and submit your CV free. To submit a CV to the database first you must select which employment category you wish to be included in. You make your selection from a drop-down list. CVs are removed after two months. You can edit your CV after entering your personal reference number and password. The site has even set up two of its own newsgroups, alt.jobs.jobsearch and alt.jobs.uk-jobsearch. Vacancies placed on the site are mirrored into these as well as other relevant newsgroups. The site has a tariff of (modest) advertising costs for recruiters. All vacancy advertisements remain live for one calendar month. We searched for teaching vacancies (13), and media (80). The results came partly in the form of actual vacancies, and partly in the form of recruitment agencies which handle vacancies in that particular field. The presentation of the site is rather functional and they do not tell you much about themselves, nor how big their database is.

JobServe
http://www.jobserve.com
If it's an IT job you're after then look no further than JobServe. With a no-nonsense search utility, you'll quickly be cutting back the chaff and getting right down to the process of seeing what jobs are available to meet your specific skills. JobServe also gives you the opportunity to have suitable job opportunities downloaded to your email address daily. JobServe puts a lot of store in its history, which, in internet terms, at four years, is an absolute lifetime. JobServe gives you a great list of accessible agencies who use their facilities, giving you access directly to find the job for you.

Job Site
http://www.jobsite.co.uk/
Job Site has thousands of vacancies in IT, science, engineering,

Top job sites and careers services

management, health and education. Its site statistics when we visited showed 23,849 vacancies monthly, 3,705 live today, and 73,148 daily emails. You can search by sector including IT and computing, science, engineering, commercial, management, professional, healthcare, education, government, and jobs abroad. You can check out a large number of recruiters A-Z, and see at a glance how many current vacancies they have. You can read the latest careers news, explore featured companies, view the featured jobs, get jobs by email, distribute your CV, and check out some of the top web sites recommended by JobSite. This site is a must if your job lies in the areas covered.

Jobwatch
http://www.jobwatch.co.uk/
Job Watch offers hundreds of jobs, updated daily, throughout the South-East. Its jobs database covers positions in Oxfordshire, Berkshire and Bristol/Bath. It says that new jobs are added every day. In addition to its vacancies database and CV submission facilities, the site includes a useful resources section featuring useful information for job hunters, such as advice on interview technique, CV construction, training schemes, and a bulletin board. It also runs a Job News section featuring the latest updates for job hunters, news about expanding companies, industry news and press releases from the Department of Trade and Industry. This is a useful local site which is trying to offer a little bit more.

Jobs and Positions for Scientists
http://info-systems.com/info/aljoben.html
This page contains general sources about open positions and requests as well as some interesting specialised lists for the natural sciences, especially biology, chemistry, maths and physics. The site did not seem to have been updated for quite a while, but it should still be worth a visit, although some of the links may be broken.

Jobs for Scientists
http://www.ajob4scientists.com/
This site is designed for those involved in research and development, including chemists, life scientists, and engineers at all education levels. It is designed to connect you to thousands of companies throughout the world. It allows you to be identified by a multitude of criteria at the exact moment when a company is looking for you. However, you need to register and obtain an ID and password before you can search for vacancies. There are some useful links on the site, plus a link to a companion site, Jobs for Engineers.

Jobs Unlimited
http://www.jobsunlimited.co.uk
Formerly Recruit Net, this is a project of *The Guardian* newspaper. You can access all its job and course advertisements from this site, whose pages we found quick to load. To help you find your ideal job, you are invited to set up a personalised career manager – its search engine will trawl through the database for you and store any suitable ads ready for

Top job sites and careers services

you to read every morning. The service is available free of charge. You can also search through all the course ads published in the paper. By registering you can gain access to all areas of the site, and to other Guardian Unlimited sites being planned. Or you can enter the site as a guest and browse for 24 hours before registering.

Kings College Careers Service Links Page
http://www.kcl.ac.uk/kis/college/careers/links/links.htm
This is a long address, but well worth noting because it will lead you to a massive treasure trove of 2,300 links to UK and international careers information. One of these is to employer web sites, a section which gives you more than 800 employers (additionally classified by industry). Most of these employer sites have their own recruitment information. You will also find hundreds of career resources relevant to your degree subject, links to some 400 professional bodies and trade associations, resources for working overseas, and loads of other information. This site is an unmissable resource.

Lab Staff
http://www.labstaff.co.uk/
Lab Staff was founded in 1990 and developed the concept of the temporary science professional. They invite you to send in your details by email. It says that its database of scientists is currently over 28,000 and the largest of its kind in the UK. There appeared to be quite a few vacancies shown on the site, which we found rather cumbersome because of its frames.

LawCareers.Net
http://www.lawcareers.net/
Here you can find fairly detailed information and advice on becoming a solicitor or barrister, plus a searchable directory of firms offering training contracts and chambers offering pupillages. This useful site is a project of Globe Business Publishing Ltd in association with the Trainee Solicitors' Group, a national organisation which represents about 20,000 law students and trainee solicitors, and which has its own web site (linked here). You can use the site to search for chambers offering pupillages and solicitors' firms offering training contracts and vacation work opportunities. You can look at case studies, news and features, courses, and visit the brochure library.

Legal 500
http://www.icclaw.com/l500/uk.htm
The Legal 500 directory is an essential reference for practising lawyers and law students. It gives lists of all the top law firms arranged by specific type of work, by name A to Z, and by size and by income (the highest earnings per partner are at Slaughter & May). These lists lead you to more detailed information about each firm, their partners, and types of work. The site also lists leading barristers' chambers and overseas law firms with UK offices. It also has a Courts & Agency Directory, and a Student Law Centre.

Top job sites and careers services

Local Authority Careers Services
http://www.open.gov.uk/dfee/ccd/csindex.htm
This site contains a handy list of the careers service areas within each local authority region. Most have email links and an increasing number also now have their own web pages.

London Careers Net
http://www.londoncareers.net/
Want to work in one of the world's most exciting cities? Then this is one good place to start. The site aims to bring you the best secretarial and clerical type jobs from all over the capital and updates the information weekly. All the jobs on the site selected from thousands advertised each week in London's four leading recruitment magazines – *Ms London, Girl About Town, Midweek* and *Nine To Five.*

Look Here
http://www.lookhere.co.uk/
Look Here is a fairly basic UK web directory which lists companies A–Z under various headings such as occupational and commercial headings. While far from comprehensive, it does provide handy links to major employers throughout commerce, industry and professions. Firms apparently pay £50 to £120 per month for a listing.

Lycos
http://www.lycos.co.uk
This is the UK edition of this well known search engine. Its home page features various Webguides, one of which is on Careers. It promotes **Monster Board, Job Site** and **City Jobs** rather heavily. A broader selection of UK links would be more appropriate and helpful from a search engine as widely used as Lycos.

Milkround Online
http://www.milkround.co.uk/
This excellent London-based site provides graduates or those about to graduate with the information they need to find their chosen job. This includes well-indexed profiles on more than 350 employers, insights into different careers, advice on applying and registering your personal details for employers. You can check out numerous links, and select the appropriate category of employment from a drop-down menu. You will also find online CV registration, employment news features, industry overviews, immediate vacancies, careers advice, sector profiles, guild guides, free email alerts, and updates on current vacancies and new employers. There are also online step-by-step guides to applying for that perfect job, creating the perfect CV, writing great cover letters, performing in interviews, and more.

Monster Board UK
http://www.monsterboard.co.uk
Monster Board is a really fantastic job seeker's resource. With around 2000 jobs available daily, let 'Thwacker', the cheeky little helpful monster, guide you through the mirade of securing a new job or career.

Top job sites and careers services

Thwacker's monster friend 'Skeeter' is also on hand to guide you through hundreds of employer profiles online. Skeeter has also had the good sense to realise that lots of job seekers want to work in specific regions of the UK and he's created a very straightforward regional company job search.

Napier University Careers Advisory Service
http://www.napier.ac.uk/depts/careers/info.html
This Scottish site gives you pointers towards vacancies, where to look for jobs, finding work, placements and courses overseas, where to look for company information, advice on the application process, post-graduate study, how to choose your next course and sources of funding.

Net Jobs (UK)
http://www.jobexchange.co.uk
With more than 120,000 hits per month Net Jobs says it is rapidly becoming a leading resource on the internet for UK recruitment. Candidates can search through thousands of new jobs each day and apply online. You can submit your CV on the web site and it will be automatically forwarded to all subscribing agencies. The site claims to have the largest listing of recruitment agencies on the internet, with links to their web sites. Actually, we counted about 70. The project is a division of Net Village, an internet service provider.

New Scientist Jobs Page
http://www.newscientist.com/sciencejobs/sciencejobs.html
The *New Scientist* recruitment database says it offers the most comprehensive listing of current scientific, technological and academic vacancies available on the web. Updated each Thursday, more than 300 science jobs are available within a fully searchable database enabling you to select and retrieve only those jobs that relate specifically to your own area of expertise.

Newcastle University Careers Links Page
http://www.careers.ncl.ac.uk/Careers/Specialist.html
Here are some well organised and quite comprehensive careers links pages put together at the University of Newcastle. They are divided into specific areas of interest, such as, biological and medical, human resources, computing, environment, media, law, accountancy, science and engineering. Whatever your subject area, you will be bound to find quite a few useful starting points on this excellent gateway site.

NISS Jobs Noticeboard
http://www.niss.ac.uk/noticeboard/jobs/index.html
NISS (National Information Services and Systems) has built up a number of different information services since 1988, all serving the UK higher education sector. Here you can find all kinds of UK university-based jobs, including postgraduate research and study opportunities and temporary positions. You can check out current academic vacancies, vacancy listings of the Association of Commonwealth

Top job sites and careers services

Universities (ACU), various careers and recruitment services and events, plus classified ads in newspapers and journals. There is also a section on temporary jobs including work placements and summer employment.

People Bank
http://www.peoplebank.com/
People Bank is a London-based online employment network and recruitment system. Its services include a job seekers' database that is searchable by employers and recruitment consultants, a vacancies database which job seekers can search to find suitable jobs, a clearing house facility called Candex for recruitment agencies, and personality profiling enabling the application of psychometrics to recruitment. Job seekers can register with People Bank online or by completing a paper registration form. Some 95,000 people have done so. You can edit your CV. The service is free for all candidates whether you are seeking permanent, contract, part-time or vacation work. The site includes an advertising tariff for recruiters. Job seekers are required to complete all the sections of its registration form. This is a rather functional site that does not go in for external careers links, news or similar features.

People Management
http://www.peoplemanagement.co.uk
People Management is the fortnightly magazine of the London-based Institute of Personnel and Development, which has 90,000 members, mainly human resources professionals in the UK and Ireland. Each printed issue contains hundreds of personnel, training and development vacancies in private and public organisations in the UK and abroad. PM Online's job section allows you to search current vacancies by job title, salary and location. We found 119 online vacancies when we reviewed the site, with only the briefest details of each. You can also ask to view only public sector vacancies.

Pharm Web
http://www.pharmweb.co.uk/
The Pharm Web appointments pages allow employers to advertise their vacancies world wide. Information is made available to potential applicants 24 hours a day and at the touch of a button. Pharm Web says it has been accessed by over 130 countries and the UK mirror site alone is receiving over a million hits per month. If you would like to know when a new job opportunity becomes available on Pharm Web Appointments then you can join the Alert mailing list. The site has sections for UK hospital, and community pharmacy appointments.

Pharmajobs
http://www.pharmajobs.com
As its name suggests, Pharmajobs offers job listings from the major international pharmaceutical companies, ranging from research appointments to senior management. As a test we picked a couple of suggested key words 'pharmacy' jobs and 'research & development' from the drop down search menu for Great Britain, but these yielded no

Top job sites and careers services

results. This rather functional site is based in Frankfurt, Germany.

Physicians Employment
http://www.physemp.com/
Operational since 1994, Physicians Employment says it is the oldest and largest online clearing house for physician appointments, with over 2,000 listings. You have to complete a registration form before you can access the site, which gives very little preliminary information about itself.

PhysicsJobs
http://www.physicsweb.org/jobs
This web site is run by IOP Publishing Ltd, which is part of the UK Institute of Physics. All the jobs, studentships and courses advertised in *Physics World* magazine are automatically placed on this server. You can quickly and easily search through the listings to view quality positions in academia, industry and commerce. The site is regularly edited so that all entries are current and up to date. New vacancies can also be sent to you by email. When we reviewed the site, there were 51 vacancies, listed in some detail.

Portfolio of British Nursing Web Sites
http://www.british-nursing.com/
This UK site provides links to about 25 selected nursing agencies and other online resources for nurses. They say more than 24,000 people have visited the site.

Prospects
http://www.prospects.csu.ac.uk/
Prospects is a section of CSU, the UK higher education Careers Services Unit. It contains information on employers, jobs, postgraduate study and career choices. Its facilities include Prospects Direct, a personalised news service for students and postgraduates in their final year, surveys of vocational training courses, publications, links to 250 top graduate recruiters, focus sections on IT, engineering, finance, sales, marketing and retail careers, with special pages on legal and teaching opportunities. The site is valuable for giving hundreds of links to major professional bodies and recruitment organisations both in the UK and internationally. This site must be an essential bookmark for all new graduates.

Proteus Careers
http://www.proteus-net.co.uk/
Founded in 1989, Proteus says it is one of the largest careers guidance support organisations in England. It has counselling centres in Ringwood, Sevenoaks, Weybridge, Bristol, London, Manchester and Birmingham. You are invited to sample its jobs database to help your career search. Updated every weekday, it receives more than 400,000 jobs a year, and claims to be one of the most complete and up-to-date resources on the internet. The database, classified by occupation categories, contains jobs advertised in UK national, regional and local

Top job sites and careers services

newspapers, and professional journals, plus vacancies notified during its contacts with head hunters and specialist recruitment consultancies, lists of pre-advertised positions from selection consultancies, and unadvertised positions from search agencies. You can also access Key British Enterprises, a company information database provided by Dun & Bradstreet, and the Executive Grapevine, a definitive source of executive recruitment consultancies. Proteus also offers an extensive compilation of internet job and company related sites. However, you must register to take full advantage of this very useful site.

Recruiters Network
http://www.recruitersnetwork.com
Recruiter's Network is the Association for Internet Recruiting, which welcomes HR and recruiting professionals. Its free services include membership, a resource centre which offers seminars, software, books, consultants, career sites, resume databases, subscription to its newsletter *Recruiting on the Web*, an online forum, and participation in Listserv. The Association is based in Milwaukee, USA.

Recruiters Online Network
http://www.recruitersonline.com
RON is a virtual network of employment firms, mainly located in the USA. It has more than 7,000 registered members, including recruiters, executive search firms, employment agencies and employment professionals. You can search for jobs, post your résumé, and read its Careers Online magazine, which contains careers links, help with interviewing and other job hunting skills. If you register, your CV will reach potentially all its members, and remain online for 90 days. Its members are organised into more than 70 occupational categories. There is also a Recruiters Online magazine.

Recruiting Links
http://www.recruiting-links.com/
All over the internet, employers are posting jobs and employment information on their web sites. Recruiting Links is a job search engine that says it will help you find jobs at these sites quickly, using a relational database of links to employers' recruiting pages. You can search it using more than 700 combinations of geographic, industry, and occupational preferences. However, our search for all health care jobs located in Western Europe produced only one employer web site. The same search for North America still only produced 13.

Recruitment Database
http://www.enterprise.net/recruitmentdb/
Recruitment Database Limited is run from the Isle of Man. Job seekers can place their full CV on the database in the category of their choice, and employers and recruitment agencies can search the whole database using specific criteria, and contact applicants direct. We found about 30 vacancies listed on this no-frills site, most of them for technical, IT and financial appointments.

Top job sites and careers services

Recruitment Gateway
http://www.recruitment-gateway.co.uk
At this very useful London-based web site you can check out employers' graduate web sites, jobs wanted, immediate jobs, the Nortel Networks job board, and recruitment agency vacancies. You can explore the appointment pages of some of the printed media, internet job shops in European and further overseas, UK careers and advice centres, a news desk, post and view your CV, and an 'add your employment' page. There are vacancies in sales, education, finance, retail, hotel and catering, languages, secretarial, public relations, engineering and many other occupational areas. The site would not win prizes for design, but it rates well as an excellent source of UK employment links.

Recruitnet
http://recruitnet.guardian.co.uk/
This is now called **Jobs Unlimited**.

Riley Guide
http://www.dbm.com/jobguide/
This is a well regarded and comprehensive guide to employment opportunities and job resources on the internet. It is a project developed by Margaret F. Riley, a job search recruiter and consultant. The Riley Guide has been online since February of 1994. Go to the site map first, to find your way around the very large number of links. You will find whole sections on general recruiters and major recruiting sites, resources for specific occupational areas, researching careers online, and lots more. Though it was primarily aimed at a US audience, this functional gateway site is valuable for job hunters anywhere on the planet.

Science Online
http://recruit.sciencemag.org/
This is a weekly online magazine produced by the American Association for the Advancement of Science. It includes many helpful contacts for candidates seeking science-based careers.

Scottish Recruitment
http://www.scottish-recruitment.co.uk
Scottish Recruitment is a weekly jobs newspaper, published from Irvine, advertising over two thousand jobs. This is its well-presented online edition. It gives easy to use links to lots of different job categories, and the links tell you at a glance how many vacancies you will find. The emphasis is on IT, engineering and technical vacancies, though clerical and administrative appointments are included.

Search Recruitment & Selection
http://www.search.co.uk/
Search Recruitment and Selection describes itself as Scotland's premier recruitment web site. There are hundreds of job vacancies, employment and career opportunities in Scotland and the rest of the UK

Top job sites and careers services

advertised every day. You can search for jobs across all the major sectors including IT, legal, accountancy, engineering, electronics, sales and marketing and secretarial. If it's your first visit you can browse through their vacancies or register by submitting your details, or advertise positions if you are an employer, and you will be contacted. Search has specialist divisions that operate across all manufacturing and commercial industries plus public sector organisations. They include accountancy, legal, information technology, electronics and engineering, sales and marketing, personnel / human resources, office services, industrial and manufacturing, construction / contract engineering. It is a member of the Federation of Recruitment & Employment Services (FRES). It has offices in Glasgow, Edinburgh, Dunfermline and Coatbridge.

Starting Point
http://www.stpt.com/business/career.html
Starting Point is one of the better known internet search engines, and this is its careers links page. However the information is US oriented and the site does not seem well geared to the UK or other non-USA locations as yet.

Strathclyde University Careers Service
http://www.strath.ac.uk/Departments/Careers/main.html
Produced by the University of Strathclyde Careers Service, this excellent site furnishes a great deal of relevant information about possible avenues of finding work, using the internet, and managing electronic applications and CVs. It contains extensive detailed lists of job sources by area and by subject, plus links to leading newspapers and periodicals with situations vacant, and more. One of the news links takes you to a portal with no less than 1,400 newspapers world wide. You could spend a very profitable hour or two here – and you don't need to be enrolled at the university.

Student World
http://www.student-world.co.uk/
Student World Ltd has developed this brightly presented and informative web site for students of all ages. It provides help, advice, chat, information, fun and online services on all kinds of topics to UK students and to students throughout the world. It plans a Jobs Online section, but this was unavailable when we reviewed the site, but it would be worth checking back.

taps.com
http://www.taps.co.uk/index.htm
So you want to know how good this site is? Look no further than taps.com's list of participating companies. It really does read like a *Who's Who* of major UK corporations. This agency is used by the BBC, ICL, BUPA, Mobil and Microsoft amongst others. You can feel confident of the ability of this organisation to secure jobs for job seekers and fill vacancies for employers. Taps.com offers jobs by email and allows searches to be made by permanent or contract work. There

Top job sites and careers services

is also a useful section on company profiles as well as several regularly updated features.

Teacher Training Agency
http://www.teach.org.uk
This official UK site gives information about becoming a teacher, whether you are a school leaver, graduate, postgraduate, or mature career changer. The site contains information about qualifications, primary and secondary school teaching, subjects, money matters, meet a teacher, your career ladder, training, FAQs, glossary, sources of vacancies, links and more. You can also check out a searchable database of courses available through the Graduate Teacher Training Registry (GTTR).

Telecommuting Jobs
http://www.tjobs.com/
Here's something rather different. Telecommuting means working for an employer, but doing so from the comfort and convenience of your own home. This site gives you the chance to explore telecommuting with employers in the USA or anywhere else in the world. Check out this site for telecommuting opportunities for artists, data entry staff, desktop publishers, engineers, photographers, programmers, sales people, web designers, writers and other skills. You can upload your own details, too. The site offers support information and services, including an online newsletter, links and resources of various kinds.

The Telegraph
http://www.telegraph.co.uk/
Online edition of the Telegraph.

The Telegraph Appointments Plus
http://www.appointments-plus.co.uk/
This is the appointments page of the Telegraph online. You can do a key word search by job category or world wide location.

The Job
http://www.thejob.com
The Job features a cross-section of permanent and contract vacancies across the UK. It spans sales, financial services, IT, engineering, professional, retailing, medical and health care, production, transportation, government jobs, and more. The site also features a graduate section, and recruitment profiles of a few large corporations and recruitment agencies. It also contains various other useful links, for example to the home pages of leading UK newspapers carrying recruitment advertising.

Times Educational Supplement
http://www.tes.co.uk/
This is the leading weekly newspaper for teachers in primary, secondary and further education. Check out the link to TES Online Jobs – it contains a database of all the jobs in the *TES* each week. This is

Top job sites and careers services

the largest source of education vacancies on the internet, advertising up to 3,000 UK and overseas jobs every week. You can browse or search the database entirely free, or you can set up a free email alert to tell you when a job matching your criteria is advertised.

Top Grads
http://www.topgrads.co.uk/
This is a companion service of the UK site **Top Jobs**.

Top Jobs
http://www.topjobs.net
Warrington-based Top Jobs on the Net was launched in 1995. Its home page depicts a series of globes, for the UK, Ireland, Poland, Australia, Switzerland, and international vacancies. In the UK section you can search categories such as executive and management, graduate, health, human resources, information technology, legal, logistics, marketing, media, other management and professional, production and operations, purchasing and procurement, retail, sales, scientific, secretarial, supply chains, telecommunications, and travel. Our search showed some uneven results. The IT section seemed to be the strongest, with 289 vacancies, executive and management yielded 42 vacancies, legal 6, and only 3 for travel and hospitality. Top Jobs say they attract an average of 200,000 visitors every month, of which, in September 1998, these job seekers made over a million searches – a tribute to its promotional efforts. The site focuses mainly on getting you to search its database but also contains some careers advice, presentations by its corporate advertisers, professional and careers links, and a companion site called Top Grads.

Tripod
http://www.tripod.com/
Hugely popular this is the main page of Tripod, a multi-services 'virtual community' rather like Geocities, where you can publish your own home page. Millions of people have now taken out free membership of Tripod. Its own home page contains a jobs and careers link leading to lots of career information and links, most of it American in content and flavour. We found many of the pages painfully slow to load, maybe because of the huge traffic on the site, and its strong graphics content.

UK Directory
http://www.ukdirectory.co.uk
Winchester-based UK Directory aims to provide the most comprehen-

Top job sites and careers services

sive guide to everything in the United Kingdom on the world wide web, and is a competitor to **Electronic Yellow Pages.** Use of this resource is free, and listing to all UK based web pages is also free. The main page is very clearly set out, in the form of a classified contents list, with numerous categories and sub-categories, to help you on your way. One of the categories is Employment, where you can easily and quickly locate recruitment agencies and internet job sites. Within this is the professional category, for example, which includes legal, finance, medical, and media. The pages helpfully tell you how many sites are listed under each heading you may want to click. This site is really an essential all-purpose book mark for UK users.

UK Employment Law
http://www.emplaw.co.uk/
This can fairly be described as the premier site for employers, employees, lawyers, HR professionals and all who need information on UK employment law. If you have any worries about your employment contract, grievances at work, actual or constructive dismissal, calculation of redundancy pay or similar topics, this would be a good place to start. To give an example, our search for information on 'redundancy pay' yielded over 500 pages of free online information. The site is a service of DiscLaw Publishing Ltd.

UK Industry
http://www.ukindustry.co.uk/
This site is a project of London-based UK Industry Web Pages Ltd. It has the ambitious aim of making available all relevant information for UK industry, including links to further reference sources. Its directory lists the home page links of several hundred top UK firms, but its no-frills coverage is very far from comprehensive and rather uneven. For example, only five welding companies and one clothing manufacturer are listed.

UMIST
http://www.su.umist.ac.uk/jobs/
This is the jobs information page of the University of Manchester Institute of Science & Technology.

University Jobs and Research Posts
http://www.jobs.ac.uk/
This is plain and simply laid out web site showing current vacancies and research posts in British universities. You can either browse the specified subject lists or you can carry out a more individual search using key words. This site is updated daily. When we reviewed it the number of jobs currently available was 459. The site is a project of UAG, a consortium of 37 universities and institutes of higher education.

University of Wolverhampton UK Sensitive Map
http://www.scit.wlv.ac.uk/ukinfo/uk.maps.colls.html
The internet magazine *Net User* says that the University of Wolverhampton's visual guide to UK colleges and universities is . . . 'by far the

Top job sites and careers services

easiest and the best way of locating and linking to a British University.' You really can't go wrong here. Sit down with a map of the UK and choose to view either colleges of further and higher education or British universities. Then by simply pointing your mouse to the geographical region of the UK, you have instant access to the college or university of your choice's home page. The map is colour-coded to help you distinguish between universities, colleges and professional institutions.

When Winners Work For Losers
http://www.myboss.com
Somewhere along the line, career hunting and the process of work must be considered fun. This site offers a light-hearted look at the world of work. You'll find some really excellent quotes and anecdotes from workers as well as the opportunity to vote your boss into their Hall of Fame.

Work Web
http://www.workweb.co.uk
WorkWeb maintains a UK vacancy database. There were 9,537 vacancies when we reviewed the site. The database is collated from many sources. You can search it either for jobs, or for agencies. You first have to specify a relevant sector such as administrative and secretarial, hotel and catering, electrical and electronics, engineering, accountancy and finance, health, human resources, and information technology. If you don't specify a UK region or salary level, the results are conveniently grouped by towns and cities A–Z. Once you have registered you can update your details, renew, or cancel the service. You can also receive a personalised daily email listing of any jobs that meet your requirements. The presentation avoids graphics and is very functional in appearance, but the size of the database makes it a very worthwhile visit.

Yahoo! Higher Education
http://www.yahoo.com/Education/Higher_Education/
Once again, Yahoo! is better known as a much used and much praised internet search engine. However, Yahoo! offers a very useful page on higher education opportunities in the UK. Covering all subjects from a listing of college and university home pages through to assistance on taking notes during lectures, Yahoo! is another excellent resource for those entering or studying in the higher education sector. A good link is also included to 'Student World UK' which lists a number of resources for students, graduates and academic staff. Yahoo!'s higher education page will be particularly useful for those currently studying in UK higher education institutions.

Yahoo! Jobs
http://www.yahoo.co.uk/
Yahoo! is the grand-daddy of search directories, and this is its UK version. On the home page, click on Business & Economy. When that page comes up, click on Employment – and away you go. When we reviewed it, there were almost 2,000 links. A feature of Yahoo! is its

Top job sites and careers services

user-friendly directory-style approach. This makes it easy to click your way towards the specific information you want. You will find an enormous amount of information here, so be prepared to spend some time, and remember to bookmark promising sites as you surf along.

*   *   *

Points to consider

1. Do you think that internet use in the UK, both by companies wishing to do business, and by personal users, would grow if the major phone companies would allow free local calls at weekends?

2. The internet is literally overflowing with useful pages of information for job seekers. As not all pages will be registered with all of the available search engines such as AltaVista, Yahoo! and HotBot, then there is a danger that you will miss out on opportunities by restricting your search to your favourite search engine. What do you think would be the advantages and disadvantages of a universal search engine being available that would recognise the world wide family of internet pages?

Case studies

Morag takes a package
Morag has been busily using the internet to try and secure a new job as she would like to return to work, part-time, after having a baby. Morag's ISP is America On Line and, since she has been making constant use of the internet over the last few months, she has decided to upgrade her current access package to include ten free hours per month access.

Gordon's keen to find a job
Gordon has decided that he would like to travel around Australia for a year. Unfortunately, since leaving university over three months ago, he has been unable to secure a full-time job. Gordon has decided that contract work is the best way for him to save as much money in as short a space of time to allow him to travel. After signing up with a major employment agency, Gordon has secured a contract position as an electronic engineer, and starts work for a six-month period at the beginning of next month.

11 Top UK employers on the internet

In this chapter you will discover:

▶ the home page URLs of some top UK employers
▶ reviews of the contents of top employer home pages.

Introduction

More and more companies, both large and small, now have a presence on the internet. Information found in these sites range from simple correspondence and contact details through to highly interactive sites offering access to company information and services.

As a dedicated internet job seeker, company home pages are critical in your search for work. In particular, if you're looking to work with one of the big boys, then you'll definitely gain access to some fantastic company information relating to history, culture and finance. And, if you're really lucky (and this is becoming more and more generally available), you'll be able to drive your truck straight into company recruitment centres and find out just what's available to suit your skills, qualifications and experience.

Company internet pages offer job seekers a number of useful benefits:

1. They give a great insight into the operation of a company. This information can be put to good use when applying for jobs and attending interviews.

2. As the companies with the most sophisticated internet pages are likely to be the biggest (they have all the smart computer nerds to build the sites!) then topical information found will be an excellent source of information relating to the business sector where the company operates. This general information can then be used when applying to join smaller players in the same industry sector.

3. Online job applications and enquiry services make job hunting so much easier.

▷ *Key point* – With the resources available via the internet relating to company and industry sector information, there is now really no excuse for arriving at an interview with little background knowledge. Get surfing, get the knowledge – and go get that job!

Army Careers
http://www.army.mod.uk/army/index2.htm
The Army is one of Britain's largest employers and has over 15,000 vacancies annually for people of all ages and abilities. Why not have a look at the vacancies available in the Territorial Army where part-time soldiers provide back-up to the regular Army. Fill in the TA Enquiry

Top UK employers on the internet

Form, submit it online and wait to be contacted by a member of the TA recruitment team.

ASDA
http://www.asda.co.uk
As you might imagine, the ASDA home page is typically bright and positively brimming over with information. The company home page has a changing headline which comments on some major company issue such as financial results. From the top of the home page, you can choose a subject and drop it into your shopping trolley. Great information is provided on the company's financial position, its environmental activity and its portfolio of press releases. 'Jobs at ASDA' is the place to go if you're looking for a job, and here you'll be introduced to the company's 'Flying Start' project as well as finding job profiles and details of where to send CVs. The ASDA site also offers some useful information and great tips on designing your CV. Altogether an impressive and very useful site for job seekers.

Barclays
http://www.barclays.co.uk
Barclay's home page details information about all banking services offered by the company, from personal banking to PC banking. If it's topical information you're looking for, making an application for employment, or attending interview, then look in the 'About Us' section and find details of current news releases, financial results and other information. The Campus Recruitment Page gives details of the company's various business functions as well as personal requirements needed for those wishing to join Barclay's graduate recruitment scheme, the 'Business Leadership Programme.' Barclay's go some way to dispel the stereotypical belief that you join the bank, work through the ranks and end up as a High Street bank manager. Go have a look at this site and see the exciting opportunities offered in modern-day banking.

Blue Circle
http://www.bluecircle.co.uk/
Blue Circle's internet pages are very straightforward in presentation and provide a good range of company information. The company history pages are particularly interesting as they provide a timeline of the company's progress through the years from 1800 to the present.

British Aerospace
http://www.bae.co.uk
When you crank up this home page the first thing that you'll encounter is a wonderful little jet fighter that continually flies across the sky at the top of the page – truly wonderful! This site offers a no-nonsense search facility that allows key words entered to be matched with appropriate site information. By keying on the word 'careers' you'll jet off to the British Aerospace graduate recruitment site.

Top UK employers on the internet

British Energy
htpp://www.british-energy.co.uk
British Energy generates electricity and provides up to 20% of the UK's electricity from eight nuclear power stations in Scotland and England. Graduate recruitment information is hiding under 'Corporate' information on the home page of this site and, as well as detailing opportunities for graduates, British Energy refreshingly include details of placements within the company for those currently completing college and university courses. Vacancies exist in the following disciplines – engineering, sciences, information technology and business.

British Petroleum
http://www.bp.com
No need to explain who BP are! Try the BPFinder in this site to find company information, financial information, health and safety issues and company activity indexed by country. You can also find details here of graduate opportunities as well as other vacancies that might exist. A point worthy of mention is that BP don't respond to speculative applications by email or post.

British Steel
http://www.britishsteel.co.uk/
British Steel is the leading steel producer in Europe. This site is very easy to navigate, is crisp and clean in its design, and is very informative. An altogether excellent site that flies in the face of fancy designs! From the main page, 'career challenges' offers information on graduate

Fig. 50. The BP home page.

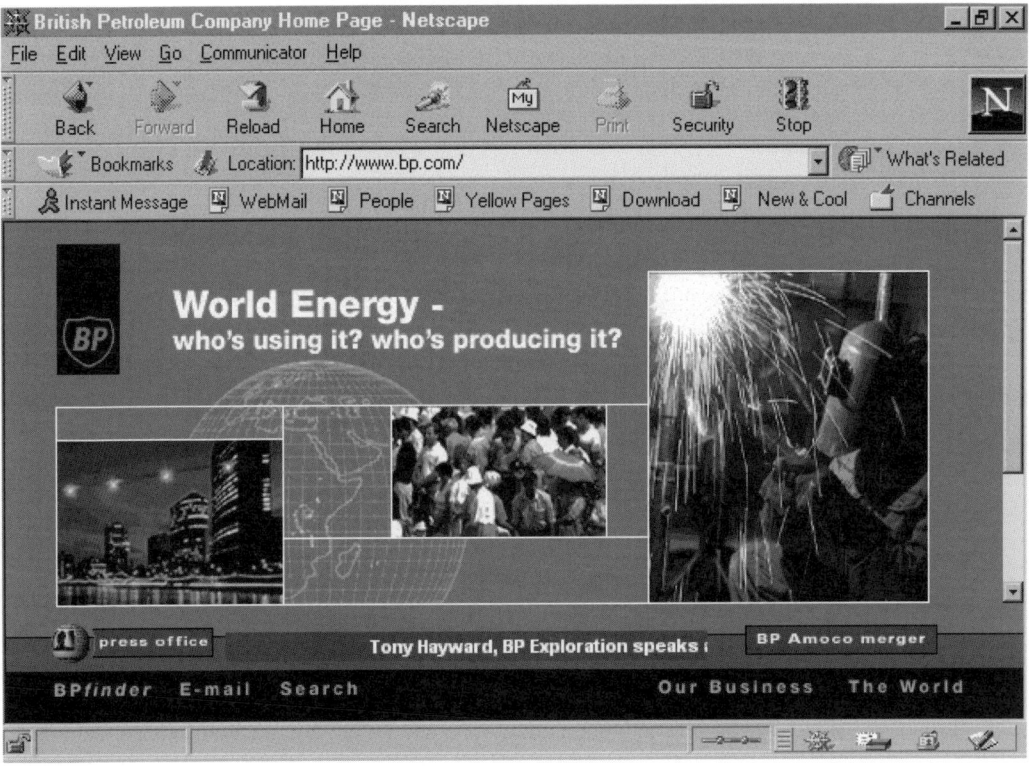

.... **Top UK employers on the internet**

opportunities by function. Graduate recruitment is explained in detail and gives information on milk-round visits, speculative applications and current vacancies. Excellent background information is also available on this site as well as a useful pack of educational teaching resources.

BTR
http://www.btrplc.com/
BTR is a world-leading engineering group comprising four main business areas, namely, automotive, control systems, power drives and specialist engineering divisions. Whilst the BTR site is basic in relation to other sites reviewed, the information is effectively presented. In particularly take a look at the site map to find the information available throughout this site.

Cable & Wireless
http://www.cableandwireless.com
Visit this site to find career opportunities throughout the company and throughout the world. Permanent and temporary jobs are included as well as details of graduate recruitment and the company's Career Management Centre.

Cadbury
http://www.cadbury.co.uk
First things first, the recipes. You've just got to try them – they really do work. The Autumn Trifle is a chocoholic's delight. Now, back to business. Cadbury's has a Graduate Recruitment Page split into operational functions which are easy to search. On clicking, each function is

Fig. 51. Cadbury's home page.

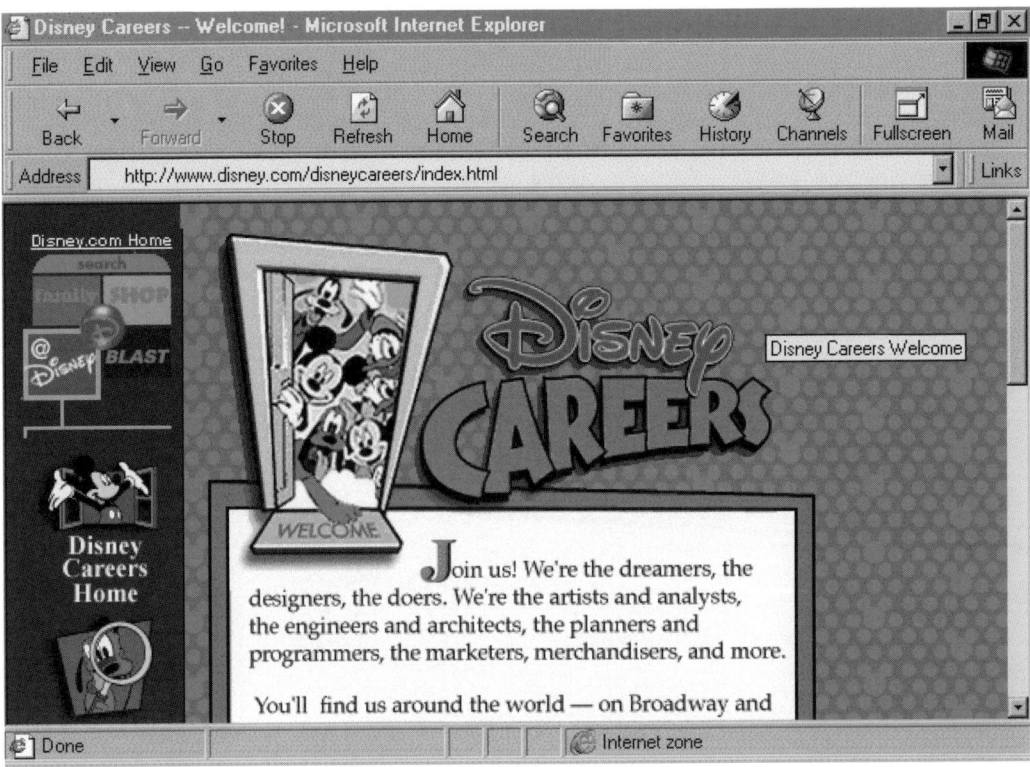

Fig 52. Disney's recruitment page.

expanded to uncover a synopsis of activity as well as the requirements that are needed to work in this area of the business. On a very positive note, Cadbury's lures prospective employees by detailing the training and support for professional qualifications that the company actively supports as well as giving information on possible career development including likely time-scales to reach particular milestones – very useful and informative. Cadbury's recruitment process is carried out annually and details of time-scales and ways to apply are also given. The only off-putting point relating to this site is the presence of chocolate bars of all shapes and sizes which appear throughout every page of information.

Disney
http://www.disney.com/disneycareers/index.html
If you've ever experienced the Disney thing then somewhere in the back of your mind you'll probably think that some day, when suburbia can be left behind, you'd like to work for them. (The author would personally be very happy selling those giant turkey legs to tourists in the Magic Kingdom in Florida!) And why not? Just take a look through the contents of this site and take the first steps to joining Team Disney. Disney offer careers covering all sorts of functions from engineers, to planners to programmers to marketeers. Employment opportunities exist throughout the world in shops, theatres and theme parks as well as in television and radio.

Top UK employers on the internet

Glaxo Wellcome
http://www.glaxowellcome.com
Glaxo Wellcome is the world's premier research-based pharmaceutical company. It operates in 70 countries and employs 54,000 people. Glaxo Wellcome provides both the pharmaceutical industry and healthcare providers with medicines and services. This site offers great recruitment information including company background, employee benefits, entry requirements and how to apply for positions within the company. Opportunities mainly exist for science graduates. The 'Milk-round' page provides opportunities for prospective graduates.

Guardian Royal Exchange
http://www.gre-group.com/
Guardian Royal Exchange provides health, general and life assurance world-wide, has over 7.5 million customers, operates in over 50 countries and has assets of £20 billion. This site offers visitors the chance to request company reports and information such as Group Profiles and Annual Reports and financial information. Of particular interest is the 'Contacts' page where you will find the address and email details of a number of contact points within the various functions of the company. Topical information is also available through the 'News' section.

Halifax plc
http://www.halifax.co.uk/
A great, no nonsense home page with hot links that cover over 25 different information areas for banking customers and those looking for company information. Four icons on the Halifax home page all offer some relevance to job seekers and cover bank financial results, corporate information, recruitment and year 2000 issues. Corporate information is very detailed covering everything from background information to details relating to the Banking Ombudsman. The Halifax recruitment page provides opportunities for graduates and non-graduates and gives details relating to applying for positions within the company.

ICI
http://www.ici.com
ICI is one of the world's largest speciality chemical and materials companies. ICI manufactures in over 55 countries in the world. Recruitment at ICI must be high on the agenda as the link to graduate recruitment can be found slap bang in the middle of the company's home page. After clicking here, and by simply choosing a country, an e-mail address label is set up for you to receive the appropriate information that you require. A nice touch on this site is the letter from the group recruitment manager for prospective applicants (this letter includes a friendly photograph of the author of the letter which gives it a certain homeliness!).

Lloyd's
http://www.lloydsbank.co.uk
The Lloyd's Bank home page is exciting, innovative and crazy! Baked

Top UK employers on the internet

beans seem to play a big role! Student and graduate information is provided in an area titled 'the Zone' and from here you can access some fantastic information on the process of going to university. From choosing an institution, applying for entry, attending a university interview and managing finances whilst studying, these pages really have it all. Whether you're a school sixth former or a more mature person looking to return to university then this site is a real must. Plenty of useful contact addresses and telephone numbers are also provided for those looking to contact the bank for employment purposes.

Marks & Spencer
http://www.marks-and-spencer.co.uk
Although it's tucked away under 'Corporate Index' and it's quite difficult to find, Marks and Spencer's employment opportunities is a real winner. Information relating to company history, shareholder information through to annual report information is included in this comprehensive account of the company's operation. If you're lucky enough to get an interview with M&S then there's simply no excuse for not being prepared. In the recruitment section vacancies are listed by function and, although each vacancy is not explained in great detail, enough information is given. Correspondence information for CV submission is also included.

NatWest Bank
http://www.natwest.co.uk/
The NatWest's home page provides an easy-to-use search routine that allows the entry of a key word to return the appropriate pages on the bank's information pages. Each page also has 'Tools' available and these can be used to contact NatWest, comment on the design of the site, request more information and display an A–Z listing of the contests of the site. This concept works very well indeed. As an aside, this site offers great information relating to NatWest's involvement in cricket.

Pilkingtons
http://www.pilkington.com/
Look under 'About Pilkingtons' for everything you'll need to know including how to apply for a position within the company as well as a list of the current vacancies available.

Post Office – Hot Spot
http://www.hot-spot.co.uk/
Hot Spot is the graduate recruitment site for the Post Office Group. It is designed to give you a brief overview of the breadth and scope of the business activities of the group and the opportunities and training programmes on offer for high-calibre graduates. The organisation recruits about 150 to 200 graduates annually, but not all of the businesses within the group recruit every year. Opportunities are advertised in the national press and here on the Hot Spot web site. The site is updated regularly, listing the current opportunities on offer.

Top UK employers on the internet

Procter & Gamble
http://www.pg.com/
The home page of this giant corporation has links to its career site which contains information about the company including orientation, careers and training opportunities world wide, and internships. Follow the links to its European career centre. The pages have more the feel of a corporate promotion than a functional recruitment section.

Railtrack
http://www.railtrack.co.uk
Railtrack's home page opens with a great quote which identifies exactly what the company does. It says 'Railtrack is the national rail infrastructure – everything the trains travel on, over, through, across, to and from', a great quote that could be rolled out at interview and which sums up perfectly the company's operation. Try looking up 'Corporate Information' to find company details, financial information and details of graduate recruitment. The graduate recruitment page offers a good step-by-step guide to jobs and careers in the company and most of your queries relating to employment should be answered as you walk through the steps. On the lighter side, 'Travel Information' answers all those questions that you can never get answered when you phone your local train station or attempt to understand a train timetable – simple things like train times, journey lengths etc. – a real winner and available for the whole of the UK.

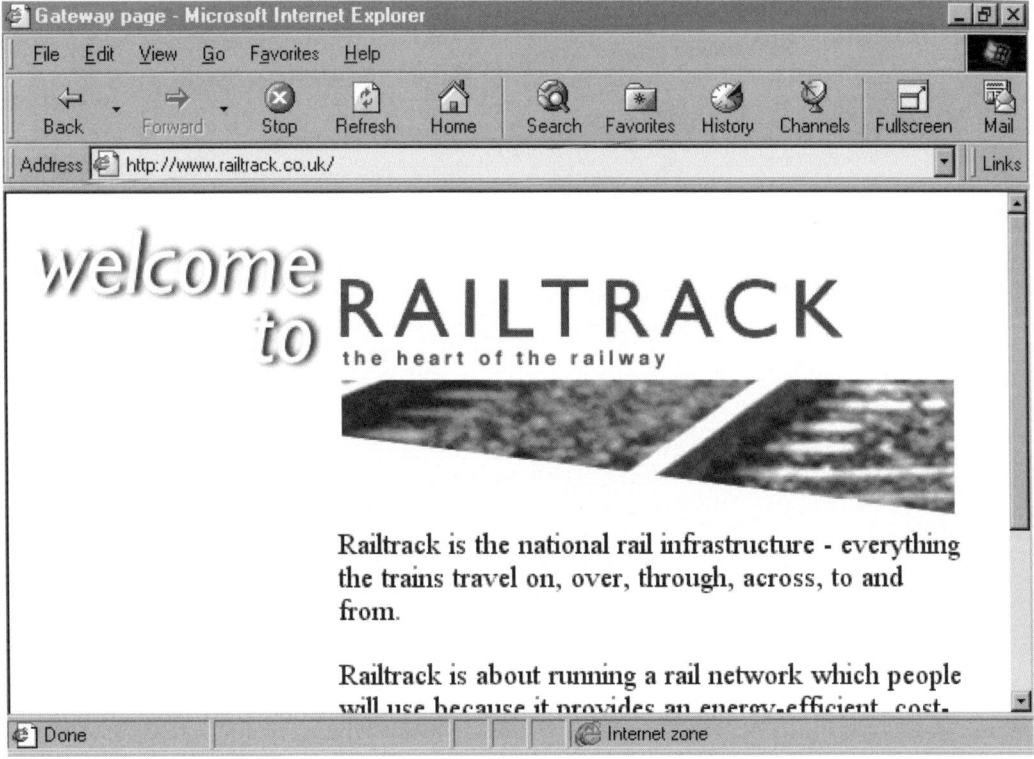

Fig. 53. Railtrack's home page.

Top UK employers on the internet

Royal & SunAlliance
http://www.royal-and-sunalliance.com

Royal & SunAlliance is the country's largest providers of insurance, pensions and investment facilities. The company has a very job seeker-friendly attitude and you can go from making general enquiries through to actually applying for a job online. You can also send your CV online to the company. Background information is available for specific job vacancies, which are listed, and all the skills and qualifications required are clearly identified. This type of site offers a very positive opportunity for job seekers as you actually apply for real-life jobs rather than respond to speculative enquiries to join various company programmes. The 'What's New' page gives you current company innovations as well as all recently issued press release information.

Safeway
http://www.safeway.co.uk

The Safeway site opens with an unusual screen – blank with nothing other than the Safeway logo and the word 'think'. This concept appears again at other points in this site. Different! From the Safeway home page three large question marks invite you to enter something – but what? No matter where you click, all roads lead to graduate recruitment information. Comprehensive information is provided about the company's graduate recruitment programme as well as general company information. The site also has a striking visual flowchart of the process you are required to follow to successfully apply for and achieve employment with the company. Information relating to employee core skills is also available.

Sainsbury
http://www.sainsburys.co.uk/

This site is bright and bursting with information. Information for job seekers is tucked away under the 'J Sainsbury plc' hotspot; however, when you finally reach it, you'll find it to be comprehensive. Look under the 'Sainsbury's History' icon to find fantastic historical information relating to the company. In particular the history tour and time-line information is useful. Job seekers will also find the statistics provided useful in an interview situation. With Sainsbury's, job opportunities exist for school leavers as well as graduates.

Scottish & Newcastle
http://www.scottish-newcastle.com

The Scottish and Newcastle home page is clearly split into the four facets of the company's business. Each facet is explained in full and covers Beer, Retail, Leisure and Corporate areas of the business. Under the Corporate area, useful information is given relating to the company's culture and style – important information for matching your own personal employment needs. There's also an online contact page that allows you to express an interest in employment with the company. At the bottom of each page a toolbar gives a detailed history 'through the centuries' of the company and again this information provides an excellent source of background reading.

Top UK employers on the internet

Shell
http://www.shell.co.uk
This is a very bright and well designed company site. Choose from a typical forecourt display board and be guided through the world of Shell. Apart from all the usual information that you'd expect to find, a couple of little fun pages exist. Try the Route Planner to plan any route, start to finish, within Europe – useful for attending those hard to get to interviews! Also, if job-hunting is becoming tedious and you need a well-earned break, try the online prehistoric game 'Quest for Oil' starring the 'Fossil' family. Great fun!

Shell LiveWire
http://www.shell-livewire.org/
Shell LiveWire helps 16-30 year olds to start and develop their own business and hosts a national competition for new business start-ups. You can use the site to pick up some valuable business advice and check out the ten most popular business ideas and their relevant fact sheets. Register online, and they will send you a free business kit which includes up to six fact sheets to develop your own specific business idea.

Shell STEP
http://www.shell-step.org.uk
Shell STEP is a national programme run through a network of agencies around the UK offering more than 1,500 work placement opportunities to second-year or penultimate-year undergraduates. Shell STEP projects run over eight weeks in the summer. The principal sponsors are Shell UK and the Department of Trade and Industry. You can apply here for a place. The programme is open to undergraduates and HND students who have completed two years of study for their first degree and who, ideally, have not had any significant work experience. Students must be under 24 at the start of their placement.

Siebe
http://www.siebe.com
Siebe's core business originally lay in marine engineering and breathing apparatus. In the early 1970's the company began to transform into the world-class controls and engineering group that it is today. Siebe's internet site is really very informative. Comprehensive information is provided relating to key personnel and board members giving personal career profiles (see the heights that you could reach!) The Corporate Presentation section allows you to view or download an Adobe Acrobat file of company information which gives you a great overview of the organisation's mission, structure and operation. A feedback form is provided where you can send an online enquiry or comment on the contents of the company internet site.

SmithKline Beecham
http://www.sb.com/search/index.html
The best way to search through the SmithKline Beecham site is to enter some keywords into the text box on this page and wait to enter the maze of linked SmithKline Beecham's sites. Under the employment

Top UK employers on the internet

pages details are given on how to mail CVs and job requests either electronically or via the traditional 'snail mail' route.

Tesco
http://www.tesco.co.uk
If it's job opportunities you're looking for, then details are hiding away under 'Information'. The main jobs listed are for IT specialists; however, this is likely to expand in the near future. Very detailed information on recruitment is given including roles, salary, benefits, packages etc. Address details for application are also given. Tesco also provide a useful FAQ section where job-seeker queries are expertly answered.

Unilever
http://www.unilever.com
This site is split into six main areas covering Unilever brands, the environment, financials, recruitment, marketing and news. The home page offers the opportunity to download a press pack which, whilst specifically aimed at journalists, provides easy-to-understand company information. The recruitment page is split into management recruitment and graduate recruitment. Contact information is provided here, as well as details of Unilever's Graduate Recruitment web site (www.uniq.unilever.com).

Vodafone
http://www.vodafone.co.uk
Vodafone is a world leader in the field of mobile communications. The main company home page is very visual and is made up of a range of clickable icons which open up detail relating to a wide range of company information. Click on the 'Career Opportunities' icon to enter Vodafone's career opportunities section where a wide range of job opportunities are on offer. Contact names and direct links are given.

Whitbread
http://www.whitbread.co.uk/
Whitbread's home page is a good, visual site. The first thing you must try is to run the 'showreel' and choose a 30-second video clip relating to part of the company's activity. A picture speaks a thousand words and these clips are invaluable. Also have a look in the resource library and research the company's history. The recruitment page provided is also very good indeed and covers recruitment for all members of the Whitbread group which includes chains such as Beefeater, Pizza Hut and Bella Pasta. Just choose the appropriate chain member, read up on the vacancies available and simply email for more information. Easy, and very intuitive.

12 Recruitment agencies on the internet

In this chapter you will discover:

▶ what services a recruitment agency offers
▶ the URLs and reviews of a number of online recruitment agencies.

Introduction

Recruitment agencies take the grief out of job hunting. Whether you scan the weekly broadsheets, check the small ads in your local supermarket or simply visit the local Job Centre on a regular basis, job hunting requires work and commitment. Recruitment agencies are specialist companies who make their living out of matching job seekers with job opportunities. The main benefit of using a recruitment agency is the fact that they do all the work for you. Normally, you submit your CV details and some information on the type of job that you are looking for, and the agency then keeps you updated with suitable vacancies – just like an estate agency for job seekers! The internet is awash with recruitment agencies and, listed below, are a few that might be worth a quick visit.

3D Recruitment
http://www.3dr.co.uk/
This is a one page site that offers you the ability to submit your CV on-line. 3D Recruitment specialises in providing employment opportunities in the Information Systems industry.

Acumen
http://www.acumen.demon.co.uk/
Acumen is a contract and permanent personnel agency which provides staffing services to the pharmaceutical, biotech and healthcare industries throughout the UK. It provides personnel for engineering, technical, scientific and manufacturing environments. The site is directed mainly at client organisations. A useful feature of the site is its links to leading UK and international chemicals and pharmaceutical employers.

Alba International
http://www.alba.net
This Isle of Man based organisation recruits for the oil and gas industries world wide. It was founded in Scotland in 1984 to service the North Sea with qualified personnel working in all areas of offshore, onshore oil and gas industry at that time. Today it has offices in Baku, Azerbaijan, Kuwait and Kuala Lumpur. Its database of candidates includes some 8,000 fully qualified and experienced oil and gas personnel to cover the requirements of the industry. The site contains some very useful industry links, including the home pages of many of the world's leading oil and gas companies.

Recruitment agencies on the net

Albemarle Interim Management
http://www.albemarle.co.uk/index.htm
Albemarle operates throughout the UK and Europe and within all industries and job functions. Albemarle specialises in the provision of interim management which is used by companies either to cover sickness, to manage specific projects or to provide temporary employment where future opportunities are unable to be accurately forecast. This type of employment might be suitable for those who like constant challenges or for experienced managers who can offer excellent skills to this type of employment. Check through this site, read through the case studies of previous interim management assignments and submit your CV online.

Angel International Recruitment
http://www.angel-int.co.uk/
Angel International Recruitment promotes the placing of temporary staff within the commercial, medical, hotel catering and driving arenas. This site has a very straightforward feedback form that can be used to declare an interest in a particular service.

Astbury Marsden
http://www.astburymarsden.co.uk/
Astbury Marsden is an established name in IT and financial recruitment. The company offers opportunities in six divisions; information technology, middle office banking, commerce and industry, corporate finance, equity research and international sectors. Each section is divided into current vacancies listed by job type and each job is explained in full.

Austin Knight
http://www.austinknight.com/
Austin Knight is a long-established player in the recruitment world. The company was founded in 1921 and has offices world wide. This site introduces 'cybercruiting' which ensures that job adverts are viewed not passively, but actively, by those who need to see them but might not normally visit third party recruitment companies. This is achieved by Austin Knight's development of client sites ensuring that advertisements are placed on company home sites as well as Austin Knight's pages. See also **Knight Net**.

Badenoch and Clark
http://www.badenochandclark.com
Badenoch & Clark was established in the UK in 1980 as a specialist financial recruitment consultancy. It now covers five areas – banking and financial services, accountancy, law, IT and the public sector. This web site offers a brief overview of its activities and includes testimonials from clients and candidates.

Balfour Associates
http://www.balfour.co.uk
Balfour is a London-based information technology recruitment agency. There is online candidate registration, and searchable database of

Fig. 54. The Austin Knight home page.

vacancies. Alternatively, you can browse for vacancies in engineering and IT.

Beament Leslie Thomas
http://www.blt.co.uk/
Beament Leslie Thomas provides a specialist recruitment service concerned with tax, management consultancy and public finance. The company stresses that it is not a generalist recruitment company thus ensuring that its expertise remains undiluted. Beament Leslie Thomas provides a pre-selection service that ensures that job seekers and clients are matched as closely as possible even before their first meeting. Contact details for the company is listed on this site. Check out 'Careerwatch' a service that provides those not necessarily desperate for a change to keep up to date with opportunities that arise. CVs are held and sent to companies only with job seeker permission – useful if you're still in employment and you don't particularly want referees to be contacted.

Beechwood Recruitment
http://www.appointmentsregister.co.uk/
Beechwood is a London-based engineering, IT and science recruitment agency, with some graduate positions.

Bio Career
http://www.biocareer.com/
The Biotechnology Industry Organization (BIO), and SciWeb, the life science home page, have combined to develop this online career resource. This award winning site is efficient, effective and an easy way

Recruitment agencies on the net

to connect job seekers and recruiters in the biotechnology industry. It provides a service for graduate students, journalists, lawyers, managers, nurses, patients, pharmacists, physicians, post-doctorals, scientists, students, teachers and web-surfers. The site includes public discussion boards to air workplace issues. You will also find a salary survey, career articles, a BIO career guide, and a web directory with links to sites with career information, scholarships, loans and relocation services. You can also select careers books from a Barnes and Noble list. HR professionals can network in the HR Contact Area. There is also a bulletin board for posting questions.

BioMedNet Jobs

http://biomednet.com/jobs.htm

This is part of the London-based world wide club for the biological and medical community. It was acquired by the UK-based information company Reed in 1997. BioMedNet's Job Exchange contains nearly 1,000 positions wanted and available in academia and commercial sectors. You can search the jobs database, add your own job advertisement or CV, check out many links to career sites, books and articles, and access other resources to help your job search. You have to complete quite a detailed online application form to register. The site is believed to have in excess of 400,000 subscribers.

Bioscience Jobs

http://www.bioscience-jobs.com/

This is an online UK-based confidential CV database for life science graduates. It specialises in employment opportunities in the biomolecular sciences. It welcomes submission of CVs, enquiries about specific posts and requests to advertise job opportunities or search its database of potential candidates. It especially welcomes skills in bioinformatics, 3D structure determination, molecular modelling, protein and peptide chemistry, structural and functional genomics, molecular immunology, and computational chemistry. Job seekers are invited to complete the online form to provide basic details of their qualifications and current experience. The service is mainly seeking candidates with postgraduate experience either in industry or basic research.

Bluestone

http://www.bluestone.ltd.uk/

Based in the City of London, Bluestone specialises in financial services recruitment. It attracts clients from a whole range of organisations from investment banks to insurance providers as well as the leading professional service suppliers. It recruits across a wide spectrum of skills for roles within consulting, managerial and technical job functions. It focuses on selective search and advertising. Its databases hold details of experienced individuals discreetly seeking new career opportunities.

Recruitment agencies on the net

Brook Street
http://www.brookstreet.co.uk
This is the web site of the 50-year-old UK temping and recruitment agency, specialising in the supply of secretarial, office and light industrial staff. It operates a local network of branches in over ninety locations from Aberdeen to Exeter. You are invited to register online, but vacancies are not listed online. There is a clickable UK map you can use to find the address, phone and fax numbers of your nearest branch. Even the London-based branches did not appear to have web sites.

Capital Markets Consulting Ltd
http://www.cmcx.com/
CMC is a recruitment consultancy for global capital markets. A semi-naked animated sprinter welcomes you to this site, which is full of useful information on career areas in investment banking. The site offers three main elements – a global graduate recruitment programme, job profile programme where you can register, and a jobs profile programme.

Capstan Teachers
http://www.capstan.co.uk/
If you are a teacher, whether UK or overseas trained, UK-based Capstan offers access to primary and secondary short and long-term posts. The site includes an introduction, guidance for students and newly qualified teachers, brief information about working in or coming from the European Union, Australia, New Zealand, United States, Canada and elsewhere. Every year, Capstan says it helps thousands of teachers to find the type of teaching post they want – nursery, primary or secondary posts, whether on a day to day, long-term or permanent basis. You can do an onsite job vacancy search. Our search for secondary school maths teachers yielded five vacancies. Little detail was given on screen about each assignment other than the area, and start date; you have to contact Capstan for more. The site has a useful 'ask an expert' page where you can find an expert on various curriculum subjects. These include US-oriented science and technology, medicine and health, computing and the internet, history and social studies, economy and marketing, professionals, personal and college advisers, library reference, literature and language arts. The site offers a miscellany of other educational links.

Career in Site
http://www.careerinsite.com/pages/home.htm
Career in Site specialises in providing solutions to employers seeking workers in high tech industries. This site is very easy to navigate through, with the most important part, the search facility, being available slap bang in the middle of the company's home page. Your search will return job vacancies listed by relevance to your keyword search. Further investigation reveals a paragraph or two on the chosen vacancies and the opportunity to apply for the positions listed.

Recruitment agencies on the net

Castle Recruitment
http://www.recruit.co.uk/
This is an exclusively IT recruitment service, based in Berkhamsted. You can check the vacancies which interest you, click a job title to see a detailed description, page down to the bottom of the form, fill in the details required and paste in your CV. You can search by reference number for advertised vacancies.

Charity Appointments
http://www.charapp.demon.co.uk/
London-based Charity Appointments says it is the longest established senior executive recruitment consultancy for the charity and non-profit sector. A small number of current vacancies are detailed on the site. It also handles fund-raising recruitment.

Charity People
http://www.charitypeople.co.uk/
This is the web site of a recruitment consultancy dedicated to the not-for-profit sector. Several dozen vacancies were listed, with full details including salary guides. It contains a substantial number of links to charitable and governmental bodies. The consultancy has offices in London and Leeds.

Christopher Keats Media Recruitment
http://www.christopherkeats.co.uk
Established in 1987, the company places staff in jobs in broadcasting, advertising, publishing, public relations, marketing and design. Brief details are given of the vacancies, which are mainly secretarial and administrative, and salaries. The site includes lists of clients in each category, with hyper links to the home pages of some of them.

City Executive Consultants Ltd
http://www.cityexec.co.uk/
City Executive Consultants (CEC) recruits for the financial services sector in the City of London. It specialises in providing candidates for investment banking, securities and fund management. Using minimal design, the site presents detailed information about current vacancies, and supplies a comprehensive CV-style response form for applicants to use online.

City Jobs
http://www.cityjobs.com
City Jobs aims to bring City of London employers and high-calibre job seekers together. Recruiters pay a fixed subscription fee to advertise vacancies, and can upload their own vacancies immediately. Once registered, job seekers can use the fast-stream application service freely. Registered candidates can keep a cut-down CV or résumé on its database and this will be the first document personnel officers see when an application is made. City Jobs was founded in 1997 by the directors of a City recruitment consultancy and Green Cathedral Ltd, a Cambridge-based internet software and new media production house.

Recruitment agencies on the net

The site includes a library, directory, and a 'City Channel' with links to travel, leisure and entertainment. The directory contains a wide selection of key financial sector, media, new-media and IT recruiters. All of these advertise at City Jobs and many have dedicated pages and presentations on the site. Others have their own information sites where you can contact them directly.

Civil Service Jobs
http://www.open.gov.uk/sesd/1998/mainstream/ukcivil.htm
The Civil Service is among the largest graduate recruiters in the country. Graduates enter the Civil Service mainly through departmental and agency recruitment schemes, although small numbers are also recruited through the fast-stream entry schemes. This comprehensive but dull web site contains an enormous list of all the categories of civil servants they wish to recruit.

Computer Careers International
http://www.cci.ie
CCI is a Dublin-based computer recruitment specialist established in 1991. You can search its database for contract and permanent positions, submit your CV using a simple applicant-friendly form, and get some CV tips. The brief details of the numerous vacancies were well classified and clearly presented.

Cooper Lomaz Recruitment
http://www.cooperlomaz.co.uk/
Cooper Lomaz are experts in the provision of a wide range of professional candidates who choose to work in East Anglia and the Northern Home Counties. This site is conveniently split into the six main recruitment areas – accountancy, computing, personnel, sales and marketing, secretarial and technical. Vacancies currently available in these areas are easily accessed from the Cooper Lomaz home page. Vacancies are clearly listed in column format detailing the job reference, salary band, job location and the recruitment office dealing with the vacancy. Each of the main job areas also has an 'About' section that, when clicked, gives a more detailed explanation of the likely vacancies that might normally exist.

Courseware People
http://www.cwpltd.co.uk
Courseware People was established in 1988 to provide a specialist recruitment service to the computer-based training industry. It originally established a client and candidate base in banking, aviation, retail and computing as well as independent training consultancies. Today, it services all aspects of technology assisted learning and multimedia recruitment. Its database of candidates numbers 6,500, covering freelances as well as people looking for permanent placements. Candidate skills including project management, instructional design, programming, training delivery and graphic design. The company has recently created a specialist internet division, Netselect, to concentrate purely on web-based businesses.

Recruitment agencies on the net

CPL Scientific Employment Services
http://www.cplscientific.co.uk/ses/
CPL Scientific Employment Services Ltd provides contingency recruitment services to companies throughout the UK. These include the supply of permanent and contract staff at all levels from technicians to managers, as well as payroll services. Its assignments are in the life science and chemical industries, including biotechnology, environment, fine chemicals, food and pharmaceuticals. The service uses a national database of more than 6,000 applicants on a no-placement no-fee basis. It is free to applicants, and has around 25-30 jobs open at any time. The company is based in Newbury, Berkshire.

Crescere Resourcing
http://www.crescere.co.uk/
Crescere Resourcing specialises in the recruitment of staff for the electronics, IT and communications industries. Crescere provides a number of online services for maintaining clients and job seekers on a database through to informal networking to fill vacancies. Check out the section on CV and interview preparation. This site offers a very intuitive search routine that allows you to electronically send your details for any job that you find interesting during your search.

Crone Corkill
http://www.cronecorkill.co.uk/
Crone Corkill provides temporary, permanent, and part-time secretaries, administrators, executives and linguists. Check through the current opportunities and find out more, or, if all that job seeking is getting you down, drive along the superhighway to Crone Corkill's 'Take 5' area and chill out and relax. Here you can leave notices for Crone Corkill staff as well as visiting some of the delicious 'recipes on the run' for those who want to cook but just don't have the time.

Dale Recruitment
http://wkweb1.cableinet.co.uk/dalerecruitment/
A very ease to use site, Dale Recruitment offers job possibilities for candidates in the computing, electronic, engineering and other industries. Set up over five years ago Dale Recruitment provides employees at all levels. Why not send a speculative CV for one of the job categories available?

Dart Resourcing
http://www.dart-resourcing.com/
Established in 1975, Dart offers permanent job and contract assignments in mainstream IT, PC, network and communications, sales and marketing engineering, management and executive. There are opportunities for applicants with skills and experience in unix, PC development and support, communications, networking, internet/html/multimedia, RDBMS, IBM midrange and mainframe, DEC VAX, Tandem, Europe and more.

Recruitment agencies on the net

DICE Online Job Search
http://www.dice.com/
DICE stands for Data Processing Independent Consultant's Exchange. This is a free service for experienced high tech computer consulting professionals, technical writers, and engineers who are looking for contract and full time work. Over 5,000 open job requirements have been posted by over 225 subscribing agencies nationwide. All position descriptions are less than 30 days old.

Douglas Llambias Associates
http://www.llambias.co.uk/
London-based DLA is a leading provider of financial, IT and other specialist recruitment services to accountancy and legal firms, industrial and commercial companies, management consultancies and banking and financial services organisations, both nationally and internationally. The site contained several hundred vacancies, presented under broad industry categories, with fairly brief details of each including remuneration levels, and online application forms. Its free services to candidates include: personality appraisals, career planning advice, market information, career guides and other literature, advice on drafting CVs, interview coaching, employer briefings, including fact sheets and annual reports, interview confirmation and de-briefings, and regular contact with progress discussions.

- Services for Clients
- Services for Candidates
- Newly-qualified Accountants
- Executive Selection
- Current Opportunities
- How to Apply

ECM Selection
http://www.ecmsel.co.uk/
ECM Selection Ltd is a specialist recruitment company which recruits exclusively for the 'High Technology Superleague.' ECM counts amongst its clients the top blue chip companies through to smaller innovative companies. ECM generally requires candidates to have at least a 2:1 Honours degree or some form of postgraduate qualification. ECM have an extended job search facility that allows you to send your CV online.

Education Jobs
http://www.education-jobs.co.uk
If you are actively seeking employment in the educational field then this site is one place to visit. You can select categories from administration, schools, further education, higher education and miscellaneous. The job details are brief but to the point.

Elite Computer Staff
http://www.elite-cs.co.uk/elite/
Founded in 1992, Elite has developed into a professional and highly regarded contract and permanent IT recruitment company. Their success results from the strength and training of their consultants and an impressive, yet controlled growth rate. They believe in forging strong, friendly working relationships with clients. This consolidates their understanding of their specific (but ever changing) contract and permanent resource requirements. Underpinning and strengthening the relationship is a strong infrastructure that incorporates powerful

Recruitment agencies on the net

recruitment software, investment in leading edge technology, extensive national and international advertising in quality journals and via a variety of internet services, and ISO9002 accreditation and membership of FRES (the recruitment body representing best practice). Elite's highly experienced technical managers, supported by a specialist recruitment team, adhere to the highest standards of quality and ethics.

Executive Recruitment Services
http://www.worldserver.pipex.com/ers/
Executive Recruitment Services specialises in recruitment for computing, electronics, defence and sales personnel. The search facility in this site allows you to choose from 227 key skills and 107 technical areas as well as determining whether you are looking for contract or permanent employment, you then search, and a list of suitable vacancies appears – simple. This site also offers an online CV service allowing you to upload your current CV.

Financial Careers Advisers
http://www.financial-careers.co.uk/
FCA offers specialist career advice to individuals with respect to employment and jobs in the financial services industry. Investment banking, securities and fund management are the broad areas covered. In particular, it advises on positions within equity and equity derivatives research, sales and trading, corporate finance and equity capital markets, investment management and research, compliance and risk management. A team approach, experience in City ways and the modern computer technology at FCA, enable each person to be advised in a sophisticated, informed and personable way. FCA offers unrivalled access to information and advice from experienced, respected and well connected professionals for modest fees.

First Choice Computer Appointments
http://www.choice-1.demon.co.uk
This is an IT recruitment agency for professionals working in or relocating to the south east of England. It places analysts, programmers, network and technical support people in local jobs.

FoodJobs
http://www.foodjobs.co.uk/
FoodJobs is a specialist recruitment consultancy for the food manufacturing and associated industries. It has been successfully recruiting staff for over ten years in a wide range of disciplines. There are links to how to find a job, current vacancies, information about food jobs, links, employers vacancy registration, and more. The numerous vacancies are well categorised, for example under engineers, graduates, production, laboratory, technologists, sales, miscellaneous, quality, planning assurance, and so on. The job descriptions are rather brief, and you will need to make a note of the reference numbers of the ones you are interested in. The site says you will need Microsoft Word to submit your CV online. FoodJobs does not distribute unsolicited curriculum vitae to firms.

Recruitment agencies on the net

Graduate Recruitment Company
http://www.graduate-recruitment.co.uk/
The Graduate Recruitment Company has a wide base of clients including PepsiCo., the BBC and the Royal Bank of Scotland. The company has managed graduate recruitment for many business areas including sales, PR and marketing, and recruitment. Positions have also been found for technology graduates in areas such as programming and user support. This site is well designed and offers a very easy to use search engine which scans through available jobs. When you find a job that interests you, it is simply then a matter of clicking the 'respond' icon at the foot of the advert. You can then simply send your Microsoft Word format CV or choose to complete an online registration form.

Health Professionals
http://www.nursebank.co.uk/
This is a recruitment company for nurses who wish to work in London and the UK. You can find out about contracts, application form, accommodation, the company, training courses, and life in London. The site gives details of registration, work permits, pay scales, accommodation, nursing books, a discussion forum, and nursing links. It is a project of the Health Professionals Recruitment Service based in central London.

Hudson York Farrell
http://www.h-y-f.demon.co.uk
HYF is an agency based in the City of London specialising in banking, secretarial and DTP recruitment. The site was being updated when reviewed.

Human Enterprise Limited
http://www.demon.co.uk/hument/
Established in 1991, the firm's objective is to assist organisations in global investment banking, internet services, publishing, advertising, communications, manufacturing, and retail with their IT requirements, predominately on a permanent basis. The firm is based in the Wapping area of London.

Insight Computer Recruitment Ltd
http://www.insight-it.com/
Insight is a London-based recruitment agency for jobs in the IT world. Its three main areas are computer operations, PC/network support, and communications systems and programming. It has several hundred contractors working for it. Only a limited amount of information was available when we reviewed the site, which was undergoing changes.

JM Legal
http://www.jmlegal.co.uk/
JM are London-based specialists in legal recruitment including secretarial and support staff.

Recruitment agencies on the net

Job Mall
http://www.jobmall.co.uk/
Designed as a virtual mall for specialist recruitment agencies, Bristol-based Job Mall includes a series of 'professional arcades'. For example there are ones for engineering, IT, education and legal appointments. Within each one there is a list of selected agencies with links to their web sites. You can also search the vacancy database, which includes up to date vacancies for those agencies with the full search facility. You select one or more of the regions, enter up to 3 key words, and click on the search button. The site is agency-oriented, and does not give advice to individuals looking for work. There is quite a good selection of recruitment agencies under each heading.

Jonathon Lee Recruitment
http://www.jonlee.co.uk/
Jonathon Lee Recruitment specialises in providing personnel for the engineering industry. Check out 'Interview' in this site to find great ways of preparing for employment – particularly useful if you're just about to, or have just, graduated.

Kate Cowhig International Recruitment
http://www.failte.com/cowhigrecruitment/
Kate Cowhig is the leading healthcare recruitment company in Europe. The company has opportunities for doctors, nurses, physiotherapists, radiographers, medical secretaries and many other healthcare professionals. Vacancies exist for workers throughout the British Isles, Europe and as far afield as Australia and New Zealand. This site has a very simple feedback form that will allow you to express an interest in either a specific job or general vacancies.

Knight Net
http://www.ak.com/
Austin Knight is a leading UK recruitment agency. Established in London in 1921, it now has offices around the world, from New York to Newcastle, Paris to Perth. There are plenty of vacancies shown on its site.

Little Angels Nanny Consultancy
http://members.aol.com/langelsnc/main.htm
Little Angels says it is the first UK free childcare and nannying information service on the internet. There are fact sheets, news updates, FAQs, and details of a few current vacancies, mainly in London. The site uses AOL's Hometown members' pages facilities.

Longbridge Consultancy
http://www.longbridge.co.uk/
An international search and consulting firm with a blue chip client base spanning the legal and financial sectors. The site was under development when we reviewed it.

Fig. 55. M&M Recruitment home page.

M&M Recruitment Limited
http://www.mmstaff.co.uk/
M&M Recruitment provides human resource strategies and recruitment solutions for the IT and engineering industries. The agency recruits for all types of jobs within these sectors. This site is very easy to look through and cuts out a lot of the fancy design, instead preferring to get you straight to the heart of the issue – getting a job. Within each sector, M&M provides a list of job types and within each job type a list of current vacancies. By simply clicking on a suitable vacancy a detailed job description is displayed detailing essential skills, qualifications, experience, desirable requirements and duties for the job in question. Should you choose to apply for any job you simply click on the button at the bottom of the advert and send your CV online. Alternatively, phone contact details are given.

Major Players
http://www.majorplayers.co.uk/
Major Players is a London-based marketing and media recruitment agency. You can check out vacancies for sales promotion and multi-disciplined agency staff, design management, new media, creatives, direct marketing, public relations, and secretarial and administrative support. The job details are fairly brief. It also offers a range of graduate trainee positions in various marketing agencies. The company offers both permanent and freelance opportunities. A useful feature of the site is its links to online directories of creative talent, design consultants and companies covering services such as design, photography, illustration, advertising, marketing, new media, writing and more.

Recruitment agencies on the net

Mansell
http://www.mansell.co.uk/
Mansell Associates provides career opportunities for those wishing to work in technical industries such as the petrochemical, aerospace and engineering industries. Facilities provided includes a comprehensive jobs database, advice on salaries, candidate profiling and the provision of interview facilities at the company's offices. This site is simple to use and provides job seekers with an easy to access list of current vacancies as well as the opportunity to send CVs online and request job specifications.

Melville Craig Group
http://www.mcg.co.uk/contents.html
Melville Craig offer opportunities covering a wide range of industries and jobs. As one of Scotland's leading recruitment agencies, Melville Craig has an excellent pedigree and offers great services to prospective job candidates. Try searching through current vacancies by keying in your required job or skill and wait for the number of job matches to appear that meets your requirements. Then follow your nose!

New Start Recruitment
http://www.newstart.co.uk/
New Start Recruitment specialises in recruitment in IT and mechanical engineering. This site is split into software, hardware, systems, test and mechanical and by clicking on any of these icons you will reveal current vacancies that are available. New Start offers a '1-2-3' to easy application that requires online registration, the sending of a current CV and then simply sitting back and waiting to be contacted by a representative of the company.

Office Angels
http://www.office-angels.com/
Office Angels offers great employment opportunities for secretaries, administrative and other office staff. Championing the case of male secretaries, and return to work opportunities for mothers, Office Angels is a great place to visit if you are looking for office-type work. At present this site only gives details of the names and addresses of UK branch offices and of manager names. However, keep your browser pointing here for future developments.

Pareto Law
http://www.paretolaw.co.uk/
Pareto's Law propounds the 80:20 principle, for example that 80% of a company's sales will be brought in by 20% of the sales force. Established in 1995, Pareto Law Plc is a company which specialises in finding top-flight graduates for sales positions in the information technology sector.

Piper Group
http://www.piper-group.co.uk/
This site offers easy access to details of the Piper Group as well as

Recruitment agencies on the net

interests for job seekers and interests for employers – a very user friendly home page. Since 1981, the Piper Group has provided recruitment services in the technical, industrial, IT and other industry sectors. Search through each division, find the list of current vacancies and then complete the detailed registration form and submit your request online.

Portman Initial
http://www.portman-initial.co.uk/
Based in the City of London, Portman Initial are recruitment specialists in IT, banking, accountancy, legal, sales and secretarial vacancies. For bankers there may be opportunities in operations staff for FX/derivatives/treasury/portfolio administration, securities and investment personnel, loans administration and credit analysis, dealers and dealer assistants, senior appointments in all markets and trainee appointments. For accountants there are opportunities for part/fully qualified accountants, derivative product accountants, profit and loss controllers, audit and compliance, accounts administrators including, payroll, ledgers, credit control.

Price Jamieson
http://www.pricejam.com
Price Jamieson are a predominantly media recruitment agency, based in London. There are opportunities in new media, design, public relations, media, direct marketing, IT, international, health, and market research. Most vacancies for graduates are in media/pharmaceutical sales, etc. The advertised vacancies on the site come with helpful full job descriptions, details of remuneration, and personal contact numbers for follow up. To keep you informed of the latest vacancies relevant to your skills, experience, qualifications and aspirations, you are invited to complete and submit the online résumé form. You should subsequently receive a message of confirmation. Price Jamieson says that all information received from candidates is treated in confidence and will not be released to any individual or organisation without permission.

PSD Group
http://www.psd.co.uk/
PSD is an international recruitment group providing specialist recruitment services for the technology, property, construction, legal, financial services, finance and accountancy and marketing sectors. Choose from the sector icons on the company's home page, and decide whether you're looking for permanent or temporary employment. Then simply choose more details from the positions listed. CVs can be submitted electronically.

RecruitMedia
http://www.recruitmedia.co.uk/
This is a recruitment consultancy based in Islington, London, for creative and technical people working on a freelance or permanent basis. You can scan its jobs pages for lists of the latest vacancies in

Recruitment agencies on the net

editorial, internet and technical, design and production, and new media sales and marketing. They require at least two years' experience. Full details are given of the vacancies, which are reasonably plentiful.

Reed Online
http://www.reed.co.uk/
Reed is a leading UK recruiting agency, and this is its main web site. Whether you are a job seeker or a recruiter you will find a wealth of information and opportunities here, including some 3,000 jobs which you can search online. There are daily updates of job vacancies. The site is divided into sections such as Reed Accountants, Reed for IT Professionals, Reed for Graduates, Reed for Insurance Specialists, and Christmas jobs. Other site features include a local branch finder, client profiles, ten minute tutorials, registration, training, year 2000 compliance, work directives, and more. When you do find the job that you're interested in, Reed Online provides a comprehensive résumé of the job that you're interested in. It's also very easy to sign up with Reed and go about securing that all important job. The site features a Regional Salary Calculator, an instant guide to comparative salaries throughout the United Kingdom. Based on your own salary and average salaries nationwide, it will tell you what you could expect to earn anywhere else in the UK.

Robert Half & Accountemps
www.accountemps.com
Robert Half & Accountemps is the largest and longest established (1948) specialist in accountancy and finance recruitment, with 225 offices world wide. Established in the UK in 1973, it now has 17 regional offices. The company has a global turnover in excess of $1.3 billion. 'Our business is to help people like you gain an edge in the recruitment marketplace whether you're looking for a permanent or temporary position, or just like to keep your options open, Robert Half & Accountemps can give you the competitive edge you need.' The site features 'The Shortlist', a selection of its current permanent and temporary job opportunities, updated weekly. You can view them under graduate opportunities, current permanent opportunities and current temporary opportunities. Other features of the site include a salary and benefits survey, candidate registration, Ontrack, its career advice service, and the *Accountemps Handbook*, a quick summary of Accountemps policies and procedures.

ROC Recruitment
http://www.roc.co.uk/
ROC Recruitment Ltd is a specialist in London secretarial and administrative appointments. It has offices in the City and West End.

S-Com CSE
http://www.scom.com/
This is a UK-based computer recruitment agency, with nineteen years' experience in the sector. It recruits for specialist markets such as telecommunications, data communications, defence, air traffic, avio-

Recruitment agencies on the net

nics and the internet. It says it has grown by 500% in the last four years. It currently has more than 650 contractors on assignments in its specialist sectors in 25 different countries. You can search for positions by international region, and by type of work. We found several hundred vacancies for example available in the UK. The job descriptions are clearly summarised and include phone and email contacts.

Secretaries Plus
http://www.secretaries-plus.co.uk/
This agency has more than 20 years' experience in the West End and City of London. It places permanent, temporary and short-term contract staff including PAs, team secretaries, college leavers, receptionists, office managers and administrators, and personnel managers and assistants.

STS Recruitment
http://www.stsrecruit.com/
Established in 1979, STS Recruitment provides opportunities for technical staff especially in the electronics and computing fields. STS Recruitment is ISO90002 registered. This site offers job seekers great advice when it declares 'to fail to prepare is to prepare to fail.' There is also information on attending interview explaining preparation, dress code, types of questions and the main reasons for interview failure.

Sure Employment
http://www.sure-employ.demon.co.uk/
Sure Employment is a recruitment agency based in Sussex, which fills permanent and temporary positions in office, IT, sales, secretarial, accountancy, legal, and technical work.

Systems International
http://ireland.iol.ie/si
Systems International provides opportunities for employment in the UK, Ireland and Western Europe for IT professionals. The company provides both permanent and temporary contracts for short and long term positions. Jobs are displayed by industry sector and there is the opportunity to complete a detailed online CV.

Tate Temp Specialists
http://www.tate.co.uk/
As the name might suggest, Tate Temp Specialists provides high quality temporary staff to a number of industries. This site offers an easy to complete online registration form which can be used to register with the company.

Time Plan
http://www.timeplan.com/
Ten years ago, Time Plan was launched as the UK's first supply teaching agency. They say that 3,000 schools have relied on Time Plan for supply cover since then, and 30,000 teachers have been recruited to fill a variety of short-term and permanent appointments. It also has an excellent 'virtual teachers centre' which has amassed an enormous

Recruitment agencies on the net

number of well-organised curriculum links. The site also provides links to teaching opportunities in New Zealand, and to business opportunities for teachers.

TSA Human Resources
http://www.tsa.co.uk/
TSA Human Resources Ltd are specialists in the recruitment of Sales and IT personnel. This site offers a great resource entitled '99 Interview Questions and Answers' which provides a comprehensive list of typical interview questions providing candidates with a really excellent job-seeking resource. Try and answer 'looking back would you have chosen a different career?' or 'Why aren't you earning more at your age?' Phewww! Sign up with TSA and find that ideal IT job.

Whitehead Mann Group
http://www.whiteheadselection.co.uk/
Whitehead Mann provides a recruitment service for a wide range of UK and international companies. Vacancies tend to be for middle to senior managers. Search through the opportunities listed and find that top job with salaries available upwards of £60K per year. Once you've found that perfect job, note the reference number and email your details back to the company. It's as simple as that.

Young Scientist
http://www.young-scientist.co.uk/
Based in Cranleigh, Surrey, this is a specialist recruitment agency for laboratory positions throughout the UK. It handles all staff levels from school leaver to senior management, though about half its positions are for candidates seeking their first one or two career appointments. It handles jobs in research and development, technical support and service, quality control and quality assurance, and pilot plant and production. The industries it covers include agrochemicals, biotechnology, chemicals, food and drink, paper and packaging, polymers, pharmaceuticals, toiletries, paints and inks, and specialities. Its services are free and confidental to candidates. The site includes sample details of a small selection of the jobs it has available.

Fig. 56. Young Scientist.

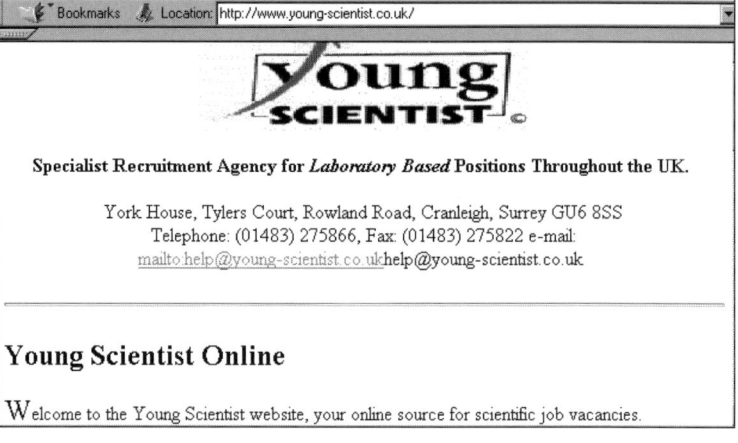

13 Overseas jobs pages

Introduction

This chapter offers a selection of web sites with information about job opportunities abroad. Inevitably, the scene is still heavily dominated by the USA, where the quality and depth and ingenuity of some of the web sites is very impressive, and hardly matched as yet by sites in the UK. No doubt this will gradually change, as UK-based publishers and recruiters get into their stride with the potential of this new technology.

Among the UK international job sites, the ones to watch include Overseas Jobs Express, and Expat Network, who are already leading information providers in the field of international recruitment through traditional media.

If you are keen on finding work abroad, in addition to exploring the site in these chapters, don't forget to make use of the major search engines and directories like Yahoo! and AltaVisa.

4Work (USA)
http://www.4work.com/
Presented in a varied magazine-style format, 4Work publishes information about mainly US career openings listed by Fortune 5000 corporate clients. Positions are searchable by state, company and position, such as job, internship, volunteer, and part time. In doing a search, your keywords can represent a skill, a location, a job title or a specific business. A feature of the site is 'Job Alert!' – a personal job search agent that you can task to search the site. To subscribe, you enter your name and email address. You are then asked to build a personal profile describing your skills, interests, abilities and to choose the region in which you would like to work.

ACES Job Offers
http://www.aces-fr.com/
This is a somewhat strangely organised French-based jobs database, which aims to cover vacancies, including science jobs, in all parts of the world. Part of it is in French and part in English. We did not find the site very easy to use, and it was hard to judge how much information was available.

ActiJob (Canada)
http://www.actijob.com/
This is an impressive and large job site for Canada. ActiJob provides you with hundreds of job opportunities for free and helps you make contact with some of the leading employers, in Canada. You can view the most recent jobs, search by keyword, browse by region or job category, check

Overseas jobs pages

out the employers by name or industry type or submit your résumé free. You can view the site in English or French. The site includes a Canadian job-chat centre. Find the drop down menu for Destinations, and click hyperlinks, to get access to loads more Canadian employment and recruitment sites ranging from government job sites to portals and guides, one of which is a directory of Canadian recruiters.

Adguide's Employment Web Site
http://www.adguide.com
This is mainly a US college-oriented recruitment site. The site is used by job hunters, students and graduates of high schools, technical schools, vocational schools, community colleges, colleges and universities. There are part-time and full-time opportunities. To be notified of free or new help wanted ads, enter your email address in the empty box and click Submit. Adguide says it is a high traffic site with about 300,000 page views per month. The site include message boards, news, and postcard service. A valuable feature of the site is its extensive list of links to hundreds of worldwide careers sites, presented in a long A–Z format.

AEA Japan
http://www.aea.or.jp/
The American Electronics Association represents the electronics, software, and information technology industries in Japan. This web site offers information on US-Japan trade agreements, a list of member companies, and a page of links to high-tech job sources for this country. Note that while this web site is in English, many things that they link to are in Japanese and your browser would need to be able to handle the characters of that language.

Alba International
http://www.alba.net
This Isle of Man based organisation recruits for the oil and gas industries world wide. It was founded in Scotland in 1984 to service the North Sea with qualified personnel working in all areas of offshore, onshore oil and gas industry at that time. Today it has offices in offices in Baku, Azerbaijan, Kuwait and Kuala Lumpur. Its database of candidates includes some 8,000 fully qualified and experienced oil and gas personnel to cover the requirements of the industry. The site contains some very useful industry links, including the home pages of many of the world's leading oil and gas companies.

American Jobs
http://www.americanjobs.com/
The site offers a free searchable database of hi-tech computer and engineering jobs with Fortune 500 companies and leading corporations. It was launched in 1994 and apparently logs up a staggering 2 million hits each month. Its online employer profiles enable you to conduct research on several hundred employers currently posting jobs on the site. This extensive background information will help you to determine which companies are right for you. You can add your résumé to its off-line database where your privacy is assured. The site says it will never

Overseas jobs pages

submit your résumé to any company or individual without your permission.

American Recruitment
http://www.americanrecruitment.com
This is a contact point for sales, marketing and retail jobs, mainly in California.

America's Employers
http://www.americasemployers.com
Developed by the Career Relocation Corporation of America, the site is based on the outplacement and job-finding assistance programmes it has provided to many Fortune 500 companies for over fifteen years. Whether you're unemployed, considering a career move, or just keeping your options open, you can use its resources to organise, expand and refine your own job search. It includes a company database, job search, a résumé bank, entrepreneurial options, career chat, relocation resources such as salary and mortgage calculators, and other job-hunting advice and information.

America's Job Bank
http://www.ajb.dni.us/
The America's Job Bank (AJB) network is the national clearing house for the public employment service. On average, more than 5,000 new jobs are received from the States each day. Additionally, thousands of employers enter their jobs directly into the system in real time. On average, more than 3,000 new jobs are received each day directly from employers. The service is funded through unemployment insurance taxes paid by employers. You can search the national jobs file or any of the state job banks, but you need to register in order to submit a résumé to AJB and save your own custom searches. The system is available to all job seekers, whether or not they have applied for services at their local public employment service. The site says it has provided details of more than 800,000 jobs for more than 350,000 applicants. Its services for job seekers include FAQs, job seeker registration, keyword search, menu search and résumé builder. There is no charge to job seekers who submit their résumés or who search the job order file for suitable employment.

Arab Information Management Services
http://www.aims-kw.com
AIMS was established in 1980 by two Kuwaiti businessmen. Today it is a leading Kuwaiti company in the information systems field with an annual turnover of US $15m.

Arbeitsamt (Germany)
http://www.arbeitsamt.de/
This is an official German employment information site. The pages are in German. There is no English translation option. The site is efficiently organised into numerous regional categories and sub-categories, with clear clickable colour maps of both regions and cities, to help you find your way around.

Overseas jobs pages

Arbetsförmedlingen Internet (Sweden)
http://www.umu.se/af
This large database of job vacancies in Sweden is maintained by the National Labour Market Board of Sweden. The site is updated daily, but you will need to be able to read Swedish to use it.

Art Job (USA)
http://www.webart.com/artjob
Established for nineteen years, this is an American newsletter issued online every two weeks, containing job listings in the arts fields. They include academic, agencies, artistic performance, conferences, international, internships, presenting and producing organisations, publications, and special features of interest. Sample listings are available, as well as subscription information.

Au Pair Job Match
http://www.aupairs.co.uk/
This is an automated job-matching service for au pairs and families. You can register free of charge and have your details forwarded to matching families or au pairs. There are advertised vacancies from agencies and employers, and a discussion forum. You can read the site in several different European languages.

Aviation Employee Placement Service
http://www.aeps.com/
This specialist site says that it is used by over 2,800 aviation companies worldwide. You are invited to enter your qualifications with a free 10-day trial. You can receive free email job alerts by entering your email address. For full facilities you must enrol as a member. The company is based in Fort Lauderdale, Florida.

Avotek Publishing
http://www.xs4all.nl/~avotek
This Dutch-based publishing company offers several guides to the European job market including the Netherlands. The site includes information on the many head-hunter directories they publish, but they also provide links to international job banks, recruiters, and other sources.

Bank Jobs (USA)
http://www.bankjobs.com/
This is a massive specialist American site for banking jobs. When we reviewed it we found it had 10,696 banking-related jobs online, plus many ancillary services, and numerous banking links.

Belgium Career Web
http://belgium.careerweb.com
Yes! This site is in English. Looking for a professional, technical or managerial job? Here you'll find many listings for high-paying, interesting positions with companies that you want to work for. There are jobs in engineering, information systems, telecommunications, marketing, accounting, healthcare and many other fields. All the companies listed

Overseas jobs pages

have profile pages with corporate, product and employee benefits information.

Best Jobs in the USA Today
http://www.bestjobsusa.com
The site describes itself as a premier employment magazine. It offers a career guide with job opportunities, career fairs and advice, résumé posting, workplace information, and company profiles. You can do a keyword search to locate thousands of positions by city, skills, position, selecting from many industries such IT, engineering, finance, business, health care and others. You can also follow a vast number of A-Z links to other employment-related sites, research a US city, access unemployment rates and cost-of-living information, population, major employers, and get a briefing on each city's economic status. The site's Corporate Profiles offers a showcase of corporate America. Each company profiles itself, giving you a chance to get to know them, link to many of their web sites and access current job listings direct.

Bilingual Jobs
http://www.Bilingual-Jobs.com
This is a service operated by International Consulting Group Inc for bilingual professionals and career seekers. Its international résumé services allow you to submit your CV directly to hiring personnel. Its lists include recruiters in major HR organisations, multinational corporations and fast-growing small companies. Bilingual Jobs will prepare your résumé in various international languages including Chinese, Japanese, Korean, French and German. The company offers complete career consulting services so you can locate opportunities worldwide. It gathers all relevant publications and articles and forwards them to you by mail or email. It can also provide you with direct telephone support. It provides links to other sites which may be valuable to international career seekers. Check out its selection of books on job hunting in Asia and Europe. It also features an international pen-pals page.

BUNAC
http://www.bunac.org.uk/
BUNAC (British Universities North American Club) has more than 34 years' experience of organising international exchange programmes. It invites you to sample working adventures worldwide. Its overseas work and travel programmes offer good value, giving you the chance to live and work legally in other countries, earn money to travel and explore independently, make new friends and enhance your CV. You click on the flag or the name of the country in which you are living for information about work abroad opportunities from that country. There are links to Australia, Canada, Ghana, Jamaica, South Africa, USA, New Zealand, and the UK. There is a newsletter, brochure order form, details of programmes, a search facility leading to a large amount of archived information, and links (not working when we reviewed the site).

Overseas jobs pages

Byron Employment (Australia)
http://www.byron.com.au/
Byron Employment Australia was one of the first internet employment sites in Australia. It operates primarily as a job listing service, and does not provide services to individual candidates or accept résumés at present. However, it offers a huge selection of jobs around Australia, posted by advertising agencies, consultants, accountants and others. You can view its extensive agency directory on screen. The jobs are sorted under accounting, banking and finance, communications, construction, engineering, government, health care, human resources, hospitality, industrial, computers and IT, legal, management, sales and marketing, schools and colleges, science and technology, support staff, and tertiary. In February 1997 BEA introduced a free set-and-forget email service, which automatically emails you details of those jobs on the database that match your search criteria. You can register your details using a simple form. Byron also includes links to other Australian employment-related resources, and includes valuable information for overseas candidates.

Cadres Online
http://www.cadresonline.com
Though slow-loading, this site looks to be a useful resource for French-speakers seeking work in France, complete with salary guide and other supportive information for applicants. You have to complete and submit an online CV, and will then be emailed details of vacancies matching your qualifications. It did not seem to be possible to do the usual kind of database job search. The site said that about 3,700 vacancies had been notified by employers during the previous month. There was no English translation option on the site.

Campus Voice
http://www.campus-voice.com/
Campus Voice offers general information and advice about study and employment in Europe, including links to useful web sites. The site was under reconstruction when reviewed.

Canada Employment Weekly
http://www.mediacorp2.com/
Canada Employment Weekly is Canada's largest career newspaper. This online edition brings you some of the 500 vacancies available each week, well organised in various categories. The site also features a career directory where you can match your qualifications with 900 Canadian employers, plus 'Who's Hiring' which ranks 4,000 of Canada's top employers in 23 occupations. This valuable site is a project of Toronto-based Mediacorp Canada Inc.

Canadian Job Catalogue
http://www.kenevacorp.mb.ca
Canadian Job Catalogue offers literally thousands of links to job sites, information and résumé banks with Canadian content. These sites are sorted into categories for easy reference. For example, there are over

Overseas jobs pages

65 major Canadian job and résumé banks containing thousands of postings, plus over 400 smaller ones containing thousands more. There are more than 1,100 Canadian occupation or industry specific sites giving free access to thousands of Canadian job postings under more than 90 separate categories, plus many regional sub-categories. The Catalogue also has Canadian job listings not on the net: local telephone hot lines and specialty associations with job openings. You can also find some 140 sites offering help and information on Canadian interview techniques, top employers/expanding companies, résumé creation and emailing, career planning, career training, employment law, employment news, helpful resources, and labour market information. When you click on a site to go to, you nearly always arrive directly at that site's employment page, which avoids having to begin a time-consuming search from home pages. If you feel Canada calling, this site is a must.

Career Bridge (Canada)
http://www.careerbridge.com
Career Bridge is an internet service designed to link companies who have job openings with job seekers. It has offices in Ottawa and Toronto. Its Career Centre is the place to begin if you are looking for employment opportunities. Before accessing the full site, you prepare and post your résumé to the internet, using the résumé entry wizard. You can then browse a database of jobs posted by employers, apply online and communicate with potential employers through your personal message centre, all for free. You can edit your résumé at any time. There are even occasional career opportunities with Career Bridge itself. The site contains profiles of about 70 leading organisations posting vacancies on the site, including such well known names as Andersen Consulting, the Bank of Nova Scotia, and the Royal College of Physicians & Surgeons of Canada.

Career Builder
http://www.careerbuilder.com
The USA Career Builder network brings together 18 leading career sites on one site for a targeted search. For job hunters there are free job notifications, a personal search agent to deliver jobs to you, hot companies, news about Microsoft and CACI, companies on Career Builder, an A-Z list of every company posting jobs to Career Builder, relocation resources, a salary calculator, apartment search, metro guides and more. For employers there is information on the benefits of online recruiting, targeting the perfect hire, posting jobs to USA Today, Medical Economics, Developer.com and more than a dozen other career sites. The company has offices in major cities across the USA.

Career City (USA)
http://www.careercity.com
This is an impressive and in depth American careers site. You can search jobs in all professions, refine your search, find out about regional job fairs, prepare and post résumés, and check out employers programmes. In the computer/hi-tech careers centre there are job listings, links to 3,000+ hi-tech firms, salary surveys, resources and hi-

Overseas jobs pages

tech agencies. A section on companies and industries gives information on 27,000 US employers, 7,000 employment services, 1,000 temp firms, with links to thousands of resources for hi-tech careers, government careers, healthcare careers and education careers.

Career Connections (USA)
http://www.career.com/
This in-depth US employment site has home page links to job seekers, employers, hot jobs, what's new, and more. Job hunters can search by company category, job location, hot jobs, keywords, new graduate/entry level, international, and résumé management. You can create, save and update your résumé. Other resources include personal career assessment, where an in-depth appraisal will provide you with a mirror of your vocational strengths. You can also download and try its all-new edition of 'Wanted Jobs', a free job-finding tool you can use to search up to 32 job sites including this one. The site also offers 'power tools for relocation' comprising a salary calculator, moving calculator, relocation planning, an auto/home insurance wizard and mortgage qualifier program. The salary calculator, for example, tells you how much you would need to make in your new city to keep your current lifestyle. The site is a project of the Heart Advertising Network, based in California.

Career Internetworking (Canada)
http://www.careerkey.com/
Career Internetworking is a Canadian online career networking resource, based in Ontario, for professionally and technically qualified applicants. Its free services include resources, strategies, tips, profiles and an open communication forum. You can browse job opportunities in Canadian manufacturing and distribution industries and meet leading companies through its 'jobs and profiles' section. Web pages, complete web sites or links to existing home pages give you company news, policies, commitments, future plans, products and services, upcoming events, plus jobs. The employers post vacancies for a 30 day period. There are sections on what's new, latest jobs, new career search, hot jobs, search by location, position, category, key contacts and online career assistance, job search tips and articles. There are some very friendly applicant-oriented FAQs on the site.

Career Magazine (USA)
http://www.careermag.com
Career Magazine is a comprehensive and attractively presented resource, designed for job seekers. It downloads and indexes job postings from the major internet newsgroups every day. Postings are searchable by location, job title and/or skills required. It also runs a résumé bank, which gives recruiters a tool to locate résumés of suitable candidates. Candidates can enter résumé information into this bank using an online form. For candidates, there are employer profiles, offering detailed information on employers around the world. There are products and services to help you manage your career, articles and news to help you plan and execute your networked career search, the career forum – a moderated discussion area where you can network

Overseas jobs pages

with others, generate leads, share experiences, and seek advice – and career links to other career-related resources on the world wide web.

Career Mart (USA)
http://www.careermart.com/
This is another all-purpose USA jobs site. Like many others it offers online job search, company profiles, email service, job advertising and résumé posting. The job search page took a while to load – well, it was Saturday – but it offered the ability to search by job categories, states, regions and international (which included the UK). The A-Z list of companies also took a long while to load, because it contained a massive number of company links in a single page, but once loaded it was easy to navigate and use. Unfortunately, many of the links were followed only to report 'no vacancies'. The site could be better organised to save surfing time. Perhaps it is still in the development stage.

Career Mosaic Japan
http://www.careermosaic.or.jp
This is a service from Career Mosaic, dedicated to services for Japan. It is in Japanese, so you will need to configure your web browser to view Japanese characters. There is no facility to read the site in English.

Career Net (Germany)
http://www.careernet.de
This is a German job service, Stellenangebote und Bewerbungen On-line. There is no facility to read the site in English.

Career Path (USA)
http://www.careerpath.com

Career Path was co-founded in October 1995 by six major American newspapers, *The Boston Globe, Chicago Tribune, Los Angeles Times, The New York Times, San José Mercury-News* and *The Washington Post*. On this site you can search the job ads of all these newspapers, search job postings gathered from leading employers' web sites, post a confidential résumé, gather information on featured employers, check out upcoming job fairs, and explore career spotlights. Career Path claims to offer job seekers the greatest number of the most current jobs available – some 263,000 when we reviewed the site. No listing remains on its database for more than two weeks, so the vacancies really are current. You can save a job search, create a résumé online that joins its extensive database of job seekers regularly searched by employers, read headline news, and gain updates on important employment trends. Career Path is free to job seekers, though some features require (free) registration.

Career Paths Online (Canada)
http://careerpathsonline.com
This is the internet version of *Career Paths Newspaper*, an official Canadian career-planning guide for designed to help students and young people formulate their career and education plans.

Overseas jobs pages

Career Spot (USA)
http://www.careerspot.com
This is a gateway to over 8,000 jobs in south Florida. The site is a service of *The Sun-Sentinel* newspaper, and can take you to lots of associated classified advertising, such as for cars and apartments, should you be contemplating a move to the Sunshine State.

Career Web (USA)
http://www.cweb.com
This is a mainly American database containing over 20,000 job openings in more than 300 companies. The home page leads you more or less straight into search mode – for jobs, or for employers. The results did not appear to be in any particular order, but they were numbered for ease of reference. You can also research employers and get lots of job-searching advice. This site's listings cover engineering, information systems, telecommunications, marketing, accounting, healthcare, and many more categories. Companies helpfully listed in bold type have profile pages with corporate, product and employee benefits information for you to review. You can also put your résumé in their database and refer it to employers. Its job-match service will notify you by email about job opportunities that match the type of job and location you're looking for. Other site features also include a career inventory section, career doctor, and bookstore (which takes the form of another searchable database).

Careers Boston (USA)
http://www.careers.boston.com
Careers Boston contains New England's largest database of jobs, with more than 15,000 employment opportunities weekly. Online listings are added daily. *Boston Sunday Globe* listings are updated every Monday.

Childcare International
http://www.childint.demon.co.uk
Childcare International Ltd is a London-based service for families looking for an au pair or nanny, and for potential au pairs or nannies looking for a family. It manages placements in the United Kingdom, Europe, Canada, and the USA.

CICA (France)
http://emploi.cica.fr
This is a French employment site offering some job and training information about the Provence-Alpes and Côte d'Azur regions. The site is naturally in French, and there is no option for English translation. It carries a European Commission WWW 1996 'Best Site' Business Award – but global standards of internet content and design have moved on a lot since then.

Computer Week Jobs Online (South Africa)
http://www.jobs.co.za/
This is a leading South African IT user publication. You can enter your

Overseas jobs pages

CV into the database free of charge. To ensure confidentiality, only recruiting agencies who subscribe have access to this database. You can search the job database free of charge. You can also access free online agency and employer directories containing corporate profiles of all corporate subscribers to the service. Its 'back office' service allows recruiting agencies and employers to load new jobs onto the job database and to access the CV database. Agencies or employers can link jobs directly to the most appropriate CVs.

Contract Employment Weekly
http://www.ceweekly.com
Established in the USA in 1969, *Contract Employment Weekly* has been an electronic magazine since 1994. It contains a large number of highly paid technical, IT and engineering contract assignments available from 500 agencies in its online database. Between 3,000 and 4,000 listings are updated every 30 minutes. About a quarter of these are viewable by non-subscribers. A contract worker is typically a highly qualified, highly paid individual who works for a contract service firm on temporary job assignment for that firm's client company. The average length of the assignment is six to nine months. Once the assignment is finished, the contractor moves on to other employment, usually for a different contract firm at another client. If you want to explore a substantially more profitable and rewarding approach to your international career, this could be a good place to start.

Creyf's (Belgium)
http://www.creyfs.be/
Creyfs recruits for temporary technical and engineering personnel in Belgium. Information on who they are and how to contact them is given in English, French, German and Dutch on this slow-loading site.

Daily Job (Hong Kong/China)
http://www.dailyjob.com/
The site gets straight to the point, with listings in Hong Kong and China, updated daily. You can view 'today's vacancies' (about 30 when we reviewed the site) or look through the rather ambitious number of categories of jobs. However, you will be lucky to find a result to match the detailed search the site makes you perform. Job details are in any case extremely brief.

Danish Employment Service
http://wwww.af.dk/
You will need Danish to use this official Arbejdsformidlingen site, which contains in depth information about job opportunities and vacancies in Denmark. It includes a job bank, CV bank service, and email updates.

E Jobs (USA/Canada)
http://www.ejobs.org
This is a handy source of information on environmental jobs and careers, developed by an American environmental analyst, David R. Brierley. E Jobs links to environmental opportunities mainly in the USA

Overseas jobs pages

and Canada. It includes careers such as environmental engineers, nature and wetlands scientists, GIS, technicians, chemists, geologists, geotechnical experts, policy and law, wildlife conservation, land use planning, and education.

Eastern & Central European Job Bank
http://www.ecejobbank.com/
This is a free service, developed in Hungary by a desperate IT company, to help companies and skilled workers find each other in the region. Job seekers can browse job listings, and post their résumés for employers to see. Employers can list their openings. Once you've registered, you'll get a password that allows your company to post jobs and access other services for employers. Employers may also want to browse the résumés that job seekers have posted with us. When we checked, there were only 16 postings in the job bank, including several for financial personnel.

Education British Columbia (Canada)
http://educationbc.com
On this smartly designed site, you can find and respond to educational employment opportunities anywhere in British Columbia and other parts of Canada.

Educational Placement Service (USA)
http://www.educatorjobs.com
Founded in 1973, EPS says it is the largest teacher-placement service in the US. It is accredited by the National Association of Teacher Agencies. With offices all over the USA it is a private concern that recruits teachers, specialists, and administrators for public, private, parochial schools and colleges. Its job search facility is by State.

EMDS (Europe)
http://www.emdsnet.com/
EMDS is an international recruitment consultancy, established in 1987. This site is designed to help you solve the puzzle of an ambitious career plan. Simply select an area of the world that interests you, click on it and a whole universe of opportunity will open up. EMDS runs the Euromanagers Recruitment Forum, an event which brings together graduates and professionals from across Europe with leading international employers. Some 600-900 candidates meet 25-50 companies twice yearly in Brussels. With offices in Brussels, London, Paris, Cologne, and Stockholm, EMDS offers a comprehensive range of services in Western Europe, and worldwide. The site gives details of recruitment events, its job database supported by 400 companies, the EMDS network and online applications, employer profiles and world regions' sponsors, and an international manager's newsletter, *In Focus*.

Emplawyernet (USA)
http://www.emplawyernet.com
EmplawyerNet is the America's leading job opportunity and career development site for the legal community. As a member, you will have

Overseas jobs pages

unlimited access to the most extensive job database in that country (more than 5,800 vacancies when we checked, including some international/European). Its staff spends all day, every day gathering job information. It doesn't charge employers to place ads, so members get the maximum possible information. It will send you job information that matches your search criteria so you don't have to search a database every day. Just check your email. The service is confidential. Law students can get 3 months free from Lexis-Nexis.

Employment Newgroups Listing
http://www.ipa.com/newsgroups.html
This is an extensive list of links to employment-related newsgroups in the United Kingdom, Australia, Bermuda, Canada, Denmark, and the United States. There are over 100 newsgroup sites to search. Many internet service providers do not support all newsgroups, partly because there are now so many of them (50,000 plus), so if you have a problem reaching a particular group, contact your provider. If you still have difficulty, you can easily access all newsgroups on the internet by finding an 'open news server'. There are lots of these, many of them free, and you can find one very easily by typing 'open news servers' into Yahoo! or your other favourite search engine. If you find a new employment-related newsgroup you are invited to let this site know. IPA Members can use QuickPost and QuickSearch in the members area to quickly post job openings or search résumé databases. Never visited the newsgroups before? – never fear, all human life is there!

Engineering Job Source (USA)
http://www.engineerjobs.com
Based in the Great Lakes area of the USA, Engineering Job Source provides job listings for engineers and technical professionals. The service is expanding, and you can now browse or search for engineering and technical jobs from all over the United States.

Entertainment Employment Journal (USA)
http://www.eej.com/
Since 1992, the Entertainment Employment Journal has been serving the career needs of thousands of professional, creative, technical, production personnel and others interested in a career in the motion picture, broadcast or cable television business. Twice a month, subscribers are informed about full-time positions and internships. The site includes a US directory of entertainment employers. Companies are listed alphabetically and by location and are organised into more than 40 major categories.

Environmental Careers Organisation (USA)
http://www.eco.org
Based in Boston, Massachusetts, ECO is a national non-profit dedicated since 1972 to promoting careers in the environment, specialising in internships, career counselling, employment resources, conferences, and green job listings. Through its stylishly presented web site you can find details of over 650 paid environmental internships

Overseas jobs pages

each year. Its alumni network is 7,000 strong. You can check out who they are and what they are doing now. If you are an environmentalist, get networking here yourself.

Environmental Careers World (USA)
http://environmental-jobs.com
Environmental Careers World describes itself as a leader in environmental and natural resources job information and career news. It was established in the USA in 1980 to help recruit top environmental talent for leading companies, environmental consultants, manufacturing industries, government agencies, non-governmental organisations (NGOs), and educational institutions. Its mission is to help people work for the environment through career news, inside tips and advice, employer interviews, career research and comprehensive job listing. The site has a section covering international environmental and natural resources jobs. These seemed to be mainly Canadian or international vacancies with US-based organisations, with a couple in the UK and Europe. The job descriptions are very detailed.

Escape Artist
http://www.escapeartist.com/
Here is an ultimate internet resource for careers overseas, especially if you would like to go offshore and escape the relentless rise of taxation. This is a web site for anyone moving to another country, expatriates, overseas job seekers, tax exiles, adventurers and freedom seekers everywhere. There are well categorised links to all kinds of useful information, for example the world's top newspapers, a world reference desk, an expatriate's book store, the world's search engines, Latin-American search engines, a countries index and stuff on global human freedom. It can help you build up your own internet commerce, with help on telecommuting, web communications, net office and web phones for expats. Find out about global investments, tax havens, stock markets of the world, offshore credit cards, offshore real estate and offshore banks. There are links to jobs overseas, embassy pages, moving overseas, an international living magazine – in fact just about everything you need to succeed as an internationally mobile and tax-free professional anywhere on the planet.

EURES Job Search
http://europa.eu.int/eures/cgi/en/jv_search
This is the job search page for the official European Employment Service, a service of the European Union. It's rather a long URL, but it could be worth the trouble. We searched for hotel and catering jobs, in all countries, which resulted in a list of about 1,600 vacancies. There appear to be only about 5,000 vacancies on the database. Since there are about 25 million people out of work in Europe, one imagines that this multi-government service has got rather a lot of catching up to do. You can view the results in batches of up to 15. The job descriptions are reasonably detailed and you can apply to the employers direct. Little effort is made at presentation. The service is not secure and the authorities can presumably monitor citizen activity.

Living & Working In Japan - Click Here
Spain - Click Here
France - Click Here
Europe - Click Here
Norway - Click Here
Countries Index - Click Here
UPGRADE - Uruguay - Click Here
Caribbean - Click Here
South America - Click Here
Mexico - Click Here
Central America - Click Here
Pacific Islands - Click Here
Asia-Pacific - Click Here
New Zealand Emigration - Click
Emigrating To Canada - Click Here
Emigrating To Australia - Click Here

.... **Overseas jobs pages**

Euro London
http://www.eurolondon.com
Established in 1990 in response to European Single Market initiatives, Euro London Appointments is a consultancy specialising in the recruitment of multilingual personnel from trainee to director level within London, the Home Counties, Europe, Asia and the Far East. With two offices in London (City and West End) and another in Windsor, it says it is the largest specialist language consultancy in the UK.

Eurojobs
http://www.eurojobs.com/
On this site you can enter your CV and submit it to a recruiter. You can use a full-colour clickable map to locate vacancies all over Europe and register with the Europe Vacancy Robot.

European Graduate Career Guide
http://www.eurograduate.com/
Eurograduate live contains an up-to-date careers database featuring thousands of graduate opportunities across Europe. There is also expert advice on career planning and how to make job applications in other countries.

Executive Grapevine
http://www.d-net.com/executive.grapevine/
Here is another long URL, but worth the trouble. Executive Grapevine is an established publisher of highly priced but comprehensive employment directories. Here you can search its database of over 5,400 companies, which includes its International Database of Executive Recruiters. The company is based in London Colney, Hertfordshire.

Expat Forum
http://www.expatforum.com/
Expat Forum is an American-based source of information, services and chat about living, working, travelling, and doing business overseas. Its bookstore selections offer choices for the best practical guides for living overseas. It does not run a jobs database. The site is a project of HR International, an independent human resources consulting firm based in Maryland.

Expat Network
http://www.expatnetwork.co.uk/
Expat Network will help you find a job overseas and will provide assistance once you are working. Established in 1989, it has obtained overseas employment for over 9,000 people using its vast pool of resources and contacts. It publishes a monthly magazine, *Nexus*, which is more than just a job supplement. It is also packed with interesting and informative articles written specifically for people who want to or who are already working abroad. The job search section of the magazine consists of around 12 pages packed full of jobs, of which a representative selection is shown on this site. Expat Network is one of the

Overseas jobs pages

essential UK contact points for people considering an international career move. The company is based in Croydon, Surrey.

Film, TV, & Commercial Employment Network (USA)
http://www.employnow.com/
This American network provides important information and resources for individuals interested in pursuing a career in the entertainment industry. It is for beginners as well as seasoned professionals. Information and resources are provided for many areas both behind and in front of the camera. If you're a producer or casting director, you can visit 'Actors Now' to view photos and résumés of talented performers. If you're wanting to break into the business, check out the employment guide or the production assistant's handbook. There are quite a few detailed job listings, information for actors, screen writers, and comedians, plus industry links.

Gemini Personnel
http://www.gemini.com.hk/
The Gemini Group was formed in Hong Kong in 1983. It says it is Hong Kong's leading recruitment company with hundreds of current vacancies, many of them with Hong Kong's multinationals. It handles all levels of placements in Hong Kong, Malaysia, Australia and London. The site includes company profile, salary survey, employment guide, an executive division, job search, candidate information, and a newsletter. It has separate divisions for information technology, banking and finance, engineering and construction, legal and professional, merchandising and general management. Overseas candidates are asked to read its online advice for non-Hong Kong job seekers.

Global Career Services (USA)
http://www.globalcareers.com/
GCS is New York-based and a human resource, technology-based consulting and recruitment firm, formed in 1996. On its web site employers can post job openings, search résumés, and find qualified and talented people in the fields of commerce, transportation and finance. Applicants can search job openings, post a résumé at no charge, and update or remove their information at any time, keeping their identity confidential if they wish.

Global Job Services
http://www.job-searcher.com/
GJS describes itself as a one-stop shop for job seekers, and for recruiters in need of outsourcing. Since there are still many people without an internet connection, and many who do have one but don't have the time or know-how to research what is available, GJS will do it for them. It claims to scour more than a million job listings on the internet to find the perfect match for candidates' skill sets. It also offers résumé writing in all formats covering traditional, computer-scannable and electronic submissions. The site gives details of hourly and other fees.

Overseas jobs pages

Grant International
http://www.grantinternational.co.uk
Grant International provides recruitment services to the international hotel and leisure industries. It employs various recruitment methods including executive search, database selection and direct advertising to ensure that everyone from pastry chefs to directors are covered. A handful of vacancies are detailed on the site, which is connected with *The Travellers' Guide*.

Grapevine International Ltd
http://www.grapevine-int.co.uk
This is an international recruitment and human resource consultancy for the hospitality industry, and was formerly part of the London consultancy Pannell Kerr Forster Associates. The service operates internationally covering most parts of the world but is particularly strong in Europe, the Middle East and the Far East. There is an online candidate registration form. A small number of vacancies are detailed on the site.

Head Hunter (USA)
http://www.headhunter.net
The statistics on this site seem pretty staggering – over 200,000 job listings online, over 64,000 jobs updated this week, 70,000 résumés online, and 60,000 different users per day. The catch – for a UK user – is that the site is US-based. Approximately 95% of jobs are based in the US, although some positions are for prospective employees who will be working abroad. Listings on Head Hunter represent the original content of its users. The database is said to be constantly cleaned: jobs are never over 45 days old, and résumés are never over 90 days old. It offers free basic posting, with a third of jobs posted by companies, and two thirds by recruiters. Given the sheer volume of notified vacancies, the site is well worth a visit. The service was only developed in late 1996, but to grow volume quickly, its founder Warren Bare modelled it after the very successful search engines, Yahoo! and AltaVista, which provide free access to all users. Will this be another multi-million-dollar sell-out to one of the IT conglomerates? We'd give it five stars if it were a British site.

HiTech Career Center (Canada)
http://www.hitechcareer.com/
This is an informative careers resource for IT jobs in Canada, produced by Kaplan Career Services which says it is the largest provider of career forums and services in North America. The site contains details of careers fairs in Toronto, Ottawa, Calgary, Montreal, and Vancouver.

Hollywood Creative Directory (USA)
http://www.hcdonline.com
This organisation publishes industry guides relating to many areas of film and television, from agents and managers to producers and distributors and many more. Its materials may be purchased in printed form, or subscribed to online.

Overseas jobs pages

Hong Kong Jobs
http://www.hkjobs.com/
This site refers to job opportunities in various fields throughout Hong Kong. The service lists many categories of employment and companies to search, but was not operational when we reviewed it.

Hospitality Jobs Online (USA)
http://www.hjo.net
Hospitality Jobs Online is dedicated to select market segments of the travel and tourism industry. It provides internet recruiting services to hotels, food and beverage establishments, travel groups, casinos, and cruise lines. The site is presented in affiliation with the Los Angeles Hotel Human Resources Association. With all its javascript and applets we found the pages slow to load.

Hospitality Net (USA)
http://www.hospitalitynet.org/
This is another USA internet resource for the global hospitality industry – 'all of hospitality on the web'. You can click on a couple of dozen job categories to find a position that might suit your requirements. As a test we searched for jobs in Catering & Convention Management, and found 26 vacancies. Each had a hyperlink to detailed job descriptions and contact details for applicants. You can also check out their employer listings. Posting entries is free to employers who register not more than 10 entries per month. The site appears to be updated weekly.

Humana International Group
http://www.humana-pm.com

Humana International in Regent Street, London, has been part of the world's largest executive search organisation, since early 1995. It provides a specialist service to the hotel, hospitality and leisure sectors throughout the world. It handles general management positions, department heads and above at hotel unit level, all positions at corporate level especially MD, FD, and operations directors. It covers all disciplines to include rooms, food and beverage, finance, IT, sales and marketing, property management, human resources and purchasing. It also handles senior consultancy within the hospitality sector. Its clients include the multinationals, medium and small organisations, independent hotels, and leading consultancies. You can submit your CV, and search its database using keywords, and selecting various international locations.

InterCareerNet (Japan)
http://www.intercareer.com/japan/
InterCareer Net Japan provides employment information for job seekers who are fluent in English and Japanese. Candidates should either have, or plan to receive, a bachelor's or equivalent degree from an overseas university, or have experience working abroad. ICN-J is a service of International Career Information Inc, an international arm of Recruit Corporation in Tokyo. Site features include net job search, profile updating, careers fairs, links, candidates' forum and membership information.

Overseas jobs pages

Intermediair (Netherlands)
http://www.bpa.nl/intermediair
This is a comprehensive jobs and career site for the Netherlands, updated every Wednesday. It contains detailed information about salaries, careers, and recruitment, based on the weekly magazine *Intermediair*. But you'll need to understand Dutch to use the site – there's no English translation. Intermediair is a project of VNU Business Publications.

International Personnel Management Association
http://www.ipma-hr.org/
The IPMA is a professional association for public personnel professionals, primarily those who work in American federal, state, or local government organisations.

Internet Career Connection (USA)
http://iccweb.com
This is another big USA site, which is both a résumé bank, and a job bank. It is a service of Florida-based Gonyea & Associates, which in 1989 created the first fully online career guidance agency. The site claims to have posted over a million ads online. You can post your résumé online for a fee of $25 for 6 months. You can edit and delete it automatically, anytime, at no extra cost. All résumés remain in the online databases for 6 or 12 months, depending upon the posting option you select and unless you delete it beforehand. ICC say they have posted over 50,000 résumés so far. Employers can search its database for individuals who match their recruiting needs. As a test we searched for 'editor' and found 70 matching résumés. To find a job, click Help Wanted, to search 1.6 million internet job postings simultaneously. This involves clicking to download a program file 'Wanted Jobs' and logo onto your desktop, a process which took us about six minutes (the file was 1.2 megabytes). You then input the type of job you want, and location, and the program goes off and simultaneously searches over 25 well known job sites for you – including MonsterBoard, America's Job Bank and CareerMosaic, for example. It then neatly lists the results for you in a separate browser window, where you can explore them. As a test, we searched for 'nurse' in 'New Jersey' and received 42 results. You click to view the details, and you can even click to upload the job details to a friend. It's a brilliant concept. If you want to see what internet technology can do, give this a try.

Inter-Work (Europe)
http://www.inter-work.com/
Inter-Work is a project of Selby Mill Smith, a firm of chartered occupational psychologists based in Bath. It has been designed for graduates, eliminating the hard work from taking your first steps on the career ladder. It says it will put your personal details and attributes in front of a lot of subscribing graduate employers in the UK and Europe without having to fill in a different form for each one. It doesn't say how many

Overseas jobs pages

employers it reaches. The service is confidential and free. You are invited to spend 40 minutes completing the personal profile questionnaires. Employers whose requirements match your profile are then supposed to get in touch with you to invite you to make an application to them. A feedback report is available. Parts of the site did not appear to have been recently updated.

Irish Jobs Page
http://www.exp.ie/
Operated from Dublin, the businesslike Irish Jobs Page claims to be Ireland's longest established recruitment web site. You can search for jobs by keyword or look at the various databases which cover for example agencies, companies, engineering, accounting, and graduates. You can browse by category, search by keyword and list by company. You can submit a résumé to either its IT or non-IT CV databases. They also have an IT world wide section for employers/job seekers looking outside of Ireland. The site includes signposts to recruiters' jobs sites and profiles of recruitment agencies, a market report on current issues in recruitment, plus advice on CVs, interviews etc. Linked pages seem slow to load.

Japanese Professional Job Site
http://www.jpjs.co.uk/
This is a résumé bank of Japanese bilingual professionals. Online registration of your résumé to JPJS is free of charge. They will publish your résumé to the global business community, but your contact information remains confidential and is provided only to those companies registered with it. The service, which includes some recruiters and company site links, has been developed by the London-based Japanese MBA Club.

Job Bank (USA)
http://www.jobbankusa.com/
This is a well-known award-winning American site, with a comprehensive directory of internet employment resources. These include a powerful job meta-search page by which you can access the internet's largest employment databases. Job hunters can search jobs, submit/edit résumé, use job scout (an email agent), check out hot-list firms and employment newsgroups, find out about career fairs, and use assessment and relocation tools. With its international search services, you can quickly find people, businesses, and other information all over the world, including the UK and Europe. Employers are invited to become members and gain access to its résumé database.

Job Connection (USA)
http://www.jobconnection.com
This USA service comprises around 200 employment recruiting firms who operate on a national, regional, state, and local basis.

Overseas jobs pages

Job Lynx (USA)
http://joblynx.com
Job Lynx says it can put your details before more than 9,000 professional recruiters who are actively searching for thousands of job candidates. It electronically enters your complete résumé into a computerised format, easily retrieved by its 9600+ registered professional headhunters actively searching for qualified job candidates. Confidentiality is guaranteed, as only headhunters have access to your résumé. The database is set up so only registered headhunters with an assigned password can access it. Résumé posters are charged fees starting at $7.95, depending on membership option and period of posting.

Job Net (Australasia)
http://www.jobnet.com.au/
Job Net offers the largest central index of computer, technology and management contract and permanent employment opportunities in Australia, New Zealand and Asia available through leading IT recruitment agencies. You can browse all the current job positions (updated daily) including skills specification and all contact details, or keyword search using its online database search facility. The current database is said to hold over 11,000 job positions. You can also join its free daily email alert service of new jobs which are delivered directly to your email.

Job Net (New Zealand)
http://www.jobnetnz.co.nz
This is a link to jobs primarily in New Zealand. You can search the local newspapers for appointments, or the New Zealand *InfoTech Weekly*. You can select the type of appointment, the newspaper source, four regions, and a dozen or so towns. When we checked, there were more than 800 vacancies on the database, the vast majority in *InfoTech Weekly*. The more general local newspapers database seemed to have very few.

Job Online (France)
http://www.cegos.fr/
This is the smart-looking French site of the Confédération Générale du Patronat Français, founded in 1926, to promote management and training in France. A level 4 browser is recommended for this site. CEGOS has 750 associates and 500 consultants. Part of the site (including client recruitment) was under construction when we reviewed it, and it has no English translation.

JobSat (Canada)
http://www.jobsat.com
This is a free service for job seekers looking for employment in Canada and select US locations. You can do résumé posting or use the job search section of over 8,500 job listings. The résumé posting section is a free web-based posting service available to all users. The Job Search section is available to registered users only. You will need to register for best access. JobSat offers recruiters the Lite Viewer, a management

Overseas jobs pages

tool to expedite the matching of job seekers with suitable employers. It screens out applicants based on criteria input by the user, who does not have to spend valuable time skimming through thousands of résumés/job postings. It also allows access to Jobsat's database.

Job Search California (USA)
http://www.jsearch.com
This site maintains databases of 40,000 companies, over 100,000 current news stories, more than 2,000 résumé summaries and 5,000 active job postings throughout southern California. It includes some rather crude self evaluation tests for candidates. We completed one as a test (21 questions) and were told we had skills in mentoring, synthesizing, diverting, negotiating, coordinating, instructing, innovating, supervising, analyzing, compiling, persuading, computing, speaking, copying, signalling, comparing, serving, taking, instructions, and helping. Well, it's what we always thought!

Job Source Network (USA)
http://www.jobsourcenetwork.com
This is another impressive and in-depth USA site with links to thousands of job sites world wide. You can do a job search, select job categories, countries of the world, and your favourite search engines, using handy drop-down lists. Another main feature of the site is the huge number of job listings in major US newspapers, which you can trawl through by name in a long drop-down menu. In addition there are loads of links of all kinds for job hunters, though the emphasis of course is quite strongly American. The site is a project of Benjamin Scott Publishing, Washington DC.

Job Trak (USA)
http://www.jobtrak.com/
Based in Los Angeles, this is another US-based employment site, intended primarily for college students and alumni. With over 35,000 visitors per day and 3,000 new job openings daily, it is one of the larger employment sites on the internet. Over the past ten years it has formed partnerships with some 800 college career centres. It offers a worthwhile source of information and links to graduate employers in the States. You will find a job search manual, and vacancies for part-time jobs, temp jobs and internships. Job Trak say that, since 1987, over 300,000 employers have used its services to target students and alumni from their choice of campuses. The fee to advertisers ranges from $18 per campus up to $395 for all 800 schools.

Job Ware (Germany)
http://www.jobware.de/
This is a professional looking online service designed for both candidates seeking a job and companies seeking staff. The site is mainly in German of course, but international applicants can submit their details on its English-language international page.

.... **Overseas jobs pages**

Job Web (USA)
http://www.jobweb.com
Job Web is a project of the National Association of Colleges and Employers. It has 1,700 member universities and colleges drawn from across the United States (and their career services professionals), and 1,600 employer organisations in the private sector. Also represented are numerous federal, state, and local governmental agencies and their HR/employment professionals. Job Web says it serves over a million college students and alumni who use its publications and services every year.

JobXchange
http://www.jobxchange.com
Dedicated exclusively to the global cruise and maritime industry, the International Seafarers Exchange sets up a direct connection among cruise and maritime companies, crewing agents, maritime schools, universities and prospective crew members. Interested in working in the cruise and maritime industry? You can review information on over 300 positions currently available, current job openings, job descriptions, salary, perks, life on board, regulations, policies, contracts, benefits and much more. It offers opportunities with cruise lines, ferries, yachts, cargo, tanker and other maritime companies seeking to recruit and hire prospective seafarers by searching its crew database of thousands. The site claims to have more than 70,000 visitors from more than 100 countries each month – it's an unmissable site in its particular field.

Jobs & Adverts (Europe/Asia)
http://www.jobsadverts.com/
This is one of the leading German job placement agencies working on the net. It offers the publication of job advertisements, company profiles and commercial ads. It numbers Siemens, Deutsche Bank and SAP among its many top clients. After more than two years' experience in the German market, the site has broadened its coverage to include Austria, Switzerland, Thailand and the USA, and other parts of Europe, Asia and Africa. When we checked, the site appeared to contain more than 12,000 job offers. As a test we selected three categories – permanent, creative jobs, and UK; this yielded three hits, of which two however turned out to be engineering jobs. The Thai database, developed in conjunction with Thai newspapers, contained more than 700 jobs. The site seems well structured and a useful contact point for overseas job hunters, though it offers few external links.

Jobs CZ (Czech Republic)
http://www.jobs.cz
We can't tell you much about this site, because it is all in Czech with no English translation facility. However, if you can cope with the language barrier, there are loads of links on the site and it would probably be quite rewarding to explore.

Overseas jobs pages

Jobs vacatures op het Internet (Netherlands)
http://www.jobs.nl/
If you are looking for job opportunities in the Netherlands this is a good site to visit, but it is in the Dutch language only. The site contains a worthwhile collection of additional Netherlands employment links.

Jobz (Australia)
http://jobz.ozware.com/
Jobz is a database of employment opportunities in Australia. Jobs are organised into numerous categories, with a link for each to aid your surfing. There may be less information than expected. Our test search for jobs in computing yielded only five results. Job descriptions were fairly brief.

LatPro (Latin America)
http://www.LatPro.com/
This is the web site of the Latin American Professional's Network, announcing employment opportunities and information for bilingual and bicultural professionals from the Americas. LatPro are not executive recruiters nor a traditional internet job-site, but a 13,000-strong membership organisation linking its members and corporate and executive recruiters searching for bilingual (Spanish or Portuguese and English) professionals. It contains review job announcements for people with Spanish and Portuguese language skills, links to the Latin American countries, and other resources. You can pay a small membership fee to receive email announcements.

Manpower (worldwide)
http://www.manpower.com/
Established in 1948, Manpower is the largest staffing and employment service in the world. With more than 3,000 offices in 50 countries, it has provided employment opportunities for millions of people. On its international web site, you can use the various clickable colour maps to find its offices in almost every part of the world. It has UK regional offices in London, Cardiff and Edinburgh, and a network of offices nationwide. It covers teleservices, clerical services and administration, driving jobs, IT services, technical appointments, nursing, production and warehousing, graduate appointments, and regional training. It offers short-term and long-term work on a temporary or contract basis, and these assignments can also lead to permanent placement offers. The site does not show specific vacancies or have any search facilities. To find out more you click on the Branch Network button to locate the branch nearest you, and telephone to arrange an appointment. The site contains a limited amount of global employment news, and there are virtually no external links. A company of this size could surely make more use of the internet.

Medical Ad Mart (USA)
http://www.medical-admart.com/
Medical Ad Mart's pages contain advertisements for positions, products and services for the medical professional. It has compiled

Overseas jobs pages

and brought online the best selection of classified advertising pages drawn from leading USA medical journals, such as *American Family Physician, California Physician, Regional Anaesthesia,* and *Veterinary Forum.*

Medical Employment Services (USA)
http://www.med-employ.com
Medical Employment Services is a USA service based on email, not web pages. Messages about new medical and nursing employment opportunities can be sent to appropriate potential candidates within a few hours of the time they are sent to the site.

MediStaff (USA)
http://www.medistaff.com
MediStaff are California-based specialists in the placement of physical therapists, PTAs, occupational therapists, registered nurses and speech language pathologists, into permanent and travelling positions across America. There are also some opportunities in the UK and in Saudi Arabia. The service is a division of World Wide Staffing Inc based in Vancouver, Canada.

MedSearch (USA and Europe)
http://www.medsearch.com/
MedSearch is a career centre, bulletin board, news group and employment site all rolled into one. With access to and data on employment opportunities, strategic partnerships, professional alliances, mergers, acquisitions, industry trends, and other issues shaping the future of health care, MedSearch provides a whole range of professional support, including a database of jobs in the medical and healthcare industries. You can also submit your résumé into their database via an online form, or send it to them by email. This very professional looking site offers a pretty comprehensive coverage of the US medical and health care fields. Its international jobs section contained more than 500 vacancies for Europe.

Microsoft Jobs
http://www.microsoft.com/jobs
This is a site devoted to world wide Microsoft employment opportunities including an area for new graduates. They say, 'Don't work for a living, work for a reason.' The jobs encompass development, research, creative content, marketing, sales, corporate operations, IT, consulting, and technical support. The job descriptions are quite detailed and you are invited to submit your résumé by email. You can also find out about recruitment events, and international opportunities.

Monster Board (Australia)
http://www.monsterboard.com.au/
If you are hoping to live and work in Australia, this is a site you should visit – a Monster Board service geared to life down under. For job seekers there is a job search facility with hundreds of jobs to choose from, with a personal job search agent to assist you, employer profiles,

Overseas jobs pages

and a résumé builder. Unfortunately the section on Australian recruitment consultants was devoid of information when we reviewed the site.

Nation Job (USA)
http://www.nationjob.com/
Nation Job is an independent network of computerised recruitment services based in Iowa. It has been providing a computerised job listing service since 1988. Its flagship service is PJ Scout. Job seekers tell PJ what they want, and this free and confidential service then automatically emails them any new jobs that match their choices. PJ is now apparently scouting for 300,000 people a week. The site includes an impressively lengthy A-Z list of links to mainly US recruiters. Be prepared to wait a few minutes while the list unfolds on your screen.

Naukri (India)
http://www.naukri.com/
Here is a comprehensive resource for job seekers and employers in India. It includes more than 5,000 job leads less than 30 days old, links to placement agencies, major employers in India, and to more Indian career resources. There is also lots of careers advice. The site is updated twice a week. Based in Delhi, Naukri currently gets approximately 700,000 hits a month, making it the most popular Indian careers site by far. You can view the statistics yourself.

Net Jobs (Canada)
http://www.netjobs.com
Net Jobs is a Canadian employment site. The jobs are listed under such categories as computer programming, engineering and technical, graphic design and arts, information systems, programmers and analysts, management information systems, networking and network design, sales and marketing, technical sales, and the transportation industry. This rather limited functional site does not extend to a searchable database, or carry many other features. We looked for positions in the category for Computer Programming and found only one vacancy. The category for Technical Sales yielded 10 vacancies.

Migrate

Visit

Study

Work

New Zealand Immigration Service
http://www.immigration.govt.nz/
As official sites go, this is quite user-friendly. Some 250,000 visitors have accessed the site in the last year. You can check out immigration requirements, the all-important pass-mark system, family categories, investor schemes, residency and citizenship, fees and forms, information for student visitors, FAQs, and more. You can download a whole series of informative booklets giving detailed information about living and working in New Zealand. If you feel serious about going, whether on a temporary or permanent basis, this site is a must.

Occupational Outlook Handbook (USA)
http://stats.bls.gov/ocohome.htm
The *Occupational Outlook Handbook* is a basic reference source for

Overseas jobs pages

careers and employment in the USA. You can use this web site to find information about specific occupations, perform a keyword search on the handbook, use the index to the handbook, and select from an occupational cluster. The handbook is published by the US Bureau of Labor Statistics.

O-Hayo Sensei (Japan)
http://www.ohayosensei.com
O-Hayo Sensei is a free electronic newsletter that lists 40 to 50 teaching – and many other English language related – positions at schools and companies across Japan. Published twice a month, *O-Hayo Sensei* presents information about salaries, skill/education requirements, duties, benefit packages, visa requirements, housing, contracts and application procedures. It also offers readers free non-commercial ads in a lively classified section, an on-going excerpt from a database of 2,000 schools, and a collection of Japan-related links.

Online Career Center (USA and Europe)
http://www.occ.com
This award-winning site is one of the most comprehensive and frequently used online job search resources in the USA. It contains a large database of jobs searchable by type and location. You can browse by US city/state, international, company, industry, engineering, health-care, human resources, and travel and tourism. You can also submit your CV. We reviewed the international section, which produced 580 jobs for Europe. These appeared in a long list in date order (most recent first). As a test we did a sub-search of 'sales' jobs, which yielded a more manageable list of 56 vacancies up to five weeks old.

Overseas Jobs Express
http://www.overseasjobs.com/
The fortnightly Sussex-based newspaper *Overseas Job Express* currently contains about 3,000 job listings and other useful job information. On its web site you can search its growing database of vacancies by keyword, or browse it by job type. An outstanding feature of the site is its guide to over 700 career, employment, job and recruiter sites in 42 countries. You can access these by clicking Africa, Asia, Australasia, Western Europe, Scandinavia, Eastern Europe, Russia, Immigration, Middle East, USA, Mexico, Canada, South America, UK and International. Advertisers are invited to reach over 100,000 overseas job seekers each month by posting their international job listings on the site. If you have any intention of working overseas, this site is a must.

Pages Emploi
http://emploi.hrnet.fr/
This site provides links to a collection of internet job sites located throughout the world. You can search by country and region, check out the top 100 job sites, link to the newsgroups or find useful mailing lists. You can also upload a copy of your CV. The site is partly in French and partly in English. There is also an English language chat room.

TOOLS TO HELP YOU GET A JOB ABROAD

● Have Overseas Jobs Express sent to you by airmail. CLICK.

Overseas jobs pages

Sales Seek (USA)
http://www.salesseek.com
This web site focuses on sales and marketing recruitment. It is a project of American Recruitment, the largest sales recruiting company in the USA. Job seekers can do a customised job search, or a quick search, and post and edit their personal profile. You have to complete quite a detailed online form first. Some 80,000 candidates have apparently posted their résumé information to its database. The site also gives useful details of upcoming US careers fairs.

Screen Actors Guild (USA)
http://www.sag.com/
This is the official web site of the Screen Actors Guild. It explains the qualifications you would need for joining this actors' union. While multi-million dollar movie deals make headlines for some stars, creating a false impression that all actors are highly paid, the reality is far less glamorous. According to the Guild's statistics, in 1996 more than 80 percent of its 90,000 members earned less than $5,000. But if you feel you have what it takes to break into this competitive field, this is a good place to start. To join, you must show proof of employment or prospective employment within two weeks or less by a Guild signatory company, and pay a joining fee of around $1,200.

Ship Jobs
http://www.shipjobs.com
Here you can find out about the big market in cruise ship jobs. Based on first-hand experience, this web site offers articles, books and videos which could help your job search and career decisions.

Showbiz Jobs (USA)
http://www.showbizjobs.com/
Showbiz Jobs is a Hollywood-based membership organisation of recruitment managers from leading companies in the film, television, recording and attractions industries seeking candidates for a multitude of industry-related positions. This well organised site includes a Jobs Board where you can look at current career opportunities with the entertainment leaders for free. You can search by company name, job category, or geographic location for the latest job openings. There are plenty of vacancies. Responding is as easy as emailing your CV direct to the respective recruitment offices. There is a $35 fee to submit your résumé for a six month period.

SmartJobb (Scandinavia)
http://www.smartjobb.nu/
This is a professional-looking resource for job-hunters wanting employment in Scandinavia. Get those Swedish and Norwegian dictionaries out, because there is no English on this site.

Softskills Recruitment
http://www.softskills.ie
Based in Dublin, this company specialises in supplying the information

.... **Overseas jobs pages**

technology industries in Ireland, Europe and the United States with graduate and professional candidates.

Student Center (USA)
http://www.studentcenter.com/
This is an American career-related information service for college, graduate students and recent graduates. It includes a 35,000 company searchable database, résumé, interview and job-hunting tips, a virtual interview, and other aids to successful career development.

Stybel Peabody & Associates
http://www.stybelpeabody.com/
This is an American board-level career resource centre 'for chief executive officers who hate to surf'. Founded in 1979, the firm works with clients seeking smooth transitions for key executives and professionals. Its core services include senior executive coaching, executive search, and senior level outplacement. Its core population consists of executives who report to boards, executives who wish to report to boards, executives who wish to serve on boards, executives who ought to be networking at board levels, and executives who want to think like members of boards. The company is based in Massachusetts.

Summer Jobs (USA)
http://www.summerjobs.com/
This site offers a very brightly presented international listing of seasonal and summer employment opportunities. We searched the jobs database for 'sports' jobs, and this yielded 20 vacancies (mostly in American summer camps). A search for 'driving' jobs produced 5 vacancies, and one for 'music' yielded 12. Employers can post jobs to the database for free. The site also contains a very useful collection of links to summer and temporary jobs, student jobs, and employment sources of various kinds. Summer Jobs is a project of Fishnet New Media.

Swiss Web Jobs
http://www.swisswebjobs.ch/
This is naturally a web site for jobs in Switzerland. It provides detailed links to employers, recruitment organisations, and offers various listings. The site is partly in German, and partly in French, but you will need to speak German to make full use of the service. An English link takes you to the Swiss section of **Top Jobs on the Net** (still in German).

TAPS
http://taps.com/
Launched in January 1996, TAPS is a prominent European web-based recruitment service. TAPS stands for The Appointments Section. Backed by a consortium of companies, it offers thousands of permanent and contract vacancies for blue chip companies. The service to job hunters is free and confidential. If you are looking for a particular type of job, you use the 'Job Search' section. You can also

Overseas jobs pages

search for vacancies by employer, by using a drop-down list of employers. If you are a graduate chasing your first job, you can check the 'Who's Recruiting' section to find out more about your potential employer. By registering you can post and edit your CV. The overall presentation is rather functional and slightly cramped, and the number of your search results is not quantified – you just have to plough through them to the end. The site includes a handy interview guide and career clinic, and has an Irish counterpart.

Theatre Jobs (USA)
http://theatrejobs.com
This is a well organised online job search system serving the North American entertainment industry. The ads are free, but as a job seeker you will have to subscribe. When we reviewed the site we found 465 job listings online. You can learn more about theatre jobs including additional services, special subscription rates, explore links to interesting theatre sites, and join the theatre jobs mailing list to receive notices of hot jobs, and discount prices.

Top Jobs USA
http://www.topjobsusa.com
This is a very extensive database of job listings concentrated on the western United States, such as Arizona, California, Colorado, Idaho, Nevada, New Mexico, Oregon, Texas, and Utah. It claims to contain over 50,000 job listings. You can submit your résumé. There is also quite a detailed links section, leading you to such further resources as US academic institutions, chambers of commerce, government sources, recruiting agencies, careers advice pages, other internet job lists, résumé banks, search engines and numerous other categories.

TV Jobs (USA)
http://www.tvjobs.com
TV Jobs provides North American employment information, résumés, jobs, professional development, station information and other resources for the professional broadcaster. It also includes a Worldwide Freelance Directory containing a searchable database of professional freelances. TV Jobs has some 1,600 broadcasting stations organised into a fully searchable index. It looks to be a pretty comprehensive and interesting site with enormous amounts of information of value to anyone seeking to develop their career in this market.

Vacation Work Publications
http://www.vacationwork.co.uk
Based in Oxford, the firm is a well-known publisher of guide books on work, travel and adventure abroad.

Vacature Overzicht (Netherlands)
http://www.iway.nl/intervac/
This site offers a comprehensive overview of jobs offered in Holland, updated every week. You will need your Dutch dictionary.

Overseas jobs pages

VIP Personnel (Australia)
http://www.vipstaff.com.au
VIP is an established (30 years) Australian hospitality recruitment specialist, listing jobs available in Australia and South East Asia. Based in Melbourne, it recruits casual and permanent placement of staff at all levels of the hospitality industry. It claims to have the largest database of hospitality professionals in the southern hemisphere. Some of the job listings seemed to be rather out of date.

Virtual Job Fair (USA)
http://www.vjf.com/
This is a USA site aimed solely at candidates with hi-tech skills. You can search the job openings of 500 employers, view employer profiles A–Z, post your résumé for high tech companies to review, browse a library of career resources, use its regional salary calculator, and more. The site says it contains more than 7,000 pages of content, 25,000 high-tech career opportunities, 110,000 résumés, details of 90 technical career events, 18 high-tech career publications, hundreds of career-related articles and thousands of career resource links. As a random test we checked under K and a company called KLA Tencor. We found it had very detailed job descriptions on no less than 294 current hi-tech vacancies, from California to Malaysia and Japan. Similarly we checked under R and a company called Rational Software Corporation, which yielded very detailed descriptions of 216 vacancies.

Voluntary Services Overseas (VSO)
http://www.oneworld.org/vso/index.htm
VSO is a wonderful charity that sends aid to developing countries in the shape of expert volunteers. VSO provides the means for men and women from the UK to work with those in poorer countries enabling skills to be shared in the pursuit of creating a more equitable world. VSO

Fig. 57. The home page of Voluntary Services Overseas (VSO). It makes an excellent starting point to search for worthwhile opportunities abroad.

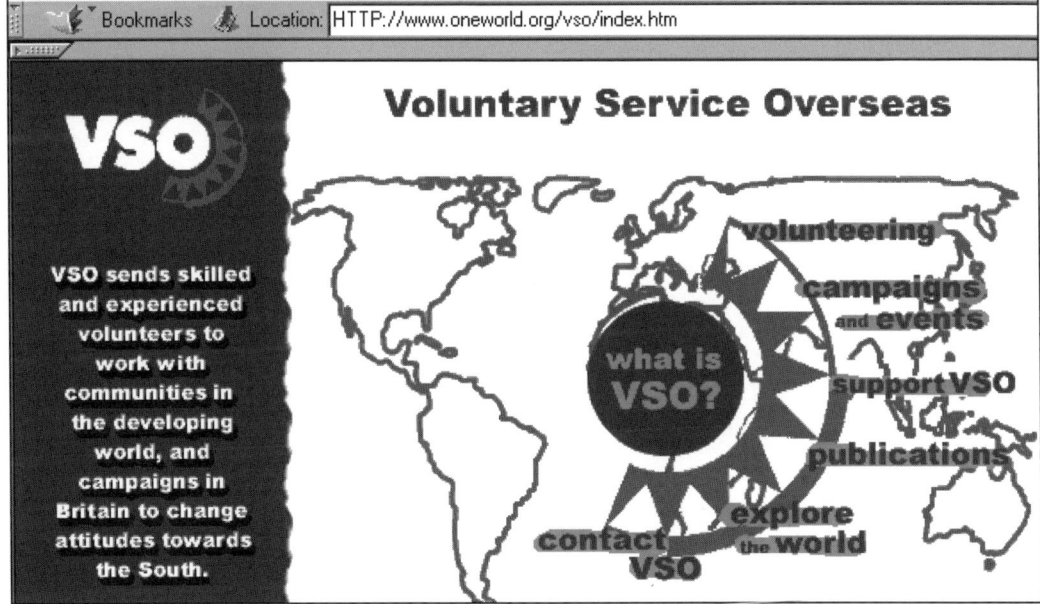

Overseas jobs pages

offers opportunities in education, health, natural resources, business, social work, librarianship, media, law, the technical trades and engineering. Visit this site and take a look at the current vacancies available then complete the online preliminary application form and find a new job that offers that little bit more. VSO should be approached after some serious thought as these worthwhile jobs require ultimate resilience and commitment often in the face of adversity and difficult conditions.

Voluntary Work Information Service
http://www.workingabroad.com/
Looking for environmental and humanitarian work abroad? Then this Switzerland-based organisation could be a place to start if you're looking for voluntary work projects in over 150 countries world wide. VWIS was established in early 1997 as an independent non-profit organisation. It offers opportunities in social and community development, environment and nature conservation, human rights, wildlife surveying and expeditions, medicine and health care, construction, sanitation, housing, education and teaching, agriculture and organic farming. There are some useful links to similar organisations world wide. Be patient, the pages can be slow to load.

Working in Australia
http://www.immi.gov.au/
This is an official site giving information about migration to Australia, published by Australia's Department of Immigration and Multicultural Affairs. It gives a practical and thorough introduction to the immigration rules, visitors' permits, permanent and temporary residence, working visits, skilled migrants, studying in Australia, fact sheets, business immigration, the humanitarian programme, retirement to Australia, Australian citizenship, government department links, and lots more. This site would be essential for anyone thinking of living or working in Australia whether short term or permanently.

World Careers Network
http://www.wcn.co.uk
'Matching students and firms worldwide', this site contains detailed information on a large number of recruiters and job vacancies. You can access a contact database of more than 10,000 employers world wide, read news, and explore links to recruiters on the net. You can also upload your CV for recruiters to access. However to use the site you first have to agree its lengthy list of conditions and obtain a personal user name and password. The site restricts access to currently enrolled students. The way it verifies that you are currently affiliated as a student is by checking your email address against a database of email patterns. The site can be read in German as well as English.

14 UK examination boards on the internet

In this chapter you will discover:

▶ what an examination board does
▶ the URLs of the most popular examination boards.

Introduction

Examination boards are public institutions set up to administer academic and vocational qualifications. These courses are then offered in schools, colleges, universities and even in the workplace with final qualifications being given by the awarding examination board.

From the point of view of those looking for a change of career or those looking to choose a new school or college course, examination board internet sites will prove a useful starting point to finding out detailed course information and entry requirements.

City & Guilds
http://www.city-and-guilds.co.uk/
This site is divided into four main sections covering examinations offered by City & Guilds (NVQs, GNVQs, SVQs), Pitman Qualifications (examinations for office based skills), City & Guild International (overseas study of City & Guilds and Pitman's qualifications), and NEBS Management (management education). Detailed information is given for each examination area and a list of subjects and courses is available. This site has a particularly good FAQ section covering every conceivable question that prospective candidates, or examination centres, are likely to ask.

EDEXCEL
http://www.edexcel.org.uk
EDEXCEL is a leading provider of both academic and vocational qualifications in England, Wales and Northern Ireland. It was formed in 1996 with the merger of BTEC and London Examinations. EDEXCEL provides such a wide variety of courses that this site is literally jam packed with course information. From GCSEs, 'A' Levels, NVQs and others, a detailed explanation is provided for students, teachers and trainers. BTEC awards have a vocational bias and are suitable for literally anyone from young people through to senior managers. Detailed information is given relating to all certificates, diplomas and NVQs administered by BTEC.

LCCI Examinations Board
http://www.lccieb.org.uk/
The London Chamber of Commerce & Industry Examinations Board offers a wide range of business qualifications and NVQs on an inter-

Fig. 58. The RSA Examinations Board home page.

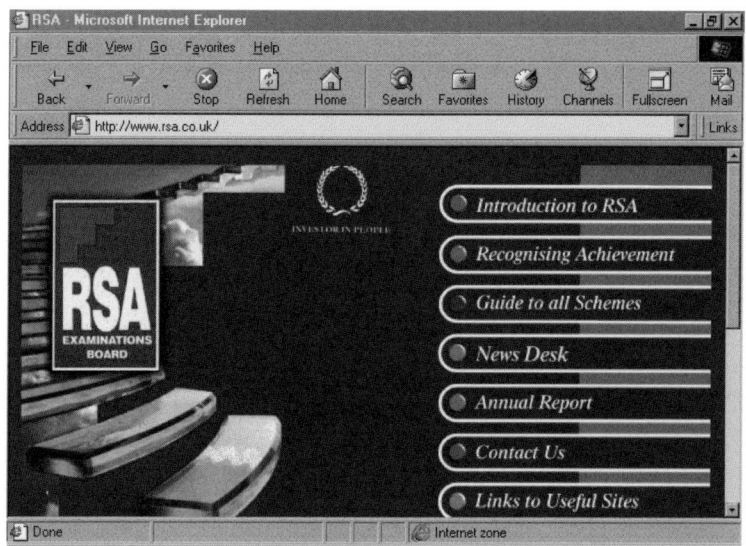

national basis. Courses are available at four levels and are taken at around 8,000 examination centres world-wide. The LCCIEB is linked with the world-wide Chamber of Commerce, and so feels that courses are developed with specific relevance to the present day needs of industry and business. From this site a very clear path is offered to those wishing information on registering a centre as an LCCIEB centre, those looking for further information on the qualifications offered, and those looking to purchase a range of study-aid publications.

RSA Examinations Board
http://www.rsa.co.uk/
The Royal Society of Arts Examination Board is the oldest and one of the largest providers of vocational education in the UK. RSA programmes number 500, and are offered by over 8,000 centres world wide. This site provides a great link to the schemes available from the RSA. These schemes cover NVQs, GNVQs, Information Technology Awards as well as many others.

Scottish Qualifications Authority
http://www.sqa.co.uk/
The Scottish Qualifications Authority is responsible for the provision of most qualifications in Scotland. Courses offered include SVQs, NCs, HNCs, Standard and Higher Grade exams amongst others. This site offers a fantastic resource for students and teachers and is jam packed with information. Worthy of particular mention is the list of courses and subjects available via a simple search routine, as well as the 'Progression Routes' page. This latter page allows you to choose an education category and develop this information further to include qualifications required for entry to courses as well as details of the type of jobs available and the likely educational requirements to secure each job. A really great site for school leavers or returners to education (even if you're not choosing to study in Scotland!).

15 UK professional bodies on the internet

In this chapter you will discover:

▶ what a professional body is
▶ the web sites of some major professional bodies.

Introduction

So, just what are professional bodies and what do they do? Well, professional bodies exist to promote their industry and their members as well as to provide a source of information, education and career development for members. If you intend working in a career such as computing, engineering or personnel then membership of the appropriate professional body can show prospective employers that you have an active interest in your industry and that you are likely to operate within a code of conduct laid down by industry professionals.

Professional bodies also lobby government and provide sources of expert information to central government, local government, and anyone requiring professional expertise in a particular area.

Some professional bodies, such as the Institute of Chartered Accountants, count membership as a prerequisite for working in jobs within a particular industry or profession.

Membership of professional bodies requires various levels of ability. This can range from simply having work experience in the industry through to the requirement to take examinable courses which can last up to four years or more. Professional bodies provide an excellent source of current research and up-to-date thinking on industry subjects and, as such, membership must be considered essential for those looking to work in industries and jobs represented by a professional body.

Many professional bodies offer some form of Continuous Professional Development (CPD) which ensures that members are kept up to date with courses on industry activities. Many of the professional bodies also afford members some designatory letters which can be used after your surname on headed notepaper, business cards and the like.

Association of Chartered Certified Accountants
http://www.acca.org.uk/
The Association of Chartered Certified Accountants (ACCA) is the largest international accounting body. It offers membership to Chartered Certified Accountants, Certified Accounting Technicians and those who hold the Diploma in Accounting and Finance. The ACCA supports a wide range of qualifications and information relating

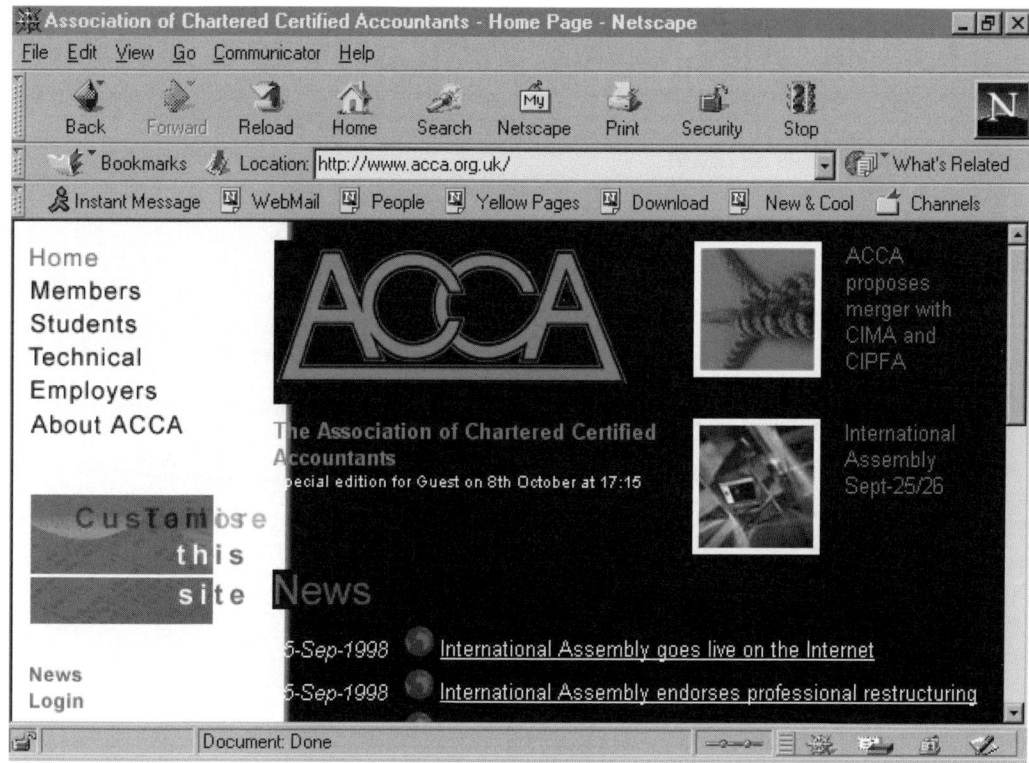

Fig. 59. The ACCA home page

to this activity can be found in this site. There also exists a section on current vacancies as well as a profile on the type of employers hiring ACCA members.

British Computer Society
http://www.bcs.org.uk/
The British Computer Society is the only chartered body in the field of information systems (IS). It exists to provide support to individual members, employers and the general public. As an Engineering Institution, the British Computer Society is licensed by the Engineering Council to nominate both Chartered and Incorporated Engineers, and to accredit university courses and training schemes. This site offers great advice to those working in the IS industry as well as students – for whom there is a lively and active membership section – as well as providing information for schools and others.

British Psychological Society
http://www.bps.org.uk/
The British Psychological Society promotes the advancement of the study of psychology. The society ensures that members maintain a high level of education and conduct. This site offers many interesting pages of information relating to the work of the society. In particular the directory of chartered psychologists is useful, as is the explanation of membership types and the list of current accredited courses available in British universities.

UK professional bodies on the internet

Chartered Institute of Bankers
http://www.cib.org.uk/
The Chartered Institute of Bankers is the leading professional examining body in the financial services industry. It welcomes not only those looking to begin a career in banking but also those already working in the industry or those with a general interest in the industry. This site offers some great resources and offers all sorts of advice on changing your career through to useful addresses and internet pages with further information on banking and the financial services industry.

Chartered Institute of Marketing
http://www.cim.co.uk
The Chartered Institute of Marketing is the world's largest professional body representing those working in marketing. Membership of the Institute results from the undertaking of a professional qualification which is available for study at over 300 colleges and universities worldwide. The Chartered Institute of Marketing has over 60,000 members. This site offers easy to use navigation icons which give you plenty of information relating to qualifications training and VQs through to current news and planned events and activities.

Chartered Insurance Institute
http://www.cii.co.uk/
The Chartered Insurance Institute is an international organisation with over 70,000 members. The Institute provides support for members and promotes high professional conduct amongst its members, those who

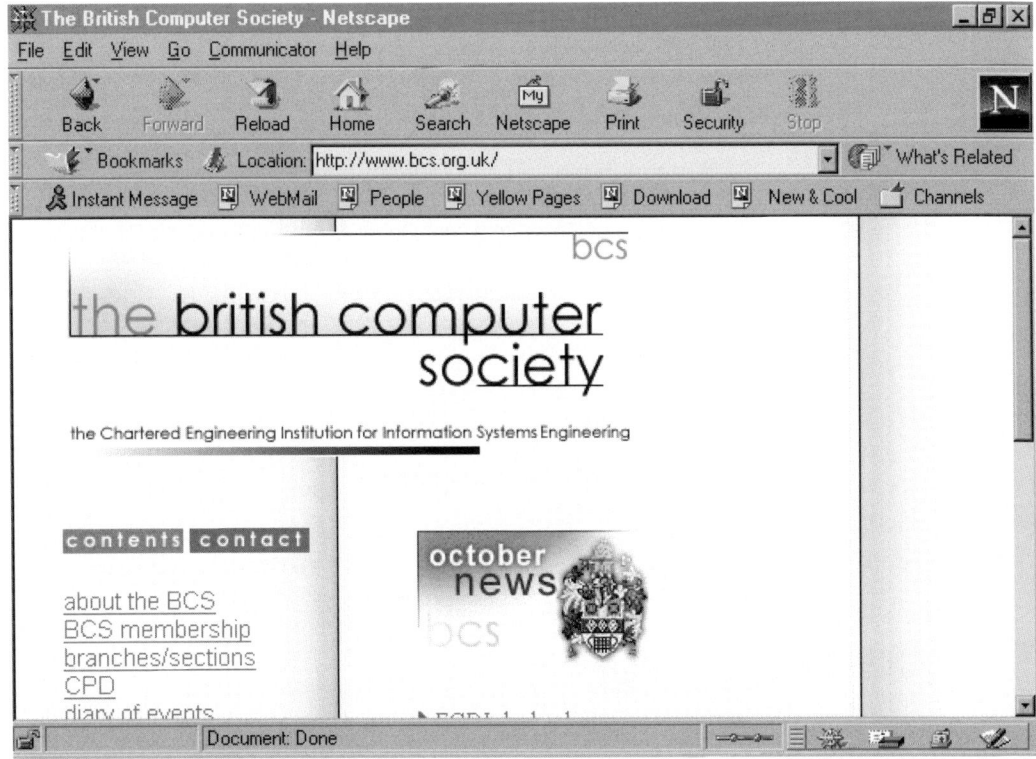

Fig. 60. The British Computer Society home page.

UK professional bodies on the internet

employ them, and the public that use their services. It administers academic examinations and supports members' continued professional personal development. Check out the Careers Information Service to find lots of useful information for those considering a career in the industry. Booklets can be requested and are provided free of charge. A list of FAQs is also included.

Institute of Chartered Accountants of England & Wales
http://www.icaew.co.uk/

The Institute of Chartered Accountants of England and Wales is the largest professional accountancy body in Europe. There are separate Institutes for Scotland and Ireland. This site gives access to services for members as well as details of careers available in chartered accountancy. A list of press releases since 1996 is also available. Interestingly, this site also provides some access and information for general members of the public in areas such as choosing a chartered accountant and the tax self-assessment procedures. Its services include Chartac Careers Services, which provides help for members on any career management issue including career planning, redundancy, unemployment, and job search.

Institute of Management Information Systems
http://www.imis.org.uk/

The Institute of Management Information Systems is one of the world's principal professional organisations for the promotion of information systems. The institute is UK based and offers a wide range of qualifications from diploma through to postgraduate courses. Courses are studied at colleges and universities throughout the world. The IMIS home page offers plenty of information for the curious, is easy to search through, and is thorough in its explanation of each area of the institute's activities.

Institute of Personnel and Development
http://www.ipd.co.uk

The Institute of Personnel and Development is the professional body which represents those working in the area of personnel and people management. The Institute has some 90,000 members and its internet site offers access both to members and visitors. For those wishing to keep up to date with current news, on-line access to *People Management*, the Institute's members' journal, gives up-to-date views and current thinking.

Institution of Electrical Engineers
http://www.iee.org.uk/

The Institution of Electrical Engineers represents the public, professional and educational interest of some 140,000 engineers world wide. These engineers work as electronics, electrical and manufacturing engineers. From this site, icons lead you through discussion and information on the publications that the IEE promotes, a calendar of events, current news, services, membership detail, activities, policies and contact details. This site also has a comprehensive search facility.

UK professional bodies on the internet

Law Society
http://www.lawsoc.org.uk/home.html
The Law Society is the professional body for solicitors in England and Wales. The society aims to improve access to the law for everyone as well as providing the principal source of services and support to solicitors themselves. The Law Society's site is easy to understand and provides access to a directory of solicitors as well as to a host of educational and members services.

Royal Institute of British Architects
http://www.riba.org/
The Royal Institute of British Architects has a membership of over 30,000 and exists to promote good practice and support its members. This site is very easy to navigate and offers informative sections on the RIBA, education, choosing an architect, and more.

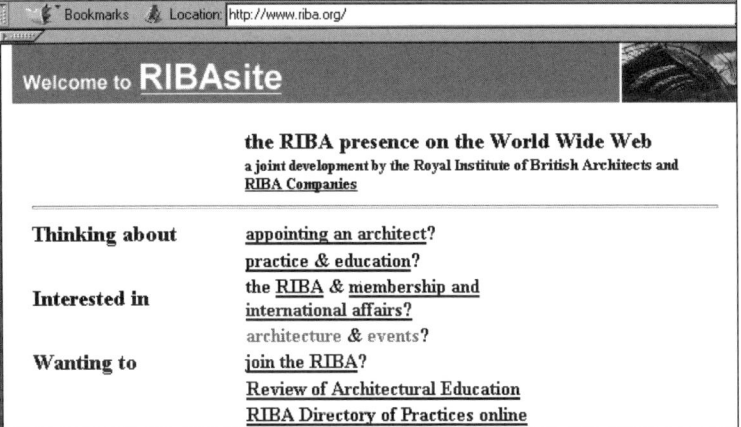

Royal Institution of Chartered Surveyors
http://www.rics.org.uk/
The Royal Institution of Chartered Surveyors has as its guiding principle a regard to the public interest. With over 90,000 members the Institution is the leading source of professional advice on land, property and construction. Take a look at the Careers page for an excellent A-Z of what a chartered surveyor actually is, to how to train for the profession, through to guidance on how to successfully secure employment in the profession. This site offers a link to the Ivanhoe Careers Guide which provides excellent careers information for surveyors.

Royal Society of Chemistry
http://www.rsc.org/
The Royal Society of Chemistry is the professional body for chemists in the UK. The society has some 46,000 members world wide and is a major publisher of chemical information. The society is a leading science communicator and supports the teaching of chemistry at all levels. From the RSC's site you can gain access to a number of useful areas such as the society's products, services and activities.

16 UK educational & professional bodies

British public education awards

BTEC	Business & Technician Education Council
C&GLI	City & Guilds of London Institute
RSA	Royal Society of Arts
PEI	Pitmans Examinations Institute
LCCI	London Chamber of Commerce & Industry

British professional bodies

BCS	British Computer Society
IDPM	Institute of Data Processing Management
BPS	British Psychological Society
CII	Chartered Insurance Institute
CIB	Chartered Institute of Bankers
CIM	Chartered Institute of Marketing
CIE	Council of Engineering Institutions
ICE	Institution of Civil Engineers
ICE	Institution of Chemical Engineers
IEE	Institution of Electrical Engineers
IME	Institution of Mechanical Engineers
ICAEW	Institute of Chartered Accountants of England & Wales
ICSA	Institute of Chartered Secretaries & Administrators
ICM	Institute of Credit Management
IOE	Institute of Export
IFF	Institute of Freight Forwarding
IPD	Institute of Personnel & Development
ISM	Institute of Supervisory Management
ACCA	Association of Chartered Certified Accountants
LA	Library Association
LS	Law Society
BC	Bar Council
ILEX	Institute of Legal Executives
RCN	Royal College of Nursing
RIBA	Royal Institute of British Architects
RICS	Royal Institution of Chartered Surveyors
RSC	Royal Society of Chemistry
IOP	Institute of Physics

17 Internet newsgroups for job seekers

A

ab.jobs
akr.jobs
alabama.birmingham.jobs
alabama.jobs
alt.building.jobs
alt.jobs
alt.jobs.overseas
alt.jobs.spam
alt.medical.sales.jobs
alt.medical.sales.jobs.offered
alt.medical.sales.jobs.resumes
aol.neighborhood.pa.state-college.jobs
at.blackbox.bbe.jobs
at.blackbox.kleinanzeigen.jobs
at.jobs
atl.jobs
ab.jobs
akr.jobs
alabama.birmingham.jobs
alabama.jobs
alt.building.jobs
alt.jobs
alt.jobs.overseas
alt.jobs.spam
alt.medical.sales.jobs
alt.medical.sales.jobs.offered
alt.medical.sales.jobs.resumes
aus.ads.jobs
aus.ads.jobs.moderated
aus.ads.jobs.resumes
austin.jobs
av.jobs
az.jobs

B

ba.jobs
ba.jobs
ba.jobs.agency
ba.jobs.contract
ba.jobs.contract.agency
ba.jobs.contract.direct
ba.jobs.direct
ba.jobs.discussion
ba.jobs.misc
ba.jobs.offered
ba.jobs.resumes
balt.jobs
bc.jobs
bda.forum.zeit.job
be.jobs
bermuda.jobs
bermuda.jobs.offered
bhm.jobs
bionet.jobs
bionet.jobs.offered
bionet.jobs.wanted
biz.jobs
biz.jobs.offered

C

can.jobs
can.jobs.gov
chi.jobs
cit.jobs
cle.jobs
cmh.jobs
co.jobs
conn.jobs
conn.jobs.offered
cuug.jobs
cz.jobs
cz.jobs.offered
cz.jobs.wanted

D

dc.jobs
dfw.jobs
dod.jobs

E

eug.jobs
eunet.jobs
euro.jobs

F

fido7.kharkov.job
fido7.kiev.job

Newsgroups for job seekers

fido7.mo.job
fido7.mo.job.service
fido7.mo.job.talk
fido7.nsk.job
fido7.rc.jobs
fido7.spb.job
fido7.spb.job.talk
fl.jobs
fl.jobs.computers
fl.jobs.computers.application
fl.jobs.computers.misc
fl.jobs.computers.programming
fl.jobs.misc
fl.jobs.resumes
fl.jobs.telecommute
fl.jobs.www
fr.jobs
fr.jobs.d
fr.jobs.demandes
fr.jobs.offres

G

git.ohr.jobs
git.ohr.jobs.digest
gov.us.topic.gov-jobs
gov.us.topic.gov-jobs.employee
gov.us.topic.gov-jobs.employee.issues
gov.us.topic.gov-jobs.employee.news
gov.us.topic.gov-jobs.hr-admin
gov.us.topic.gov-jobs.offered
gov.us.topic.gov-jobs.offered.admin
gov.us.topic.gov-jobs.offered.admin.finance
gov.us.topic.gov-jobs.offered.admin.ses
gov.us.topic.gov-jobs.offered.announce
gov.us.topic.gov-jobs.offered.clerical
gov.us.topic.gov-jobs.offered.engineering
gov.us.topic.gov-jobs.offered.foreign
gov.us.topic.gov-jobs.offered.health
gov.us.topic.gov-jobs.offered.law-enforce
gov.us.topic.gov-jobs.offered.math-comp
gov.us.topic.gov-jobs.offered.misc
gov.us.topic.gov-jobs.offered.questions
gov.us.topic.gov-jobs.offered.science
gov.us.topic.gov-jobs.offered.technical
gvnc.jobs

H

han.misc.jobs
hepnet.jobs

hk.jobs
hk.jobs.recruit
houston.jobs
houston.jobs.offered
houston.jobs.wanted
hsv.jobs

I

ie.jobs
iijnet.jobs
il.jobs
il.jobs.misc
il.jobs.offered
il.jobs.resumes
in.jobs
israel.jobs
israel.jobs.misc
israel.jobs.offered
israel.jobs.resumes
ithaca.jobs

K

ka.uni.jobs
kc.jobs
kw.jobs

L

la.jobs
li.jobs
linux.jobs
lou.lft.jobs

M

md.jobs
me.jobs
medlux.misc.jobs
mi.jobs
milw.jobs
misc.jobs
misc.jobs.contract
misc.jobs.fields
misc.jobs.fields.chemistry
misc.jobs.misc
misc.jobs.offered
misc.jobs.offered.entry
misc.jobs.resumes
mn.jobs

Newsgroups for job seekers

N

nb.jobs
ne.jobs
ne.jobs.contract
nebr.jobs
netcom.uk.jobs
niagara.jobs
nj.jobs
nj.jobs.resumes
nv.jobs
ny.jobs
nyc.jobs
nyc.jobs.contract
nyc.jobs.misc
nyc.jobs.offered
nyc.jobs.wanted

O

oh.jobs
ont.jobs
osu.jobs
ott.jobs

P

pa.jobs
pa.jobs.offered
pa.jobs.wanted
pdaxs.jobs
pdaxs.jobs.clerical
pdaxs.jobs.computers
pdaxs.jobs.construction
pdaxs.jobs.delivery
pdaxs.jobs.domestic
pdaxs.jobs.engineering
pdaxs.jobs.management
pdaxs.jobs.misc
pdaxs.jobs.restaurants
pdaxs.jobs.resumes
pdaxs.jobs.retail
pdaxs.jobs.sales
pdaxs.jobs.secretary
pdaxs.jobs.temporary
pdaxs.jobs.volunteers
pdaxs.jobs.wanted
pgh.jobs
pgh.jobs.offered
pgh.jobs.wanted
phl.jobs
phl.jobs.offered
phl.jobs.wanted
phx.jobs
phx.jobs.wanted
pnet.jobs
pnet.jobs.volunteer
pnet.jobs.wanted

Q

qc.jobs

R

relcom.commerce.jobs

S

sac.jobs
sat.jobs
scot.jobs
sdnet.jobs
sdnet.jobs.discuss
sdnet.jobs.offered
sdnet.jobs.services
sdnet.jobs.wanted
seattle.jobs
seattle.jobs.offered
seattle.jobs.wanted
sg.jobs
sg.jobs.offer
sk.jobs
sk.jobs.offered
sk.jobs.wanted
slac.jobs
slo.jobs
stl.jobs
stl.jobs.offered
stl.jobs.resumes
su.jobs
sudbury.jobs
swnet.jobs

T

triangle.jobs
tx.jobs
tx-bcs.jobs

U

ucb.cs.jobs
ucb.jobs

Newsgroups for job seekers

ucd.cs.jobs
uk.jobs
uk.jobs.contract
uk.jobs.d
uk.jobs.offered
uk.jobs.wanted
us.jobs
us.jobs.contract
us.jobs.misc
us.jobs.offered
us.jobs.resumes
ut.jobs
utcs.jobs
utexas.jobs
uw.ece.jobs

V

va.jobs
vegas.jobs

Z

za.ads.jobs

Glossary of internet terms

AltaVista
A popular internet search engine used to find pages relating to specific keywords entered.

Article
The name given to a message posted in a newsgroup.

AOL
America OnLine, one of the biggest internet service providers.

ASCII
American Standard Code for Information Interchange. It is a simple text file format that can be accessed by most word-processors and text editors. It is a universal file type for passing textual information across the internet.

Attachment
A file which may be word-processed, a database, a spreadsheet file or graphic file, and which is attached to an email message.

Bandwidth
The width of the motorway that gives you access to the internet. The higher the bandwidth, the wider the motorway, the faster traffic can flow.

Baud rate
The measure of data transmission speed in a modem.

Bookmark
A file of URLs of your favourite internet sites. Bookmarks are very easily created by simply bookmarking (mouse-clicking) an internet page when you decide that it is useful.

Browser
Software that allows you to browse through internet pages and download useful information. Internet Explorer and Netscape Navigator are by far the most popular browsers available.

Company profiles
This refers to details relating to the financial performance, ethos and activity of a company. Useful for job seekers looking to research a company's background.

Crash
What happens when a computer program malfunctions, causing the operating system of your PC to perform incorrectly or completely stop operating altogether.

CV
Curriculum Vitae. The main document used by a job applicant to provide prospective employers with information relating to qualifications, work experience and personal skills.

Glossary

Cyberspace
Popular term for the 'place' where you go to surf: the magical world of computers and telecommunications on the internet.

Domain name
The domain name of an internet site identifies the organisation or computer hosting that internet site, followed by an identifier detailing the type of site. For example, chamsheath.gov would probably be a government organisation called chamsheath.

Download
The term used to describe copying a file from the internet to your desktop PC or laptop. The opposite term – copying a file from your computer to one on the internet – is upload.

Email
Short for electronic mail, a message sent across the internet to an individual or group of individuals.

Email address
The unique address given to you by your ISP. It can be used by others using the internet to send email messages to you. An example of a standard email address is BrendanEd@aol.com

Encryption
A powerful form of coding anyone can use to protect the privacy of communications on the internet. The best known version is American software called PGP (Pretty Good Privacy), available free.

Excite
A popular internet search engine used to find pages relating to specific keywords which you enter.

FAQ
Short for Frequently Asked Questions. It refers to text files held in newsgroups and on internet pages that give answers to the questions people most commonly ask about the newsgroup or web site. Always read FAQs before leaving any message relating to the problem that you are experiencing, or the question that you wish answered.

File
A file is a specific set of related data such as a word-processed document, a spreadsheet, a database file, a graphics file, or a sound file.

Firewall
A firewall is software that can be used by your ISP to stop the flow of certain files into and out of their network.

Flame
A more or less hostile or aggressive message posted in a newsgroup, or to an individual newsgroup user. If these messages get out of hand, they are termed 'flame wars'.

FTP
Short for file transfer protocol. The method normally used to send files back and forth across the internet.

Glossary

GIF
Short for graphics interchange format. A compressed file format used on the internet to display files that contain graphic images.

GUI
Short for graphic user interface. It describes the friendly screens found in Windows and other WIMP environments (Windows, icons, mice, pointers).

Home page
The index page of an individual or an organisation on the internet. This page usually gives links to related pages of information and other sites.

Host computer
A computer that is directly connected to the internet. When you sign up with an ISP you have access to your ISP's computer which is the host computer for your access.

HotBot
A popular internet search engine used to find pages relating to specific keywords entered.

HTML
Short for hyper text mark-up language. It is a kind of word-processing language used by internet users to develop pages which can be uploaded and viewed across the internet using a browser.

HTTP
Hyper text transfer protocol. You'll see this acronym at the start of every web address, for example:

http://www.zzzzz.com

It is the standard way that HTML documents are transferred from host computer to your local browser when you're surfing the internet.

Hypertext
A link on an HTML page that, when clicked with a mouse, results in a further HTML page or graphic being loaded into view on your browser.

Internet
A broad term for the expanding network of global computers that can be accessed in a standard manner.

Internet account
The account set up by your internet service provider which gives you access to the world wide web, electronic mail facilities, newsgroups and other value added services.

Internet Explorer
The world's most popular browser software, a product of MicroSoft.

Internet Service Provider
An organisation which offers internet access to users, usually for a fixed monthly charge. Services typically include access to the world wide web, electronic mail, access to newsgroups, as well as a number of other services such as news, chat, and entertainment.

Glossary

ISDN
Integrated Services Digital Network. A high speed telephone network that can send computer data from the internet to your PC faster than a normal telephone line.

Java
An internet programming language developed by Sun Microsystems.

Job profiles
Details of the functions and activities of a particular job. May also include educational requirements for those wishing to apply for the job.

JPEG
Short for Joint Photographic Experts Group. JPEG is a specialised file format used to display graphic files on the internet. JPEG files are smaller than similar GIF files and so have become ever more popular – even though there is sometimes a feeling that their quality is not as good as GIF format files. See also MPEG.

Lurk
The slang term used to describe reading a newsgroup's messages without actually taking part in that newsgroup.

Mailing list
An electronic facility of the internet. For example, when you surf through the job pages on the internet and decide upon an agency who you would like some more information from, you join their electronic mailing list. This means that any new information that might be of interest to you is downloaded to your PC automatically. You can normally quit a mailing list by sending an email message to request removal.

Mirror site
An exact copy of another web site. Some FTP software providers set up mirror sites to handle the heavy traffic of software downloads.

Netiquette
The unofficial rules and language popularly used to ensure acceptable communication via electronic mail and newsgroup communication.

Modem (MOdulator/DEmodulator)
This is either an internal or external piece of hardware which when plugged into your PC, and into a standard phone socket, gets you access to the internet.

MPEG
The file format used for video clips available on the internet. See also JPEG.

Net
A slang term for the internet.

Netscape
After Internet Explorer, the most popular browser software available for surfing the internet. Netscape has dropped dramatically in popularity in the wake of the rise of Internet Explorer. However it has recently been taken over by America OnLine for $4 billion.

Glossary

Newsgroup
A special area of the internet ('usenet') where anyone can discuss things around a specific subject of common interest. The discussion takes the form of posting messages, which everyone in the newsgroup can then read. There are upwards of 30,000 active newsgroups on the internet.

Online
The time you spend linked via a modem to the internet. You can keep your phone bill down by reducing online time. The opposite term is offline.

POP
Point of Presence. This refers to the number of local dial telephone points available from your ISP. If your ISP does not have a local access number or POP, then don't sign up – your telephone bill will rocket.

Post
The common term used for sending ('posting') messages to a newsgroup.

Protocol
Technical term for the method by which computers communicate.

Server
Any computer on a network that provides access and services to other computers.

Shareware
Software that, although free, comes with a moral obligation to send a small donation to the author should you continue use of the software after a trial period – usually between 30 and 90 days.

Signature file
A computer file which normally contains your address details, and which you can add to email and newsgroup messages. Signature files need be created only once and can be appended as often as required.

Spam
Popular term for electronic junk mail – the act of sending unsolicited and unwelcome email messages across the internet.

Snail mail
Popular internet term for the standard postal service that reliably turns up at your front door every morning!

Surfing
The act of browsing the internet, particularly pages on the the world wide web.

TCP/IP
Transmission Control Protocol/Internet Protocol, the heart blood of the internet.

Thread
A collection of related messages in a newsgroup. Once a new message is posted, several people may reply to it and to each other – these connected messages are collectively known as a thread.

Glossary

Uploading
The act of copying files from your PC to a server or other PC on the internet. Most commonly used to describe the act of copying HTML pages onto the internet via FTP.

URL
Short for uniform resource locator: in plain English, the full address of a particular world wide web page.

UNIX
A grand operating system that's been around for years and that is still used in many mid to large systems. Most ISPs use this operating system.

Web authoring
Creating HTML pages to be uploaded onto the internet. You will be a web author if you create your own home page on the internet.

Webcrawler
A popular internet search engine used to find pages relating to specific keywords entered.

World Wide Web
The user-friendly face of the internet characterised by millions of web pages, usually containing bright colours, hyperlinks, sounds and even video clips.

WYSIWYG
What You See Is What You Get. If you see it on the screen with bells and whistles on it, then when you print it on your printer those bells and whistles should still be there!

Yahoo!
A popular internet directory and search engine used to find pages relating to specific keywords entered.

Zip/unzip
Many files that you download from the internet will be in compressed format, especially if they are large files. This is to make them quicker to download. These files are said to be zipped. Unzipping these compressed files generally refers to the process of returning them to their original size on receipt. Zip files have the extension '.zip' and are created using WinZip software or a similar package.

Further Reading

BOOKS ABOUT CVs

How To Compile Your Perfect CV by Michael Brown (Ellerton Press)

How To Write A Powerful CV In A Hurry by Jill Walsh (Lewisham CV Service)

How To Write A Successful CV by David R Boulton (First & Best in Education)

How To Write A Successful CV by Joanna Gutmann (Sheldon Press)

How To Write A Winning CV by Allan Jones (Arrow Books)

Killer CVs & Hidden Approaches by Graham Perkins (Pitman)

The Perfect CV by Tom and Eileen Jackson (Piatkus)

BOOKS ABOUT INTERVIEWS

Successful Interview Skills: How To Present Yourself With Confidence
by Rebecca Corfield (Kogan Page)

BOOKS ABOUT THE INTERNET AND THE WORLD WIDE WEB

10 Minute Guide To The Internet And The World Wide Web
by Galen Grimes (Que Publishing)

All You Need To Know About The World Wide Web
by Davey Winder (Future Books)

Browsing The World Wide Web With Word For Windows
by Tim Tow (Que Publishing)

Complete Idiot's Guide To The World Wide Web
by Peter Kent (Alpha Books)

10 Minute Guide To Internet Explorer 4
by Joe Lowery (Que Publishing)

30 Minutes To Master The Internet
by Neil Barrett (Kogan Page)

Accessing The Internet
by John Smith (Thomson Publishing)

Advertising On The Internet
by Robbin Zeff (Wiley)

All You Need To Know About Internet Jargon
by Davey Winder (Future Books)

All You Need To Know About UK Internet Service Providers
by Davey Winder (Future Books)

Further reading

BOOKS ABOUT HTML

10 Minute Guide To HTML
  by Tim Evans (Que Publishing)

Complete Idiot's Guide To Creating An HTML Web Page
  by Paul McFedries (Alpha Books)

Advanced HTML Companion
  by Keith Schengili-Roberts (Academic Press)

Beyond HTML
  by Richard Karpinski (A. Osborne)

Index

Internet Source Book Career Center, 108
Interview Network, 108
interviews, 90-94
IT jobs, 76, 77
Ivanhoe Career Guides, 66

JANET, 61
Job Finder, 36, 75, 108
Job Hunt, 109
Job Hunter, 72
Job Resource, 59
Job Search, 37, 109
Job Seekers Network, 59
Job Serve, 76, 77, 109
Job Site, 73, 109
Job Watch, 110
Jobs & Positions for Scientists, 110
Jobs for Scientists, 110
Jobs Unlimited, 110
junk email, 31

Kings College Careers Service, 111

Lab Staff, 111
Law Career, 111
Law Society, 191
LCCI Examinations Board, 185
Legal 500, 111
Line One (BT), 18
Lloyds, 129
Local Authority Careers Services, 112
London Careers Net, 112
Look Here, 112
lurking, 87-88
Lycos search engine, 22, 112

mail boxes, 32
Marks & Spencer, 130
Microsoft FrontPage, 51
Microsoft Mail, 28
Microsoft Network (MSN), 18
Milkround Online, 112
modems, 11
Monster Board, 37, 38, 74, 112

Napier University Careers Service, 113
NatWest, 130
Net Jobs, 75, 113
netiquette, 31, 34, 85
Netscape browser, 17, 19, 25, 46
Netscape Communicator newsgroups, 78, 84
Netscape Page Composer, 52, 53
New Scientist Jobs Page, 113
Newcastle University Careers Links, 111
news server, 82

newsgroups, 78-88
newsgroups for job seekers, 195-198
newspapers online, 71
NISS Jobs Noticeboard, 113
Nuntius news reading software, 83
nursing, 115

occupational profiles, 65, 96
Office Angels, 148
open news servers, 82
Open University, 63
Outlook Express, 80, 84
overseas jobs, 153ff

People Bank, 75, 114
People Management, 114
Pharm Web, 114
Pharmajobs, 114
Physicians Employment, 115
Physics Jobs, 115
Pilkingtons, 130
Post Office, 130
postgraduate education, 63
posting to newsgroups, 78
Pretty Good Privacy (PGP), 26
privacy, 26
Proctor & Gamble, 131
professional bodies, 187, 193
Prospects (CSU), 115
Prospects Web, 58, 64
Proteus Careers, 115

Railtrack, 131
Recruiters Network, 116
Recruiters Online Network, 116
Recruiting Links, 116
Recruitment Database, 116
Recruitment Gateway, 117
Reed Online, 74, 149
referees, 35
Riley Guide, 117
Royal & SunAlliance, 132
Royal Institute of British Architects (RIBA), 191
Royal Institution of Chartered Surveyors, 191
Royal Society of Chemistry, 191
RSA Examinations Board, 186

Safeway, 132
Sainsbury, 132
Science Online, 117
Scottish & Newcastle, 132
Scottish Qualifications Authority, 186
Scottish Recruitment, 117
Search engines, 20
Search Recruitment & Selection, 117

server, 27
shareware, 83
Shell, 133
Siebe, 133
signature file, 30
smileys, 30
SmithKline Beecham, 133
spam, 31, 86
spell checker, 30
Starting Point search engine, 118
Strathclyde University Careers Service, 118
Student World, 118
surveillance, 26

tags (HTML), 15, 44-46
TAPS (The Appointments Service), 36, 75, 118
Teacher Training Agency, 119
Telegraph, The, 119
Tesco, 134
Times Educational Supplement, 119
Top Grads, 120
Top Jobs, 74, 120
Tripod, 120

UK Academic Sites, 61
UK Directory, the, 120
UK Employment Law 121
UMIST, 121
uniform resource locator (URL), 19
Unilever, 134
universities, 63
Universities & Colleges Admissions Service (UCAS), 61
University Jobs & Research Posts, 121
University of Wolverhampton university maps, 62, 121
uploading pages, 47
usenet, 78-88
user name, 27
UUNet, 18

Virgin Net, 18, 82
Vodaphone, 134

web authoring packages, 50
Webcrawler search engine, 23
web space, 16
Whitbread, 134
Work Web, 37, 75, 122
world wide web (WWW), 13, 15

Yahoo! Higher Education, 122
Yahoo! internet directory, 24, 62, 122
Young Scientist, 152

Index

Accountancy Magazine, 95
Accounting Web, 95
AGCAS, 55, 65, 96
AltaVista search engine, 21, 96
American Department of Defense, 13
AOL (America OnLine), 17, 39, 40
AOL email, 32
AOL ftp screen, 47
AOL newsgroups, 82
application forms, 89
Army Careers, 124
ARPANet, 13
ASDA, 125
Association of Business Schools, 63
Association of Chartered Certified Accountants (ACCA), 187
Association of Graduate Careers Advisory Services (*see* AGCAS)
attachments to email, 39, 40, 69

Barclays, 125
Biz, The, 96
blind carbon copies, 29
Blue Circle, 125
bookmarks, 59
Bridges, 96
Bristol University Careers Service, 97
British Aerospace, 125
British Computer Society, 188
British Energy, 126
British Petroleum, 126
British Psychological Society, 188
British Steel, 126
browsers, 25, 46, 47
BT Internet, 82
BTR, 127

Cable & Wireless, 127
Cadbury, 127
CanDo Disability Careers Network, 97
Career Builder Network, 55
Career Guide, 97
Career Lab, 97
Career Mosaic, 56, 67-68, 98
Career Resource Centre, 98
Career Solutions, 98
Career Zone UK, 99
careers service, online, 55
Careers Service, 60
Careers Services National Association, 99

Cascaid Careers Software, 99
censorship, 81
CERN Laboratories, 13
Chartered Institute of Bankers, 189
Chartered Institute of Marketing, 189
Chartered Insurance Institute, 189
City & Guilds, 185
Collabra Discussion Groups (Netscape), 77
company profiles, 71
Compuserve, 18
Construction Site, 100
Continuing Education Gateway (CEG), 57
Cornwall & Devon Careers Service, 100
CVs, 33ff
cybercafés, 18
Cymru Prosper Wales 100

Datagold, 100
Demon Internet, 18, 82
Disgruntled, 101
Disney, 128
domain names, 27
Downing Street, 14

Earthworks, 101
E-CV, 101
E-Jobs, 101
EDEXCEL, 185
education, college sites, 60
education, continuing/postgraduate, 63
education, university sites, 60
Electronic Recruiting News, 101
Electronic Yellow Pages, 102
email, 16, 26ff, 38, 39, 69
emoticons, 31
Employers (UK), 124ff
employment agencies online, 72-73
Employment Index, 102
Employment Newsgroups Listing, 103
Employment Service, the, 103
encryption, 26
examining bodies, 193
Excite search engine, 21, 22, 103
Executive Grapevine, 103

FAQs (frequently asked questions), 87
favourites (bookmarks), 59
Federation of Recruitment &

Employment Services, 104
feedback, 49
flame wars, 86
forms, 49
Forte Free Agent (news reader), 83
free speech online, 81
freespace, 17
FTP (files transfer protocol), 47

Galaxy search engine, 104
GET Directory of Graduate Recruiters, 104
Gis-a-Job, 104
Glasgow University Careers Service, 105
Glaxo Wellcome, 129
Graduate Agency, 105
Graduate Fair (London), 105
Gradunet, 106
Grapevine, 106
GTI Careers Journals, 106
Guardian Royal Exchange, 129

Halifax, 129
Heriot-Watt University Careers Service, 106
Hobsons careers publishers, 106
home pages, 43
Hot Dog, 50
hotspots, 13
HotBot Jobs, 107
HTML, 14, 44
HTML Writer (software), 50
hypertext links, 13

ICI, 129
Impact Publications, 107
Infoseek search engine, 22, 107
Inside Careers, 107
Institute for Employment Research, 107
Institute of Careers Guidance, 107
Institute of Chartered Accountants (ICAEW), 190
Institute of Personnel & Development, 190
Institution of Electrical Engineers, 190
Internet Architecture Board (IAB), 13
Internet Explorer (browser), 17, 19, 20, 25, 50, 83, 85
Internet Recruiting, 108
internet service providers (ISPs), 15-18

207